THE BED TRICK

THE BED TRICK

Sex and Deception on Trial

Izabella Scott

Atlantic Books
London

First published in hardback in Great Britain in 2026 by
Atlantic Books, an imprint of Atlantic Books Ltd.

Copyright © Izabella Scott, 2026

The moral right of Izabella Scott to be identified as the author
of this work has been asserted by her in accordance with
the Copyright, Designs and Patents Act of 1988.

All rights reserved. No part of this publication may be reproduced, stored in
a retrieval system, or transmitted in any form or by any means, electronic,
mechanical, photocopying, recording, or otherwise, without the prior
permission of both the copyright owner and the above publisher of this book.

No part of this book may be used in any manner in the learning,
training or development of generative artificial intelligence technologies
(including but not limited to machine learning models and large
language models (LLMs)), whether by data scraping, data mining or use
in any way to create or form a part of data sets or in any other way.

1 3 5 7 9 8 6 4 2

A CIP catalogue record for this book is available from the British Library.

Hardback ISBN: 978 1 80546 254 5
E-book ISBN: 978 1 80546 255 2

Printed and bound by CPI (UK) Ltd, Croydon CR0 4YY

Atlantic Books
An imprint of Atlantic Books Ltd
Ormond House
26–27 Boswell Street
London
WC1N 3JZ

www.atlantic-books.co.uk

Product safety EU representative: Authorised Rep Compliance Ltd., Ground Floor,
71 Lower Baggot Street, Dublin, D02 P593, Ireland. www.arccompliance.com

For GK

The truth is messy, incoherent, aimless, boring, absurd. The truth does not make a good story; that's why we have art.

Janet Malcolm,
The Crime of Sheila McGough (1999)

Contents

	Author's Note	xi
	Prologue	1
1	Miss X on the Stand: Consent	15
2	Rape on the Stand: Myths	39
3	Gayle Newland on the Stand: Deception	54
4	The Closet on the Stand: Sexuality	77
5	Identity on the Stand: Fraud	104
6	Kye Fortune on the Stand: Avatars	124
7	The Dildo on the Stand: Bodies	154
8	The Blindfold on the Stand: Touch	171
9	Kye Fortune on the Stand: Impostors	196
10	The Reasonable Person on the Stand: Legibility	212
11	Storytelling on the Stand: Fiction	228
	Epilogue	253
	Notes	260
	Acknowledgements	319

Author's Note

This is a work of non-fiction. My primary sources were the trial transcripts for the UK criminal trials *R v Newland* (2015) and *R v Newland* (2017), and other documents embedded within them. My request for these transcripts was granted in 2020. Access to trial transcripts is part of the principle of 'Open Justice', which is written into UK legislation and requires court proceedings to be open to the public.

A range of reporting restrictions work alongside 'Open Justice' legislation, to protect and anonymize complainants (people making a complaint) in sexual offences cases. The restrictions apply to this case. The woman making the accusation was automatically granted lifetime anonymity the moment she filed her case. In this book, her name is replaced with a pseudonym, 'Miss X', and various dates, locations and other details have been either omitted or blurred in accordance with this legislation and other reporting guidance.

Prologue

A woman is in the witness box. I cannot give you her name. She is simply a letter, a blurred face: 'Miss X', a woman in her twenties. It is September 2015, and the third day of a sex offence trial. The setting is a Crown court in northern England.

Miss X's cross-examination by the defence barrister, a man named Nigel Power, is in full swing.

For a witness, the cross-examination is a dreaded part of any criminal trial, and particularly of sex offence trials. A complainant's allegations will be disputed, as a defence barrister tests their story, undermines it, tries to show the jury that this witness might not remember correctly, might be unreliable, might even be making it all up, a liar.

In court, complainants tell their story first, and Miss X's case has been heard across two days. A prosecution barrister named Matthew Corbett-Jones has introduced her allegations and the charges against the defendant. Miss X alleges that the person in the dock, Gayle Newland, tricked her into having sex on multiple occasions by pretending to be someone else: a man named Kye. She says she was deceived into having sex that she would not otherwise have agreed to – sex that appeared to be heterosexual, but that she later discovered was homosexual because Gayle was not Kye and not a man. Miss X says she did not know who she was having sex with because she was wearing a blindfold.

Towards the end of the second day, the prosecution barrister is replaced by the defence barrister. Nigel Power, representing Gayle Newland, begins his attempt to pick holes in Miss X's account. Question after question, his aim is to seed doubts in the jury's mind. Miss X is examined about her previous sexual history – quizzed on how many men she has slept with. The questions a barrister can ask a witness in relation to sexual history have to be screened in advance, as a result of feminist advocacy during the 1990s. Today the cross-examination proceeds in two directions. First, Power attempts to discredit Miss X's claims about the blindfold. She admits to spending perhaps a hundred hours in Kye's company over five months, and having sex with Kye between ten and twenty times. She says she felt and touched and heard her lover, but never saw him, and had not known who she was really with. 'Every single time I met up with Kye I had a mask on and I had a scarf on top of it,' she explains, in what becomes a refrain.

Power tries to make the blindfold, which is the crux of the allegation, seem improbable, even silly. Could she really have been wearing a blindfold every minute, he asks? Did it never slip? Didn't she want to get a glimpse of the person she was consenting to, all those times? 'You can see how it looks ridiculous, though, can't you?' he says at one point. Miss X replies, 'If I'd known that there was a woman with a strap-on, having penetrative sex with me, I would *not* have carried on.'

PROLOGUE

The second direction of Power's cross-examination concerns that strap-on. In his proposition, sex with a dildo feels different to sex with a penis, and Miss X must have been able to tell the difference. This is where Miss X's sexual history comes in, because if she'd had sex with many men before, with a range of penises, then Power reasons that she should have known what was what, and couldn't have been fooled by Gayle as she alleges.

It's Power's job to represent Gayle, who disputes Miss X's account, saying that the allegations are false, that Miss X never wore a blindfold and always knew who she was having sex with. They were best friends, says Gayle, and lovers in the closet. Kye was a shared fantasy that had been going on for years. There is no anonymity guarantee for defendants, and unlike Miss X, Gayle's face is not blurred. From the first day of the trial reports appear in news outlets, first locally then across the country. Those articles featured photos of Gayle, seen entering the court in the morning or leaving in the afternoon often with a file in hand. The captions included Gayle's name, age and full address.

The court has not yet heard Gayle's version of events. That's to come. But before Power argues a defence, putting forward a different story, he is given the opportunity to counter Miss X. And that's what he is doing – trying to dismantle Miss X's story, one that after two days of demonstration is currently in the mind of the jury. As the minutes creep by, his questions become more technical, and more explicit, as he digs into the various sexual encounters between Miss X and Kye. Who was on top? Was there foreplay? When did Kye get his penis out? Where were Miss X's hands?

At times Miss X is reluctant to answer. 'I thought everyone here knows how sex progresses,' she says at one point, 'I didn't know you wanted it – count by count.' But Power does. That's how the court measures it, count by count. And this sex isn't 'typical' sex – which means it's difficult to read; it isn't legible. Courts like archetypes, reasonable persons engaged in reasonable activities. Here, in the courtroom, the blindfold and dildo are atypical, unreasonable, illegible. 'But this isn't – this isn't ordinary sex, is it?' he replies. 'So I think you should work on the basis that not everybody knows – how it works.'

An hour in, Power's questions begin to focus in on the difference between rubber and flesh, the touch of a dildo versus the touch of a penis. Miss X is asked to describe the feel of Kye's penis. Wasn't it strange that it was always erect? Didn't it feel hairless and unlike a crotch? And what about the testicles, weren't they hard and immobile? Miss X gives way to the volley of questions, divulging information that she doesn't want to offer, that still feels private, despite the scrutiny of the police investigation, and the exposure of the trial.

> MISS X. —I could feel, I could feel them slapping against me. If you really wanna know the nitty-gritty details. When I was on top bouncing, I could feel them slapping against me. So that's why I thought it was a real guy that I was sleeping with.
>
> POWER. And that's just the biggest lie you've ever told, isn't it?

PROLOGUE

A. No, it's not.

Q. When you were on top of Kye, could you feel what the area around the base of the penis felt like?

A. Not really. My, my, my vagina is not fingertips. I could feel what I could feel.

There are limits to what can be understood about sex from the outside. To a certain extent, the court is listening to what Miss X and Gayle have to say about the sex they had, or thought they had. But trials are storytelling contests. The lawyers are trying to persuade the jury of one version of events, or the other. They are making a case, producing stories – competitive stories that use extremes in order to win. And in its quest for resolution, the trial is given a plot.

*

Gayle Newland was found guilty in 2015, and again at a retrial in 2017.

The convictions surprised me.

I first encountered the case during a heatwave, as the second verdict came in. Reports explained that Gayle had been accused of an old and rare offence called 'sexual fraud', one that I'd previously encountered only in fiction. This narrative plot has been named the 'bed trick'. Shakespeare made it famous, a favourite device of his, in plays replete with lovers switching places in the dark. There are many iterations across myth and folklore, but in life a consummated bed trick is rare.

I have long been fascinated by this plot, which caught my

attention as a student of literature many years ago. I pored over bed tricks in *The Canterbury Tales*. In one of the tales, told by an estate manager called the Reeve, a student tricks a wife in the dark. When he hears the wife go outside in the dead of night 'to piss', the student sneaks into her bedroom and steals the baby's cradle, moving it to the foot of his own bed. The wife, making her way back in the dark, gropes her way to the cradle. Unable to locate it, she believes she's in the wrong bedroom and realizes how easily she could have got into another bed. Finally, she finds the cradle with her fingertips and gets into bed with her husband. But of course, it's the student. They have sex and, in this comedic tale, she is amazed by her husband's newfound stamina. (As Chaucer put it, 'On this good wife did he vigorously lie/No such merry time she'd known in years gone by'.)

In stories, bed tricks are told to entertain. Night-games are a theme of medieval folktales, in which brides slip a drugged pig into bed on the wedding night, or clasp fish-heads between their thighs. In Italian *opera buffa*, suitors masquerade as strangers, tricking their sweethearts in tests of loyalty that go terribly awry. Bed tricks also feature in adventure novels, dark comedies and works of magical realism. They surface in films too, such as the cult musical *The Rocky Horror Picture Show*, in which the mad Dr. Frank-N-Furter deceives a naive couple, Janet and Brad, one after the other in the dark (hilariously Janet thinks it's Brad and Brad thinks it's Janet).

I was drawn to the intriguing suggestions made about intimate misrecognition. The plot suggests that, in bed, anyone might be mistaken for anyone else. I was compelled by this curious proposition. Could bodies be so

PROLOGUE

indistinguishable in the dark? Mine? My girlfriend's? Held within this suggestion is another radical idea: that all bodies are not just indistinguishable in the dark, but alike. In other words, all those characteristics that seem to set bodies apart – from race and gender to physical quirks – are collapsed by the bed trick. The plot suggests that, in the dark, all bodies are just the same.

Gayle's trials appeared to show life imitating art – the two protagonists caught in a web of artful patterns, playing out a counterintuitive bed trick plot. This drew me in further. The boundary between reality and fiction is something I think about, as a writer, all the time.

I was intrigued by the allegation and ultimately by the verdicts. I wanted to understand how a jury had been convinced by a plot so rare in real life.

There were two objects at the centre of the trials and the reporting. The first was the blindfold. Miss X was ridiculed for agreeing to wear it every time she met up with Kye. The second was the dildo. I was particularly alert to the way queer sex was being represented and judged. The excitement and horror that surrounded the object disturbed me, as Gayle was described as a 'lesbian sex abuser', seeking 'bizarre satisfaction' by any means.

News outlets obsessed over one further detail: Gayle had been studying Creative Writing at the time the events on trial took place. Did this make the allegations more credible, as reports seemed to suggest? Was Gayle 'an imaginative and persuasive liar', as one report indicated, able to pull off this wild, long-running, two-year scam?

My curiosity soon ossified into unease. For the most part, reading about the case was very sad. The two women were jeered and laughed at, their secrets and intimacies turned into spectacle. I wanted to get beneath the reporting. I wanted to go back in time and watch both trials from start to finish. But more than that, I wanted to *read* them. In Janet Malcolm's literary reinvestigation of a criminal case, *The Crime of Sheila McGough*, she begins by looking at the trial transcripts. 'The transcripts of a trial at law – even routine criminal prosecutions and tiresome civil disputes – are exciting to read,' Malcolm promises. In the UK, every word spoken at a criminal trial is captured for the public record. When transcribed, each day produces a document around 25,000 words in length. Bookending the trial are pre-trial meetings and sentencing days, also on record if you know how to find them. Over a year, I assembled an archive.

Malcolm was right. The transcripts for these trials were 'exciting' to read. Finally, I could read the accounts of Miss X and Gayle in their own words. But this was a rape trial. To read the transcripts was to find an awful portrait of sex offence law, and a system that is not so much broken as cruel. I encountered two vulnerable people – two students, formerly best friends, both in their early twenties. A jury is told that one person is telling the truth, and the other is lying. Gayle either goes to jail or walks free.

*

Was there something else behind my desire to devote so much time to these trials?

Researching the case dredged up a long-suppressed memory. It began to surface, quite unexpectedly, when I was looking through old emails. On a whim, I had been digging into my inbox, to see what I had been doing on the dates that

PROLOGUE

were important to the case – such as the day Miss X filed her complaint, and the day Gayle was arrested. Once upon a time, I'd dutifully tagged my emails with various labels. These tags now seemed amusingly innocuous, providing an unexpected index of my preoccupations as a young woman: 'art project', 'blog', 'camera case', 'exams'.

But then one label jolted me. It was titled 'court case'. And what I had forgotten – or (let's face it) repressed – was this: many years ago, during my second year of university, I received a court summons.

The document had arrived by post in February 2008, summoning me to give evidence in a sex offence trial. The allegation was 'attempted rape'. 'All the witnesses in this case have already been examined except Izabella Scott,' the document read. 'Her examination in our court is essential for the interest of justice.'

The letter was typed on thin grey paper and arrived from India. My name appeared again and again. I was being compelled to give evidence at a trial. But, as in a nightmare, the date of the trial – in 2007 – had already passed. I was studying English Literature, training to be an expert reader, to interpret words on a page. But this document was different; I felt that I couldn't read it, that I didn't understand.

The sheet of paper had a binding, real-world power. The summons made clear that if I failed to turn up (which I had), a warrant could be issued for my arrest. There was clearly a mistake – some miscalculation by the court, an error. But I felt paralysed, responsible, afraid.

The document identified me as 'the principal witness', 'the informant' and 'the victim'.

The fact was, two years earlier, I had gone to a police

station, in a country that was not my own, to report an attempted rape. I was travelling alone through a beach town called Puri in eastern India, and I was nineteen years old. While there, a local man held me down and tried to rape me, while I screamed and kicked. Somehow, I got away and I found a police station. According to my diary, which I turned to now, I was given a cool drink, I was listened to, I was believed. But the procedure quickly turned violent. An hour later my attacker had been found and I was asked to identify him. In a cruel circling, a sickening narrative structure, we were back at the same spot where, not long ago, I'd struggled and yelled. (A haunting detail: he hadn't fled.) Now *he* was being beaten in front of me. Now *he* was on the floor, crying out. Everything was reversed, and now I seemed to have all the power – the police asking me, 'Miss, are you satisfied?' as they landed each kick.

In the following days the complaint was made public, reported in various newspapers, including *The Sunday Times* back home. I was mortified; before I'd had time to process it, the story had been taken out of my hands. In one report, I was reading a novel, which the man 'tore up' before trying to rape me. In another, I was dozing when the attack took place.

For a while, when I returned home to the UK, it was all anyone would ask me about. That summer, a teacher from my old primary school stopped me in the street to get the story first-hand. Soon after, a neighbour called the family landline, and asked me, with a dreadful frankness, 'Were you raped?' It was a horrible, local sort of fame. My departure for university at the end of the summer couldn't have come soon enough.

PROLOGUE

The incident was public, but the court's attempt to summon me to trial, surfacing years later, was secret and felt unbearable. This was not the only court summons I received. Over the next three years, new documents would arrive, year after year, each one summoning me to give evidence in court, on a date that, torturously, had already passed. I would contact the Home Office, the Foreign Office, and dispatch letters to the Indian court judge, explaining why I was unable to give evidence and my desire to withdraw the complaint. No matter what I did, the summonses kept arriving. As I studied, went out with my friends, partied, fell in love – my assailant awaited trial, in a distant beach town, in a cell.

It was as if there were a void into which my letters vanished. Every new summons made it clear that no correspondence from me had ever reached its destination. The legal machinery, once ignited, felt inhuman, unstoppable. I grappled with these documents, literature that I couldn't negotiate. There was something surreal about being caught between legal systems, between diplomacies. I wanted to drop the charges, to end it. I longed to release myself from the past, and from him. We were tied together by his attack, by my complaint, by a case that was, as each summons put it, 'lingering for disposal'.

As time went on, my memory of the event condensed. I didn't recall the attack so much as the aftermath. I remembered him beaten and bloody on the ground. I remembered him weeping as the police threw him into a cell. What had I set in motion? Privately, I began to berate myself as a clueless tourist who had lodged a complaint, regretted it and vanished into thin air. I fantasized about flying back there, finding the judge or jail, speaking to someone (even him), face to face.

Then, in April 2010, during my finals, one of my letters finally reached the judge in Puri – and it was over.

For years, I never spoke about this; I think I hid it from myself. I realize that even during the process of trying to drop the case, I was burying it. I didn't confide in anyone besides my parents – not in my friends at university, nor even my sisters. Unable to face it, or reason with it, I shoved it in a mental box and locked it away.

For a long time, the impetus behind my interest in the law eluded me, even as I worked for a human rights lawyer, straight after I graduated. Even as I returned to university, this time an art school, and began writing about crime.

But inevitably it was always there, in my voracious reading of court reporting, especially around sexual offences and rape trials, and in my interest in other people's legal examinations, a psychic spot. The criminal cases that interested me had unclear, murky dynamics – stories of uncertain, encrypted relationships that I wanted (needed) to understand.

Years later, after gathering the transcripts for Gayle's trials, I started a PhD. I would spend the next three years taking apart the transcripts, working closely with a legal scholar. I studied the history of sexual fraud and its literary equivalent, the bed trick; the criminal trial; and the difficulty of proving and prosecuting rape.

What you are about to read is the result of these years of research, as I strove to understand Gayle's case and puzzled over how to tell it. Often, I felt unsure if this was a story I should be telling, and of my purpose in telling it. At the end

PROLOGUE

of this endeavour, I now see that I was driven forward by the experience sleeping in my subconscious and by the documents from Puri that I couldn't understand. (Perhaps all this time, I've been learning to read them.)

During the process of writing this book I have often felt close to Miss X and Gayle, in different ways. Both were students in their early twenties when the events on trial took place – events that occurred in their final year, when term ended, just after their final exams. I felt I could relate. Like Miss X, I had been a complainant. Though I'd suppressed the legal process, I'd not forgotten the aftermath of my attack, and I felt I knew the gravity of going to a police station, alone, to lodge a complaint. At the same time, I felt close to Gayle; I'm a lesbian too, and I was conscious that not so long ago the law penalized queer desire. Gayle's difficulty explaining her sexuality in court made sense to me. But the reality is, I know Gayle and Miss X only through the transcripts. In those documents, one person's word is pitted against the other, as both are accused, time and time again, of lying.

In fiction and drama, the trial is a popular format. This is partly due to its inherent narrative cohesiveness, structured by phases of revelation that all lead towards the verdict – which can make for riveting entertainment. But in real life, this system, in which two sides battle it out, most forcefully through the cross-examination, can feel vicious. In a sex offence context, it can feel like a hunt for the liar. Writing against this structure, I have tried to be on both their sides, in a way the trial – which produces opposing stories – never could.

At certain points in this book, there are scenes in which I evoke the accounts from one person's perspective and then the other's. To write the scenes, I relied on the transcripts, in which Gayle and Miss X's voices are recorded alongside the evidence presented at trial, including a vast log of text messages. At the same time, I pushed at the limits of these records, which are accusatory and incomplete, shaped as they are by the requirements of the law and the rules of evidence. Often, I tried to get behind and beneath the records, utilizing my imagination and closely scrutinizing what was said. All the while, I was starkly aware that it is the most serious of matters, concerning real people and current law.

Throughout this book, my aim has been to show the mechanics of a rape trial – to open the bonnet, to show how it works. Importantly, I also put storytelling on trial. I think about the stories that grip us in life, but also in court. I wonder why some stories are more believable than others. I ask: when is the bed trick plot enjoyed as just a story? When is it taken seriously and prosecuted as rape? And why do we enjoy bed tricks in fiction – but punish them in life?

In the end, *The Bed Trick* considers what is under examination at these trials, and also, more widely, at any criminal trial; this includes my trial, the one that never came to be.

1

Miss X on the Stand: Consent

The Crown v Gayle Newland.
Chester Crown Court, 2015;
Manchester Crown Court, 2017

Sex is usually a private act – though it's hard to generalize about something so idiosyncratic, something different each time. It often takes place behind closed doors, often between only two people. The sex under scrutiny at these trials happened in hotel rooms, and at a flat where Miss X lived alone. There were only two people in the room, the defendant and the complainant. Neither documented the sex in any way. There was no hidden camera. I wasn't there. Nor were the solicitors, barristers, the judge and jury, or anyone else for that matter. This means, when it comes to the sex on trial, there are only two accounts: one from Miss X, one from Gayle Newland.

In the UK, criminal trials are structured as a competition between two narratives. One side represents the accuser – at this trial, Miss X's complaint. The other side represents the accused – in this case, Gayle Newland's defence. To 'take the stand' is to appear in a witness box and to give testimony before a jury. The barristers, representing each side, will examine their witnesses on the stand. That's the nice part. Examination is followed by cross-examination, where it's the barrister's task to spoil the other side's story, to trip the witness up. All the while, a jury looks on.

People accused of crimes are presumed innocent, until proven guilty. It's a core legal principle. The defendant is in the dock; the trial is named after them (i.e., The Crown v Gayle Newland) and it's their fate being decided, their freedom or incarceration. But by this logic, they have nothing to prove. A defendant is there to respond to accusations, to put up a defence. They have the right to remain silent. They can choose whether to take the stand or not. A barrister can speak for them.

Meanwhile, the complainant has a different role. If a case does make it to trial (there are many hurdles; not being believed is a typical barrier), it is taken on by the state, or Crown. A complainant like Miss X will become the principal witness. She is there to explain what happened. Since nobody else, bar the defendant, saw or felt what she saw, she can become the trial's main evidence. And as the evidence, she has to be tested. Her testimony will be met with intense scrutiny, a hostile cross-examination. Counterintuitively, and particularly challenging in sex offence trials, often it feels like the *complainant* is on trial.

When Miss X takes the stand to be grilled by Nigel Power, this is exactly what happens. In the harsh spotlight, before an audience, he tests her credibility, the credibility of her story. So often, rape trials come down to two reports, as one person's word is pitted against the other. Power's accusation – 'that's the biggest lie you've ever told, isn't it?' – exemplifies the defence strategy: to seed disbelief. Miss X's conduct is on trial, her behaviour, her desires. So is her ability to persuade, as jurors are asked, finally: *do you believe her?*

Since the 1970s, a range of special measures has been introduced to try to make rape trials easier for complainants to bear. This is an acknowledgement of how grim it has always been. The promise of lifetime anonymity, automatically given to Miss X, entered legislation in 1976. It makes it a criminal offence to publish her name, or any information that might identify her, in relation to the trial. This is a powerful protection – but it lacks force on the day of the trial.

Miss X appears in court twice. On the morning of the first trial, before proceedings begin, the barristers meet with Judge Roger Dutton, who is hearing the case, to run over the day to come. A reporting restriction order, already invoked, prevents the publication of Miss X's identity – but Power suggests that the trial might need extra reporting guidance. The fact that Gayle and Miss X went to university together, and were at one time best friends, complicates matters. Naming the defendant will spoil the anonymity promised to the complainant, Power suggests.

In some ways he was right. The decision to name Gayle inevitably exposed parts of Miss X's life. Power was obviously representing Gayle, using this line of argument to try to get his client some protection, but he also seemed to grasp the heat this case might draw – is drawing. Already, there are photographers at the court doors. Power encourages Judge Dutton to give 'some guidance' at least, 'in relation to the sensible reporting of the case', but Dutton resists. He's breezy; he believes in the sturdiness of the law and the decency of journalists.

By the second day, it's clear the press is not acting sensibly. Reporters have flocked to the entrance of the Crown Court, congregating in the car park out front, which serves the court and the buildings either side. Miss X has been photographed walking in.

'That has caused her some considerable distress,' the Crown barrister, Matthew Corbett-Jones, now explains to Dutton. She is in tears and anxious about giving evidence, he explains. Journalists have taken a picture of her – a picture of her face. Clearly, it's not as she was promised.

Dutton is surprised, a little enraged. 'There is no purpose,' he splutters. And indeed, there is none. It's a criminal offence to violate Miss X's anonymity; the act of publishing a photo, like this one, could result in jail time. Photos are being taken of Gayle too, who is similarly distressed, as Power informs Dutton – but there is no clear way of objecting to this. Defendants are fair game, and they are rarely protected by reporting restrictions. That's the law.

Before the day commences, Dutton will have to reassure Miss X that the photographs taken of her can't be used, ever, and she is under the protection of the law. Even so, the incident highlights the frailty of special measures like this one, when it comes to that day in court. Anonymity is a right that can only be reaped after the hearing has taken place. Criminal trials are open to the public. Press, family members and other viewers can all sit in the public gallery. Anyone attending this trial will learn Miss X's name in the course of the proceedings, because anonymity isn't immediate. Miss X's name isn't beeped out every time it's mentioned by the judge or the court clerk, by her barrister, by Gayle. Anonymity by law is a reporting restriction. Her name is removed afterwards – by a transcriber, who replaces it with an 'X'; by the reporters as they formulate their articles.

Other special measures, further attempts to protect complainants from the sex trial's harsh focus, also prove to be weak. The screening of questions around sexual history is a case in point. A month before the trial, Power met with Corbett-Jones and Dutton for a pre-trial hearing. The judge ruled that sexual history questions were 'absolutely inevitable' in a case of this kind, and the same line of questioning was allowed again by the new judge at the retrial.

One of the features of reporting rape includes telling your story over and over again, as it is tested through phases of investigation (to the police) and prosecution (to lawyers), and finally in court. A special measure introduced in 2003 tries to overcome this. In a shift away from a reliance on live testimony and the performance of a complainant on the stand, this measure allows statements recorded by police during the early phases of a complaint to be played during the trial. Miss X's full account was videoed in 2013 in the days after her initial statement. These DVDs, running to two and a half hours, are played at both the trial and retrial, and become evidence-in-chief as soon as they are viewed. In some ways, this measure is a relief for complainants. Miss X doesn't have to tell the story yet again from beginning to end. She doesn't have to carry the burden of reliving the account in every detail. The DVDs speak for her. But, of course, the DVDs can't be quizzed or questioned. Once the hours are up, Miss X has to take the stand – and take their place. The transcripts record Power and Miss X sparring, hour after hour. She has to do this twice, because there are two cross-examinations, one at the trial and one at the retrial.

Power is there at the second too, focusing on the dildo, often going in for the kill: 'A penis that you had sucked, a penis that didn't leave any semen. It's just not a real penis. And you knew,' he accuses.

By the retrial, Miss X has opted to give evidence from behind a curtain, a measure available to vulnerable witnesses by request. A curtain, drawn around the witness box, blocks the public gallery and the box in which Gayle Newland is held from view.

Retrials are rare, and while this is a second chance for Gayle Newland, who is on bail from jail, having been found guilty the first time, it's an ordeal for Miss X. As the legal record proliferates, it creates trouble for defendant and complainant alike. The doubling provides opportunities, unique to a cross-examination, for catching a witness out. At every turn, the barristers are trying to undermine the credibility of the other side's evidence. Miss X's original DVD accounts are played once again, but this time, when she is cross-examined by Power, he has the transcript of the first trial to check her words against – to catch her out. Any differences in her testimony, any slips or errors or misremembering, will be used to convince the jury that she is unreliable, a liar.

In a sickeningly familiar scene, Power and Miss X traverse the same ground as they did in the first trial, only this time for a new judge, a new jury. Miss X is served the old questions: why couldn't she tell a dildo from a penis, hairless rubber from tender flesh?

It's June. Reporters describe a heatwave in Manchester where the retrial is being heard. The courtroom's air conditioning is broken. Wigs are removed, everyone is sweating. Miss X, who is being cross-examined by Power, appears tired, frustrated, tipping towards breaking point. She sighs a lot, loses her temper.

'Were you aware of his testicles?' asks Power. She's been here before.

'When you're having sex, it's not the first thing you think of,' she replies. 'You don't think: oh, I'd better put my hand down and check for balls.'

Power ploughs on: but when you were on top, having sex, didn't you feel them – the testicles? He's persistent with these questions, and precise. She doesn't realize, but he's trying to catch her out – and it works.

'I didn't feel anything,' Miss X says. 'I thought I was having sex with a guy.' Now Power steps up the attack.

'All right. I'm going to ask you what you said about this in the last trial and, in fairness to you, I think it's probably easier if you have a copy of the transcript, all right?'

That transcript is circulated, and Power begins to read out the old dialogue.

'Question: "The testicles weren't moving around during sex, were they?" Answer: "When I was on top, they felt like they were" . . . Is that true?' Power asks.

'If it's what I said at the time, then that must have happened,' Miss X says, worn out. 'I can't remember the very small details.' Power's ambush continues.

'Question: "What, the testicles?" Answer: "I could feel, I could feel them slapping against me. If you really wanna know the nitty-gritty details, when I was on top, bouncing . . ." Now, obviously you'll accept that you said that, but was it true?' he asks.

'The only reason I came here is to get justice,' she hits back. 'Everything that I've said is true.'

THE BED TRICK

In a few minutes' time, Power will move on to her sexual history, as he did previously – asking Miss X about her experiences with 'real' penises: how many men she'd slept with, what their penises felt like, if they varied in shape, size, sensation. But before that, he holds up the dildo for the court to see.

It's not the actual one used during the liaisons, which is missing, but a duplicate. Power has had the prosthetic penis on his desk at the ready, asking his legal team to place it there 'discreetly' that morning. Now he holds it up: a neon pink dildo. The shaft and balls are textured with veins. It excites the public gallery. ('You can almost smell the rubber,' one journalist salaciously reported.) Miss X, behind the curtain but in Power's sightline, is aghast.

> POWER. Just give me one moment please? . . . You see, the strap-on wasn't recovered, but one's been bought that's either identical or very similar, all right? Now you've seen this bef—
>
> MISS X. Yeah, you did this to me last time, yeah. (Witness distressed.)
>
> Q. Yeah, I was about to say you've seen this before. I'm not going to ask you to look at it.
>
> A. (Witness distressed.) Yeah, cos you think it's hilarious. You think this bad movie here that's my life, you think it's a joke. (Witness distressed.)
>
> Q. You see, this strap-on hasn't got testicles that could

slap wet against your bottom as you were having sex, could it?

A. Well of course they could cos if I'm on top and you're wet, everything feels wet, doesn't it?

Q. But they're fixed in place, they can't slap about. It's just, it just didn't happen, did it?

This time round, reporters have been restricted from publishing anything about the trial, until it's been decided. Judge David Stockdale, who is hearing this retrial, appears a little more media-savvy, refusing a petition to lift the restrictions put forward by members of the press. Immediately after the jury delivers its verdict, finding Gayle guilty for a second time, articles appear in news outlets across the UK; miles south of Manchester, in London, I will be reading them for the first time, curious and disturbed. The dildo will form a large part of the reporting, as it did at the first trial. Power had brandished the dildo then too, circulating the box it came in, and holding up the replica, identifying the testicles, which he describes as prosthetic, non-human, hard.

Across two trials, two years, the dildo sustains the focus of the court, the media, the public – as if looking at it, analysing the strap-on, sensing it, will help answer some of the key questions of the trials. Did Miss X know? Should she have known? Known it was a dildo, feel it was plastic, and thus, by extension, feel and know she was having sex with Gayle?

In the reporting, Miss X is anonymous, an 'X'. But when it comes to the trials, she's the star. As her cross-examinations show, despite decades of feminist advocacy – despite amendments, special measures and other reforms – complainants remain in the spotlight, the evidence to be tested.

And the reason for this intense scrutiny is, of all things, the law of sexual consent.

Miss X's consent, or lack of it, is a central focus of the trials. In a speech known as the opening of facts, for example, given on the first day of the first trial, the Crown barrister invokes the word 'consent' no fewer than thirty-nine times. 'The complainant did not knowingly consent,' he says. 'She was not consenting to penetration', 'At no time did Miss X consent', 'She did not give this defendant consent'.

I had long thought of consent as a magic rule, a feminist milestone in the history of rape law, and a success. But that was before I studied the rape trial. In the broadest sense, consent law was part of an important shift in the legal interpretation of rape. In past centuries, rape was understood as a crime of force – perceived as damage to a man's property, the property being a virginal daughter or a wife. Under this rubric, only violent attacks (comparable to breaking and entering) were legible as rape to the law.

But a shift in interpretation across the twentieth century culminated in a revision to the Sexual Offences Act, altering the definition of rape. In a 1976 amendment, rape was redefined by whether 'a woman' did or did not 'consent to it . . . at the time'. (It would take another two decades for the law to recognize anyone other than a woman, or anything other than a vagina, as a victim of rape.)

The amendment marked a critical staging-post in a process – still ongoing – of redefining rape and the extent of its harm, and better understanding all the ways a person can be violated. This process was furthered by revisions to the Sexual Offences Act in 2003, which built on consent, defining rape as a violation of sexual autonomy – that is, a violation of personal freedom, of choice, and thus a violation of selfhood, identity, perhaps even humanity.

But the rule used to draw the line between sex and rape has flaws. The problem is, when consent is the right to choose, where sex is wanted and rape is unwanted, the question becomes: 'what did the person choose?' And in a courtroom, this results in a heightened focus on the complainant – importantly, on how they conveyed their consent; on how their consent, or lack of it, was delivered.

The 'yes/no' formulation that always follows is a simplification. It is so limited when it comes to navigating sexual intimacy. Miss X's complaint is a case in point. It's more complicated than a simple 'yes' or 'no'. She explains in her DVD statements that she wanted to have sex with Kye, that she desired him, chose him. 'Lying there,' she says of the first time they had sex, 'I was just so happy . . . I felt grateful.' But she says her eyes were shut beneath a blindfold; she couldn't see, and didn't know what she was really choosing. Consent's 'yes or no' gives way to other questions. When is a 'yes' not really 'yes'? What do you need to know about somebody to freely, truly choose them?

The problem with consent's question, 'what did the person choose?', is that it imposes bright lines where there are none. And one of the reasons for this imposed clarity is that consent is heavily influenced by another field of law

– contract law. Both areas of law centre on an agreement to which two parties or more consent.

Contract law solidified during the industrial revolution, to make promises legally binding to aid trade. For a contract to be valid, it must be formed in precise steps. A proposal must be offered and accepted, the terms sufficiently certain and agreed. Crucial to the valid contract is a stage known as 'the meeting of minds', where the two parties reach a mutual agreement, and a new shared or joint intention is produced: the agreement itself. If promises are not met, one side can sue the other by asking a judge to examine the paperwork or other available evidence, to decide who's in the wrong and what the remedy should be.

Borrowing this logic, sex offence law conceptualizes the pair, the agreement, and imagines a public sexual contract, one applicable to all. The Sexual Offences Act 2003, the latest to date, sets out the terms of that contract, one we engage with, consciously or not, every time we have sex. If something goes wrong, and if one person makes it public and files a complaint, the sexual contract will be scrutinized – first by the police, then by prosecutors, finally by a judge and jury.

Determining consent follows the logic of the contract: was there an agreement, a meeting of minds? Did both parties sign, say yes? Did they do so freely, by choice? Did they know what they were signing?

But sex, or most sex, does not involve a written contract, only an implied one, arising from words, gestures, murmurs, touch. There's no paperwork to scrutinize in the aftermath, no terms or signatures to assess. (Nor would it help to actually have a contract; experiments in literalizing consent's contract have created more problems than solutions.) Instead there are people. Usually two people, reporting on something that happened in private between them.

*

Once it's been investigated by the police, Miss X's complaint is reviewed by the state, in the form of the Crown Prosecution Service (CPS), which decides whether Gayle should be charged. This is the process by which a crime against an individual is nationalized, and becomes a crime against the state: The Crown v Gayle Newland, *R v Newland*.

In her DVD accounts, analysed by the state, Miss X says she consented to the sex on trial and enjoyed it. She was in her twenties at the time, an adult. She desired her boyfriend, Kye Fortune, also an adult, and was deeply in love with him. They were engaged, partners for life, ready to sign marriage contracts. Before meeting in person, they spent thousands of hours on the phone, and later, though she was blindfolded, a lot of time in each other's company – many afternoons, whole days, perhaps a hundred hours. They had talked of where they would live when they were married, the family they'd make, what their kids would look like. They had, Miss X emphasized, a 'normal' relationship – a word that becomes a refrain during the trials. There were some terms and conditions. The blindfold, for example, that Miss X says she agreed to wear at all times (which she refers to as Kye's 'terms'). But the state has no business in the details of how adults choose to have sex – as long as there *was* such an agreement, and as long as they are of sound mind, signing freely and no one is harmed.

But the contract, says the Crown, was fake. Miss X was operating under a colossal deception. From a contract law view, she was a victim of fraudulent misrepresentation. All Miss X's love, her consent, all her signatures and yesses, were operating under a false belief, because Kye – the name on the contract – wasn't Kye. When Miss X pulled off the blindfold, she claims she found her best friend Gayle having sex with her, not Kye. Several days later she filed a complaint. She told the police who interviewed her that she had consented to a different person, and ultimately a different act. She said she had been raped by her best friend pretending to be her boyfriend, her fiancé – a man she now realized didn't exist.

*

In order to charge Gayle Newland, the police and the Crown prosecutors have to boil down Miss X's experience to an offence, or set of offences, described in the Sexual Offences Act 2003.

Before 2003, the CPS would have found it difficult to mount a rape charge (or the equivalent) against Gayle. This is because the definition of rape was terribly narrow. Only men could rape. The law, fixed in books and evolved in case law, did not recognize, or refused to name, rape by another actor, or rape by something other than a penis. Penetration without a penis would generally be prosecuted under another lesser offence, such as the (now abolished) crime of indecent assault.

But in 2003, the Sexual Offences Act was amended – this time, almost totally rewritten. The offences were made gender-neutral, and rather than defining crimes via identities – 'men' raping, 'women' being raped – the new provisions focused instead on sexual acts. In the process, the protagonists of sexual crimes were adapted. A new cast of actors was introduced. Genitals and orifices were assigned key roles – the traditional penis and vagina appearing alongside the anus and the mouth.

Using this new ensemble, the definition of 'rape' was expanded to account for all the ways a body could be raped. But 'rape', which is Section 1 of the Act, remained limited in one way: a flesh penis was required to do it. The new offence was viewed as gender-neutral, because, unlike any previous definition, a woman could rape, since a woman can have a penis. But people without flesh penises, women or otherwise, can't.

To describe the phenomenon of rape *without* a penis lawmakers would have to find new words, indeed a new section – eventually named 'assault by penetration', Section 2. The new offence had almost the same wording as rape, but more guilty parts were introduced: objects, tongues, digits and other body parts could unlawfully penetrate; victims could include mouths, anuses and vaginas; prosecutors would have to name the 'particulars' in the indictment.

The charges against Gayle, outlined in an indictment, are read out at the trials. Every count in a sex trial has 'particulars'. The pair is identified, with the date and location of each offence and, importantly, their body parts or other actors are named.

Gayle does not have a flesh penis. The sex on trial is sex with a dildo, sex with fingers and hands, sex with a tongue. Section 2 is identified by police and prosecutors following Miss X's account, and it is from here that the indictment is formulated. At the first trial, Gayle is charged with five counts of assault by penetration – the 'particulars' being in this case 'the vagina of Miss X' was penetrated each time. In four counts it was penetrated by 'a thing, namely a prosthetic penis', and in one count with 'a part of the body, namely her tongue'.

In the indictment and at the trials, the police, the prosecutors, the court and Miss X together identify Gayle Newland as a woman. During the trials, it will become clear that Gayle Newland also, for about a decade, had spoken online and eventually lived part-time as Kye Fortune, a man. When Gayle enters the court each day, watches from the box and appears on the stand, this gender variance is not presented. Gayle Newland appears in court as Gayle Newland using 'she/her' pronouns. Gayle's appearance corresponds to the single sex and gender fixed in state papers, her student ID: female, a woman.

A specific legal story is figured using Section 2 of the Sexual Offences Act. This story concentrates Miss X and Gayle into parts: a vagina, a prosthetic penis, a tongue. In much of this story, the pair are boiled down to genitals. Miss X is a vagina separated off from her self. Gayle Newland is, for the most part, represented by a pink dildo, one that in both trials Power will hold aloft – a strap-on without a body, the 'thing' not consented to.

At times the myopic focus makes reading the trial transcripts bizarre. There's an absurdist quality to the body parts, cropped off their personages, becoming accuser and accused – as in Nikolai Gogol's short story 'The Nose'. In the tale, a government official wakes up to find his nose is gone; he reports it to the police, who try to arrest the nose, which has developed a life of its own and keeps evading capture.

Here in court, the Crown represents Miss X's vagina. Power represents Gayle's tongue, and the pink prosthesis sits at his elbow.

*

Miss X's story, told in her own words, goes beyond the story of consenting to a penis not a dildo, to a man's tongue rather than a woman's. It's a story about a person named Kye. A handsome, half-Asian man she met online, also a student. It's a story about a deception and a betrayal that went on for years. Two years in which she thought she was falling in love with Kye, when all along she was being deceived by her best friend Gayle.

She gets to tell the full story in the DVDs, played at trial. This was her full statement, given to the police in 2013, in the days after her initial complaint. In the recordings, she told police that she'd been raped by her best friend, pretending to be her boyfriend. The deception had been going on for months. It was a week since they'd last had sex: the night she said she'd discovered the truth.

That night, in June, Miss X called 999 at 7.30 p.m. The call was logged, and it's part of the prosecution's evidence. The call lasted twenty seconds. When the operator asked Miss X if it was an emergency, she said it wasn't; the operator advised her to call the police instead. The thing that had just happened – the deception that she narrates to the police in her full account – was something difficult to describe on the phone. It wasn't, and was, an emergency. She wasn't in danger or injured. This was an emergency without force, rape by lies – a boyfriend revealed to be an impostor, a friend revealed to be a snake.

That 999 call attests to the moments right after Miss X says she discovered Kye was not Kye – the moment she realized that the contract was fake, that her choice had been taken away, and that sex was reclassified as a violation, an assault.

She explains in the DVD accounts and in the transcripts that Kye came over that Sunday night at 6 p.m. He'd been coming to her flat every Sunday for the past few months, and they had a system in place for his arrival. She trusted him fully. She didn't love wearing a blindfold, but she loved him, and it was the only way he said they could be together. But that summer night, in June, she began to question her trust. 'Something just felt different,' she says. She means this expansively – a mood, something in the air. But, sometime before 7.30 p.m., it also became literal, because something *felt* different; she couldn't see, and the first way she detected something wasn't right was by touch.

Reading Miss X's account of that evening, I think about the slipperiness of desire, trust, how easily sex can skid towards something else, unwanted, and how fluid consent is (unlike a contract).

Maybe they eat something, maybe he puts on the radio – she has no specific memory, only general memories of what they'd do on those Sundays together while she was blindfolded – but at some point things start to heat up. He guides her towards the bed and asks for a blow job. She describes not wanting to give him head, but doing it anyway, Kye being too rough, shoving it in her mouth, choking her, and how she gets upset, pulls away, protests. Then he apologizes and cuddles her. They lie back on the bed and it gets heated again. Now they're on the sofa and Miss X is on top, which is how they both come. Miss X reaches round the back of Kye's neck for more grip, and this is where she says her perception of him starts to shift. Now something felt different in a literal sense. For the first time in all these months, her touch didn't match with what he'd established, what she'd imagined. Her fingers told her that his head wasn't shaved, as she expected. In fact, she felt the opposite: his hair was long and fine. She describes it as silky and artificial, 'like a Barbie doll's hair'. The moment before she pulls off the blindfold unfolds in fragments. She remembers her ring getting caught on the back of his head, on something woolly, and he said that he was wearing a hat. She remembers how the blow job didn't feel right – when he choked her, the way his testicles scratched her chin. Suddenly it doesn't add up, suddenly her trust is slipping away. She sits back on the bed and, without telling him what she's going to do, she pulls off the blindfold, rips it off, and sees the person she's having sex with, with her own eyes, for the first time.

Miss X describes this as a devastating moment. It wasn't Kye in front of her, it was her best friend Gayle – but it wasn't Gayle either. She says, 'it wasn't Gayle and it wasn't Kye. I just didn't know who this person was. This was just a stranger to me who had just had sex with me.'

*

Gayle's version of events, and indeed of the relationship, is different. There was a dildo – Gayle freely says that she purchased one; the original box is an important piece of evidence for the defence, its purchase date used to demonstrate a contrary timeline of events. But the difference, in Gayle's story, is the blindfold: there was none. In Gayle's account, Miss X saw her lover, chose her lover. Gayle says that she knowingly consented every time to sex with Gayle and Kye, because there was no Kye without Gayle; they were the same person.

Many rape trials are lopsided. Defendants can choose to take the stand – or not. A barrister can speak for them. But Gayle takes the stand and tells her side of the story. Gayle undergoes examination, cross-examination and re-examination, telling her story to the court, to the jury, to the public gallery, allowing me to read it years later too.

In court, Gayle explains that she lived as Gayle and also as Kye. She'd been doing so for almost a decade. For most of that time, Kye lived online – that is, until she met Miss X.

Gayle's relationship to Kye is in crisis throughout both trials. During the first examination, Gayle tries to tell the story of how Kye came to be, but the court will find it difficult to hear. Judge Dutton interrupts Power in the middle of the examination several times, to ask Gayle a question. He can't get his head around it.

'I want to understand exactly what you are saying,' he says at one point, late into the first trial, its fourth day. 'Are you saying that . . . that Miss X knew all this time that she was in fact corresponding with a man called Kye, who was actually you?' Gayle, who has been explaining just this for the best part of a morning, replies in the affirmative. Dutton makes a note and then interrupts again. 'So you told her? . . . You spoke about it more than once?' Gayle again affirms. She's almost bamboozled; it's what she's been saying since she took the stand yesterday afternoon: 'Yeah of course . . . Yeah. Yeah. Yeah, of course.'

The issue is that Gayle's narrative lacks order. She sometimes describes being Miss X's 'girlfriend', and sometimes being Miss X's 'boyfriend'. To claim to be both, boy and girl, not one or the other, is difficult for the court and Dutton to register.

Since the Gender Recognition Act 2004, a person can legally reassign their gender. That person must first seek medical approval. Gender dysphoria, the current diagnostic label, identifies a list of symptoms, including 'a strong desire for the primary and/or secondary sex characteristics of the other gender' – primary characteristics being genitalia, the desire for a penis or vagina, secondary being breasts or facial hair, etc.

Gender certification, though hard won, is not always a home for gender fluidity. It offers shelter for people wishing to affirm their gender, usually described as 'the other gender' (i.e., one or the other), through legal and medical means. Gayle has never on public record identified as trans; she had not begun a process of certifying Kye before either trial. On the stand, she describes Kye as temporary, someone she lived as part-time, a role from which she moved 'in and out'. Before the first trial, when her story emerged, splashed over local and then national news sites, she did not have any clear social recognition of her fluctuating gender identity. During the trial, she relays the secrecy that shrouded Kye, especially in the early years, when she was a teenager, in chatrooms and on Myspace, speaking as a boy. She explains that being a lesbian, and being Kye, were her greatest secrets – something that, before meeting Miss X, she could never find a way to tell.

Adding complexity to this account, the man she identified as is half-Asian. Gender identity aside, racial questions hang over Gayle's identification as Kye. She is white and British. The photos that appear in Kye's channels, where Gayle spoke as Kye, show a half-Asian man. To make matters even more complicated, these photos belong to a real person, an Asian-American man named Carlo, whose images Gayle admits she had been repurposing, without his consent, for almost a decade.

Gayle's description of that summer evening is also devastating. The setting is the same. It's an almost identical scene – Gayle, Kye and Miss X are together at Miss X's flat – but the story is different. There's no blindfold and everyone's eyes are open, but the evening is equally explosive. A coming-out story collides with a secrecy pact, igniting a brutal fallout between Gayle and Miss X, who are secret lovers and best friends. According to Gayle, by June, she and Miss X were deeply embroiled in a secret romance, one that had been going on for two years. Both found being lesbian difficult to accept, and they were united in the closet. They were also united by Kye, who provided a way for each of them to make their sexuality bearable – both call it 'normal' – a way to be together as boy and girl, rather than girl and girl.

Earlier that year they'd begun having sex. Gayle bought a dildo and they'd spend Sundays at Miss X's flat, hanging out and being intimate. It's now two years in, and Gayle wants to come out to her family, to whom she's close despite her secret – but Miss X doesn't want to. They argue on the phone because Gayle's breaking the pact, but Gayle insists on telling her family, making Miss X angry.

MISS X ON THE STAND: CONSENT

That evening she goes round to Miss X's flat. They had left things in a bad place yesterday, and Gayle wants to make up, make it okay, and things seem to go all right at first. They don't talk about the argument and slip into their Sunday routine – but Gayle notices that Miss X isn't herself; she's a bit distant, quiet.

After watching TV and cuddling, they start to have sex. Gayle puts on the strap-on, becomes Kye – and Miss X still seems quiet.

There's no blow job in this version, but they start on the bed, as Miss X also recalls, and then move to another spot – in this account it's a chair. Miss X is on top, like she said, but she's acting a bit off, seems so much quieter than usual, and Kye notices, asks if she's okay. Miss X says she's fine and they say they love each other. As they finish having sex, just before Kye takes off the strap-on and becomes Gayle, Miss X starts shouting.

'She just switched, like, *switched*,' says Gayle during examination. There are a lot of filler words in her speech, which make her sound hesitant, unsure. Her vocabulary is stuttering and repetitive; she's often asked to speak up. 'Erm, like, acting or, or acting like she was almost shocked, like, startled, erm'. Gayle remembers Miss X saying, 'What the hell! What's this? What're you doing?' as she stood there, half Kye, half Gayle, removing the strap-on, feeling confused, starting to get scared. 'I just remember I kept saying, "What, what, what do you mean? What . . . Like, what d'you mean?"' The rest of the scene unfolds in fragments, just as Miss X's version did: Miss X runs into the bathroom, calls 999, hangs up, comes out, gets dressed, pushes Gayle away, over, down the stairs, as she rushes out. Gayle, hurt from the fall, follows and they argue in the street, say terrible things to each other. They are captured on CCTV footage, which is played at the trials; there's no sound, just two fuzzy figures gesturing at each other on the street, breaking apart. Then Gayle gets in her car, has a panic attack. She drives around manically, eventually to a bridge over a canal, where she gets out and jumps.

2

Rape on the Stand: Myths

Several days after the fight, Miss X went to a police station to file a complaint against Gayle. The response to her report was immediate: twenty-four hours later, Gayle was arrested. Her bedroom was searched. That evening, she was interrogated. Soon after, the police launched 'Operation Imperia', a code name for the investigation into Miss X's allegations, which would eventually lead to charges and finally the trials.

The road to trial was typically long, more than two years until September 2015. That period included endless stages and tests, statements and pre-trial hearings. And finally the trials, when Miss X and Gayle arrive in court to step into the harsh spotlight – twice.

Making a complaint to police, let alone a trial, requires immense resilience. Reading Miss X's statements and examinations, it is clear she found the process punishing. But the case, from a rape justice point of view, was exemplary. An investigation, charges, a trial, a conviction – it's not what most victims experience. In fact, a 2021 UK government report, the *End-to-End Rape Review Report on Findings and Actions*, revealed an appalling statistic: only 1.6 per cent of rape reports result in a charge. That's a tiny percentage. And it's only in relation to those who report rape in the first place (less than one in five, research suggests). Nor is this news, exactly. 'The figures for prosecuting rape have always been worryingly low,' the review notes.

Against these odds, Miss X was believed at every stage – first by police, then by prosecutors, and finally by a jury. Why was Miss X's case exemplary, and why do 98.4 per cent of rape complaints reach a dead end? The 2021 rape review, like the many reports that preceded it, corroborated what feminist advocacy groups had been pointing out for years: the vast majority of rape victims are failed by the justice system. The review suggested the entire apparatus was beset with problems at every stage, from police procedure ('improvised' decisions) and the prevalence of 'rape myths' (the perceived credibility of an allegation), to the expectations about 'the perfect case' and the tortured rules of proving sexual offences.

Perceptions about 'real' rape shift through time. In recent years, persistent prejudicial assumptions, such as the notion that 'real' victims fight back or report immediately, have been demonstrated by mock jury studies. Although the rape trial's (infamous) 'cautionary instruction' was abolished in the 1990s – warning jurors that rape was an 'easy charge to make but difficult to defend' – suspicions linger.

Rape is not an easy charge to prove. 'No injured party [is] more distrusted than the rape victim', writes Joanna Bourke in her book *Rape: A History from 1860 to the Present* (2007). Rape (along with murder) has been a fixation of criminal law, a class of crime about which there can be 'no controversy', the legal thinking goes: any 'civilized' society would criminalize the act. As such, rape is viewed as a *mala in se*: not wrong because it is legally wrong, but because it is inherently wrong (an 'evil'). Why, then, is it so hard a charge to make?

Bourke points to a central problem – the credibility of the victim, and credibility of the act. Histories of rape often turn to the Victorian period, because acts created in these years form the backbone of criminal law today, significantly the Offences Against the Person Act of 1861, of which the Sexual Offences Act is a more recent offshoot. In this period, rape was outlawed, considered an evil act. And yet, Victorian legal thinkers wondered, what precisely *was* an act of rape? There were vying theories about a true rape act – who could be raped, and how.

Rape in this period was defined as 'carnal knowledge of a woman, by force and against her will'. Force was the critical element. A victim had to prove continuous physical resistance to prove rape. This crime of force was very wrong. But, the thinking went, it rarely *did* happen.

In fact – jurists and doctors argued – the act of rape was extremely difficult, if not impossible, to achieve. A popular notion known as 'the vibrating sword' theory posited that it was 'almost impossible' to rape a woman who resisted (in the words of one jurist writing in 1831), just as it was extremely difficult to sheath a sword in a vibrating scabbard. This notion was repeated time and time again in nineteenth-century textbooks of medical jurisprudence, notes Bourke. In these texts, doctors spoke of the power of a woman's pelvic muscles, which were almost insurmountable when it came to forced entry.

These theories suggested that women merely needed to

'vibrate' their pelvis to repel an attack. If a woman *was* to be raped, it was generally agreed that one man could not do it alone; to stop a woman's pelvic muscles from 'vibrating', perhaps four men would be necessary to hold a victim still. This eliminated most complaints. The logic was circular: women who claimed to have been successfully 'raped' by a single man had not actually resisted, and therefore were not actually 'raped'.

By this logic, most reports were not credible. Women were lying.

The belief that women lie about rape is a pernicious rape myth with deep roots. It can be traced back to the biblical Book of Genesis, a collection of ancient stories, local myths and popular lore. The parable of Potiphar's wife tells the story of a false complaint against the young and fair Joseph. Potiphar's wife, who does not have a name, accuses Joseph of rape when he refuses her advances. She is the scorned, revengeful woman, lying to hide her sin, while Joseph is the true victim.

Lying women also feature in bed trick tales. Stories like Chaucer's Reeve's Tale are made comic by the suggestion that wives actually enjoy sex and like being deceived – and who, in the bed trick's fantasy, know what is going on and are in fact feigning surprise.

By the Victorian era, bed hopping was a trope of adventure novels. Swashbucklers like Alexandre Dumas's *The Three Musketeers* were riveting to read, crammed with perilous duels and secret trysts. In one episode, Dumas's hero D'Artagnan tricks his enemy, Milady, in a darkened room by hiding in a closet and pretending to be her lover. Daring feats were inspired by the lives of mythic figures like

Casanova, the erotic adventurer, whose lavish memoirs were published in the 1820s.

To Victorian jurists and physicians, most rape accounts were not credible. The act appeared as improbable, perhaps, as a real-life bed trick. And yet, the opposite was true. As early as the 1830s, one kind of rape was recognized as credible: rape by deception.

In cases reaching courts, Victorian wives explained they had been cheated into sex – not by force (an account that required multiple men) but by trickery. These were bed tricks come true but stripped of humour, as virtuous wives complained they had been deceived in the dark by strangers pretending to be their husbands.

Take the testimony of Mary Capell, reaching court in 1838. She was staying in a lodging house and explained that her husband, Thomas, got into bed after her. It was very dark, and there was no oil lamp beside this unfamiliar bed. When he reached for her, she submitted. The dreadful discovery only came afterwards, when he lay there spent. It wasn't Thomas but a stranger.

Other wives described the moment of apprehension after lovemaking was complete – stroking a husband's hair, hearing an unfamiliar voice in the dark, seeing a foreign shadow slip out of the room.

Fascinatingly, in these decades, stories of husband impersonation appeared to be more credible than accounts of 'regular' rape. A spate of cases led to some rare convictions. The new, credible scenario was this: a wife's superhuman pelvic muscles stilled by way of a trick.

Why did these reports hit home when so many other accounts did not? For a judge assessing Mary's case, 'the fraud' legitimized her allegation. It explained how the stranger had got around her defences and thwarted her (pelvic) 'resistance'. Another judge came to a similar conclusion: 'resistance is prevented by the fraud of the man who pretends to be her husband', he stated.

At first, tricked wives were compared to blind women, or seen as victims of a kind of property offence comparable to 'theft in the dark'. But increasingly, the crime was understood as a form of fraud. One judge drew an analogy with a man signing a contract, which had been secretly whisked away when his back was turned and substituted for another. 'It cannot be said that he agreed to the terms of the latter document ... although his signature appears thereon,' he reasoned.

Rape by deception spoke to contemporary anxieties about the dangers facing women, but also the proliferation of fraud. A series of financial scandals unfolding in the 1850s stirred up fears about 'white-collar crime', as it would later be named, committed by subtle charlatans posing as persons of respectability. In these years, new legislation regulating Victorian bankers emerged out of a growing fear of, and obsession with, types of fraud.

Bed hopping also worried husbands for another reason, seeming to tug on primitive fears around paternity. Before DNA testing, it was impossible to ever be sure of fatherhood, unless you married a virgin and secured a 'good' wife who would never commit adultery. But what happened if she was tricked in the dark?

Sexual fraud was legislated against in 1861; its scope was then crystallized in a judgment of 1888, which set out the deceptions that counted (made distinct from 'seductions' that did not). This Victorian judgment remained the basis of sexual fraud law over the next century.

Then came 2003, when rape by deception law was rebooted in the new Sexual Offences Act. Though it retained a Victorian wording, the offence was refigured under the rubric of consent. New provisions, titled Section 76 – still in place today – set out circumstances where consent is gained by deception and is thus not consent. Here, sexual fraud law was amplified and bestowed with special power. If employed at trial, it triggers an exceptional rule, which makes rape and assault by penetration easier to prosecute.

Section 76 is used to convict Gayle at the first trial.

Rape justice reviews, probing the 'worryingly low' prosecution rate, explain that many cases fail the evidence test. This stage takes place after police have investigated, often months after an initial complaint. At this stage, prosecutors examine all the evidence and decide whether to take a case forward. The step requires CPS lawyers to ask whether there is a 'realistic prospect of conviction', and whether a jury is 'more likely than not' to find a defendant guilty. It's a calculation, and ultimately a judgement. Cases without enough evidence (or enough of the right evidence) are considered unprosecutable. Some prosecutors blame this common complication on the nature of the offence: usually two people, reporting on something that happened in private between them. Given these conditions, rape is sometimes referred to as 'a black box'. This description suggests the internal workings of rape are hidden, because nobody can see into the private room in which it so often takes place. A third party – a detective, a courtroom – has nothing to go on, except what each person says.

And Section 76 makes all the difference by affecting the likelihood of conviction. Because, unlike any other section of the Act, it changes the rules of the trial, altering what a Crown prosecutor must prove.

*

For so many complainants, reporting a sexual offence to the police can lead to nothing. It is the beginning and the end, the opening and the close.

Miss X's initial complaint is missing from the transcripts. The videoed statements recording her second interview take place a few days later, after Gayle's arrest. This is her witness statement. Already, the complaint has reached the next step.

On the night of the fight, she is last seen clashing with Gayle. They stand below a traffic light, which signals mindlessly: go, change, stop. Their postures suggest conflict. Eventually Miss X turns and runs, while Gayle stands there for a moment before slowly walking to her car.

After the CCTV footage, there is a gap. Miss X doesn't go to the police station right away. She speaks about this period occasionally in her statements and refers to it on the stand. Importantly, there are also phone records presented at trial, which track the calls and text messages sent in this fraught period.

To write the following scene, I pieced together the hours and days between the fight and Miss X's complaint. By spending so much time with the transcripts, I felt I could imagine what Miss X felt. At times, I tried to resist the limits of the records, breathing into openings even as the evidence held me close.

RAPE ON THE STAND: MYTHS

*

Miss X is out of breath but she runs up the stairs. After fumbling with the key, she gets into her flat. Then she leans against the door, vibrating with fury. She is so angry that it scares her. The emotion is disorienting, and she has no idea what to do next. The emergency operator said to call the police. But she doesn't. Instead, she sits on the floor where it all happened. There are memories everywhere – the bed, the sofa, the chair. She spent so many hours here with Gayle, so many hours here with Kye.

'You raped my heart,' she texts Gayle, 'you raped my life'. She is full of white-hot rage, a furnace of emotions. She begins to torture herself by remembering little details. She remembers Gayle coming round on her birthday, bringing flowers from Kye. She remembers how they'd gush over the engagement, Gayle saying 'you two are made for each other' and promising to walk her down the aisle.

Her head is pounding. She sends more messages saying furious things. Then her phone rings but she doesn't pick up. It rings and rings.

She feels poisoned and broken. She isn't close to her family. Who can she tell – the police? A nurse? She thinks about getting an examination but she can't bear to. She'll have to explain everything. Disgust rises in her. She's got nothing to show anyway, not even a scratch. Just the engagement ring, his letters, the doting texts. The damage is all on the inside. And Gayle is the one with the bruises; Miss X remembers pushing her down the stairs, watching her fall.

Mindlessly, she starts cleaning the flat, ripping off the bed sheets and scrubbing the walls. Afterwards, she kicks herself. She feels like she can't do anything right.

Days pass. When she tells herself what happened, it sounds unbelievable, absurd. She knows she's got to tell somebody, but she's scared they'll laugh. She's scared they'll think she's stupid. A fool. How can she ever explain it? Every day she thinks about going to the police station. She knows the building – she's walked past it a hundred times. But she's embarrassed. When she imagines telling the police, she imagines a room of men.

It was normal! – how can she explain that?

The final term of university is over and her friends have already left town. But Miss X has a job so she's decided to stay. She wants to forget so badly and when she goes into work, it feels like a relief at first. She smiles at her colleagues and asks them about their boyfriends. She is bubbly like she always is. But inside, it is different. She's a mess. The rage is imploding into a rot of self-loathing and she is having dark thoughts. Internally, she's chiding herself for being an idiot. Hating herself for going along with it – the years, on and on. It's eating her up, like a worm in her gut.

Can it be rape when it felt like love?

Every day, there are messages from Gayle, apologizing for the fight or begging Miss X to take her back. Sometimes Miss X replies, but she's repulsed by the exchange.

She knows it was rape – it's got to be. But she wonders how a woman can do that to another woman. She wonders if anyone will believe her, believe what Gayle's done.

When Gayle reaches her at work, blabbering down the phone and invading her workplace, something in Miss X snaps.

'I'm here because I've got to stop her,' she tells a female police officer, as she files her initial complaint. 'She's dangerous. She's mental. She could do this to someone else.'

RAPE ON THE STAND: MYTHS

*

If a rape complaint fails the evidence test, the CPS won't prosecute, no matter how serious or sensitive it is. This means no charges, no trial and no verdict.

But why is rape so difficult to evidence?

Unlike murder, the forensic aftermath of rape can be inconclusive. Sometimes police struggle to verify whether a crime even took place. The 'black box' of rape points to the way that, often, there is little first-hand evidence (called 'direct evidence'), beyond a testimony, for the prosecution to present.

On top of this, the way rape and assault by penetration are defined in law can pose complications. The 2003 Act organizes offences around lack of consent. In so many ways, the logic of consent cuts to the dirty heart of the offence, offering a much better understanding of what rape is, what it violates; but in practice, when consent is formulated as a negative, it can make offences difficult to demonstrate. In order to prove an assault happened, the prosecution has to demonstrate something *not* happening: consent. And it's hard to prove a negative – harder to prove that something *didn't* happen, rather than did happen, because it's harder to measure or observe something that didn't occur. There's less evidence to assess. Most sex trials aren't about demonstrating whether sex happened, but about demonstrating consent – or lack of it. What's more, reflecting the two sides of the agreement, proving these offences demands proving a negative, twice: the complainant's lack of consent, but also, crucially, the defendant's lack of belief in the complainant's consent.

Prosecutors tell their stories under constraints – at every sex trial, arguing a narrative in relation to the Sexual

Offences Act, as the sexual contract is scrutinized. Assault by penetration is defined in four parts called elements, labelled 'a', 'b', 'c' and 'd'. To prove the offence, a prosecutor must work through the elements. 'A' and 'b' are often (though not always) simple to establish: that penetration took place; that it was intentional and sexual (what is known as the *actus reus*, the guilty act). At both trials, neither of these points are contested. Both Gayle and Miss X agree the liaisons took place. It's the next two elements of the offence that are in dispute – both of which relate to lack of consent.

After hearing the examinations, cross-examinations and arguments, the jury will have to decide it's sure that Miss X didn't consent (part 'c') and that Gayle *did not reasonably believe* in Miss X's consent but acted anyway (part 'd'). Proving a state of mind can be difficult because the agreement, or lack of it, is intangible. There's no paperwork to examine, no signatures to assess – only memory, testimony, what a complainant and a defendant say. These last elements tend to block conviction; some prosecutors refer to this barrier, laid in the 1970s, as 'the consent wall', due to the central role consent plays.

And Section 76 changes this. The special rule relates specifically to the consent parts, 'c' and 'd'. If triggered during a trial, it allows a prosecutor to bypass these tricky elements by negating consent.

At the first trial, it's Corbett-Jones's job to prove the elements of the offence. When it comes to 'c' and 'd', he will have Section 76 in mind. It is a gift to the prosecution. The Crown will try to show it applies and trigger it, while the defence will attempt to avoid it at all costs.

Section 76, which is found towards the end of the Act,

is rarely triggered. Judge Dutton says as much to the barristers in a private get-together – a tête-à-tête called matters of law, which is a convention of any trial. It takes place on the fourth day, when all the evidence has been presented. The jury is sent out of the room, but the mics are still running. 'I never thought, actually, that in the whole of my career since the 2003 Act was passed, I would ever use Section 76,' Dutton confides. The section is narrow, Victorian, rare. Its phrasing dates back to 1888. When triggered, the section allows a prosecutor to sidestep the consent parts, and to get around the tricky elements, which help to keep prosecution rates 'worryingly low'.

*

Why does consent, the magic rule, also create a barrier, a wall?

Since the 1990s, a complainant's word is legally enough to prove lack of consent ('c'). But even when jurors do believe complainants – and often they do – it's only half the job, because absence of consent alone is not enough. There are two consent parts, two negatives to prove. And the last element ('d') is the trickiest of all, relating to the defendant's state of mind – what is known as *mens rea*, the guilty mind.

Responsibility is a central tenet of criminal law. In order for a defendant to be found guilty of an offence, the prosecution must prove intention. If a person didn't mean to do something, if it was a mistake, they're not guilty of the offence – or at least, guilty of a lesser one. When it comes to sexual offences, the guilty mind is famously hard to demonstrate because it's impossible to see into somebody's head. Unless a defendant gives evidence at trial – and frequently they do not – the prosecution may have nothing to go on, because states of mind rarely leave an evidential trace.

To this day, the difficulty is this: if a sex trial overcomes 'c' and takes a complainant at their word, it still faces the significant hurdle of 'd'. A defendant can simply give no narrative at all, and their barrister can focus on undermining the complainant and arguing the allegation is not *certainly* true. If the defendant does take the stand to claim an honest belief in consent, the strongest evidence of their mindset tends to be their word too. And this is where trials can get stuck – unless there is some remarkable direct evidence that shows the defendant has a guilty mind . . . perhaps they recorded themselves in the act (rare); perhaps they bragged about it in a text to a friend (also rare). Very often, sex trials turn on this final element – the defendant's belief in consent – haunted not by the question of whether a complainant refused, but whether their refusal was clearly conveyed. If jurors come to believe a defendant didn't *know* the complainant wasn't consenting – didn't hear them say no, didn't see any signals saying no – and accepts those errors as reasonable, then it's not rape, it's not assault by penetration. It's a terrible misunderstanding, but it's not a crime.

Together these last two elements (and especially the last) make rape and assault by penetration difficult to prove.

And this is where Section 76 comes to the rescue. The special rule smashes into 'c' and 'd', breaking consent's wall. Instead of proving negatives, Section 76 offers the Crown a short cut. The rule means that Corbett-Jones only has to prove the first two elements of the offences: that intentional penetration took place, and it was sexual. He can then skip the last two elements, and focus instead on something else:

deception. If he can demonstrate that Gayle tricked Miss X about the sex she was having (the phrase in the relevant part of Section 76 is 'intentionally deceived' as to 'the nature' of the act), then that's it – she's guilty. It's the end of the consent question and a conclusion of Gayle's guilt: all four elements of the offence will have been proved. With Section 76 in play, the trial's core question shifts from 'did Miss X consent?' to a new one: 'did Gayle Newland deceive?'

3

Gayle Newland on the Stand: Deception

Defendants take the stand second.

Gayle watches the trial unfold from the dock. She's there on the first day, when the indictment is read out, and the Crown gives its opening speech. She's there for Miss X's DVD statements, and she watches Miss X's examinations unfold.

The Crown is bringing forth a complex and rare charge – that Gayle effectively tricked Miss X into signing the sexual contract. Tricked her best friend into sex that she would not otherwise have agreed to. Why else would Miss X call 999, run into the street, go to the police? Why else was a dildo box found in Gayle's bedroom? Why else is this trial happening, this ordeal, except for the reasons Miss X says?

When Gayle finally leaves the dock and begins her examination, replacing Miss X on the stand, it's day three of the first trial: Wednesday, 9 September 2015.

Unlike a complainant, the accused is visible. There's no anonymity protection for defendants. Photos of Gayle are taken each day as she enters and exits the courtroom. By

GAYLE NEWLAND ON THE STAND: DECEPTION

Tuesday, before she's taken the stand, news items appear online, and the case goes viral.

Most defendants have nothing to prove; the burden of proof rests squarely on the prosecution. But with the shadow of Section 76 hanging over the trial, that changes. In order to prevent the section applying, the *defence* must now show that Gayle has not been intentionally deceptive. The special rule refocuses the trial onto Gayle, and onto deception.

By 4 p.m., it's only Miss X's story that has been heard and questioned. Now it is Gayle's turn – and the chance to put forward her story in her own words.

To avoid the Section 76 short cut, her own evidence is now crucial.

As Gayle undergoes examination, the defence barrister, Nigel Power, draws out her story. She denies Miss X's allegations, saying the dildo was consented to, her tongue was consented to, and everyone's eyes were open.

Hidden sexuality is at the centre of the trial. On the stand, Gayle describes a life of secrecy. As long as she can remember, she was gay; 'I've always known,' she says – but she didn't have the words. She says she couldn't be herself, and she struggled with secret feelings.

That's when Kye came into the picture, when she was thirteen years old. As Gayle explains it, if she could be a boy – speak online as a boy, appear online as a boy – then she could feel 'normal', 'comfortable'. Throughout school and up until the first year of university, Gayle says she appeared straight to her family and friends. Nobody knew who she was on the inside, and online – a lesbian. No one knew of this whole other life she had, expressed through Kye.

But with Miss X, says Gayle, it was different. 'She knew from the get-go, from the very, very beginning,' she explains.

Was Gayle intentionally deceptive? That is the question at the heart of the first trial. The problem is, her defence turns on a deception of sorts: the closet. To prevent Section 76 applying, Gayle must open up the closet and explain Kye. She must illuminate her interior life to make it less suspicious and less obscured.

Examination is followed by the dreaded cross-examination. Gayle is grilled by the Crown barrister for most of Thursday and Friday morning. Matthew Corbett-Jones is out to prove sexual trickery, and demonstrate a false sexual contract – intentional deception, fraud. He turns to two exhibits – love letters to Kye, written by Miss X, in the weeks before she made the complaint. One letter reads:

> To My Loving Fiancé. These two years have flown by. Definitely because we are having so much fun and are so in love. You are my everything and more. Waiting for you was worth it. You are my other half, my everything, the light in my heart and the rhythm it beats to. I'll be with you for ever and all time.

There is a copy of the letter in the evidence bundle, for the jury to see. After reading it aloud, Corbett-Jones steps up his attack.

'What caused that person to suddenly contact the police and tell the police that you had been sexually abusing her, posing as a man?' he asks. In the preceding days, Miss X has claimed that she was tricked for two years by Gayle, faking it as Kye. In her testimony, Kye's whole story, his whole life

– the thousands of text messages, thousands of calls – was a fiction: behind it all was Gayle, perpetuating a plot.

For Miss X's account to convince, Gayle needs to be a uniquely good plot-maker, exceptionally persuasive, a seductive spinner of tales. Corbett-Jones asks Gayle about her degree – she was studying Creative Writing and Marketing at the time. 'So creative writing is one of your skills,' he suggests. Pointing to Kye's Facebook account, and turning again to the bundle of evidence, he begins to claim that Gayle controlled Miss X through Kye, and through a plot.

At this point, it's Thursday afternoon. Gayle is weary on the stand. She stutters a lot. There are 'erms' in her responses. Often she's asked to speak up. The transcriber, who has listened to the recording, repeatedly writes, '(defendant distressed)' or '(defendant very distressed)' or '(inaudible)'.

Miss X lost friends, Corbett-Jones continues, left a job – all masterminded by Gayle, playing two roles, a best friend and Kye. Over two years, she is accused of using her creative writing skills to manipulate Miss X by expertly inventing the character of Kye. She is accused of creating an atmosphere of paranoia by playing the role of an overprotective boyfriend, warning Miss X away from colleagues and friends – from everyone, that is, except Gayle. And ultimately, she is accused of using a fiction to control Miss X, to 'play her like a puppet', as the barrister will phrase it.

'I don't see how that's possible?' Gayle pushes back. 'I can't make someone do anything they don't wanna do. Everyone has their own free will.'

But Corbett-Jones is advancing a specific story, one with explicit dynamics: the powerful and the vulnerable, master and puppet. In this narrative, Gayle is the cunning writer, pulling the strings, deceiving Miss X with the threads of Kye. Miss X, meanwhile, is the manipulated party, overpowered by Gayle's fiction – naive, vulnerable, duped.

Slipping between tenses, Corbett-Jones accuses, 'She believes – she believed that you were a man.'

But Gayle, refusing these powers, says she couldn't have controlled her friend, or reality, in this way. 'Why would she believe that? Why would she believe that? ... She's an intelligent young woman. She's a very, very intelligent young woman. Why, why would she ever believe that?'

*

Section 76 changes the focus of a trial, and says deception voids consent – but why?

Sexual fraud law is rooted in the Victorian era, when rape was understood as a crime of force. But consent-rule jurisdictions continue to recognize that deception can turn sex into rape. In today's terms, deception is understood to 'vitiate' consent – a legal word that means to impair or destroy legal validity.

For philosophers, the answer lies in autonomy – because deception disrupts personal autonomy. Autonomy is the right to make informed decisions about your body. In a sexual context, there are two sides: positive sexual autonomy, which is the right to have sex with whom you want (as long as they want it too); and negative sexual autonomy, which is the right to say no, at any time. This makes consent – saying yes, saying no – an exercise in sexual autonomy.

And deception meddles with this – it erodes a person's autonomy, warping it. That's why it 'vitiates' consent. Because deception takes away the freedom to choose, and it distorts the choices available.

The general principle is deception vitiates consent. But deception is a loose word, a concept in motion, inflected by time and place. It's slippery, there's a scale. Philosophers of deception have made a distinction between 'active' and 'passive' deception – the first, to actually invent information, to intentionally lie; the second, to conceal, to withhold a piece of information, to not correct an assumption. And when it comes to deceptive sex, what does deception mean? What lies or omissions count?

Modern UK sexual offences law has by and large focused on 'active' deceptions – explicit lies, rather than hidden ones. But the question of exactly which 'active' deceptions spoil consent is one that has troubled modern sexual fraud law across this century.

People lie all the time, especially when it comes to intimacy, seduction, sex. From a purist view, any lie could undermine sexual autonomy, and turn sex into rape, because lies distort a person's choices, and damage their free will. Some legal philosophers contend that there is no lie too trivial, as long as that lie is 'active' and as long as it is a deal-breaker – that is, if it makes a meaningful difference to whether a person consents to sex. As argued by the scholar Jonathan Herring, 'I love you', told as a lie to seduce someone into bed, violates sexual autonomy; it distorts someone's choice; therefore, the act that follows isn't sex: it's rape.

But this position is unpopular and, in practice, unrealistic. In real life, total sexual autonomy can feel like a crazy, impossible standard, and legally the deceptions that count have always been qualified, with some frauds recognized as criminal (like husband impersonation), and others (promises of marriage) seen as 'minor wrongs'. These definitions reach back in case law, shaped in precedents decided when rape was understood as a crime of force, and before the consent model came to be.

Deception fascinated Victorians in a society alarmed by fraudulent practices and the dangers facing women. Fraud, it was increasingly reasoned, could trick women out of resisting sexual advances. Victorian case law reveals two kinds of fraud emerging as significant. Alongside husband impersonation, another sequence of cases featured a new, shocking culprit: Victorian doctors. These cunning practitioners, sometimes quacks, were accused of pretending sex was not sex, that it was something else – a medical procedure. The victims were naive virgins who submitted to an operation or procedure, without knowing what it really was.

These were nasty accounts, shocking abuses of power. In a case from 1850, a young woman believed that she was undergoing medical treatment, rather than sex; she lay on the examination table, without any idea what she was submitting to. In another case from 1877, a man, posing as a surgeon, convinced a young woman that sex was a necessary operation, a way to break 'a string' inside of her body and to cure her fits. She let him 'operate' on her, without knowing what the act really was. More cases followed; all featured young women tricked into sex by men in positions of power.

Deceptions about the very 'nature' or 'purpose' of the act, as the wording went, were clearly understood as rape, resulting in a chain of guilty verdicts since the first case reached court in 1850. Adding to the legal lucidity, the power dynamics of these cases were stark: cunning doctors, quack or otherwise, wielding specialism and knowledge to prey on naive virgins – their innocence plausible in an era that actively refrained from educating women about sex.

Worryingly, other cases were reaching the courts too, following the discovery of chloroform, which began to be used on patients during surgery in the 1850s. Reports in the press described allegations of attempted rape using the substance. The accusations centred on one group with unparalleled access to the drug: doctors.

In 1888 came the crystallizing judgment, which decided what types of fraud might destroy consent. A judge named James Fitzjames Stephen sought to stipulate the scope of sexual fraud. 'The maxim that fraud vitiates consent is too general,' he worried. 'If fraud vitiates consent ... many seductions would be rapes'. As a result, his judgment tightly restricted sexual fraud to two types – fraud relating to 'the nature of the act itself' (the doctors), 'or as to the identity of the person who does the act' (the husband impersonators). This dichotomy, fixed in law, would become known as 'fraud in the factum' and 'fraud in the inducement'.

In practice, the judgment was rarely invoked. These cases were oddities, and yet they held an outsized place in the imagination. On the one hand, accounts of real-life bed tricks, stirring up a cocktail of fear and (narrative) delight. But also, on the other, less ambivalently, they raised a concern about, and abhorrence of, unscrupulous doctors.

Across the twentieth century, cases involving physicians continued to reach courts. Irregular as they were, the allegations proved persistent. And they were not restricted to the UK. Take *People v Minkowski* (1962), a case from California, in which a series of young women had consented to what they thought was a pelvic examination. As the girls lay on the examination table, with their feet in the stirrups, the doctor had used a speculum and then inserted his penis. While the definition of rape inspired debates, cases such as these were considered unambiguous. As a judge stated, referring to the Minkowski case, these women had consented to 'an act of an altogether different nature ... penetration by a medical instrument'.

Perhaps understandably, when these cases did occur, they attracted media attention, often in excess. Turning on a total breach of the Hippocratic oath, these horrible, compelling stories spoke to the archetype of an evil doctor, a timeless figure, a kind of folk devil.

The trial of Thomas Courtney in 1992 is a good example. Courtney had for many years posed as a Harley Street gynaecologist and founder of a charity for HIV-positive women called Womb. He portrayed himself as a national expert on AIDS and lived off donations given to his charity. Police would later describe him as the 'perfect rapist' – respectable, charming, plausible. At trial, a series of former patients, all vulnerable women, explained how Courtney had turned gynaecological examinations into sexual acts. He was found guilty in December 1992 and sentenced to seven years.

It was cases like these that kept the narrative of 'fraud in the factum' alive.

And alive it was, ten years later, when the Sexual Offences Act was being rewritten. The Act was touted as 'a new code of sex offences [for] the new century', which would 'set the boundaries' for society by way of consent. Importantly, it included the first statutory definition of consent, defined by way of sexual autonomy, the key words being 'freedom', 'capacity' and 'choice'. The terms of consent were also added, circumstances that can vitiate the agreement – including Section 76.

This section was at once old and new – old because it reflected the 1888 judgment, with two parts labelled 'a' and 'b' (one for deception about the act, another for impersonation). And new because it was given extraordinary status: during a trial, Section 76 could trigger a rule, called a presumption.

Presumptions are legal instructions telling a court where to begin, and what to assume in the absence of evidence. Some rules are written into the procedure, such as the 'presumption of innocence' – the instruction for juries to assume a defendant is innocent, until they are shown to be guilty. There are others too, such as the 'presumption of sanity', which says a defendant is to be presumed sane, unless shown otherwise.

In criminal law there are two kinds of presumption. The first is 'rebuttable', which is a legal word meaning that a presumption can be proved otherwise. The presumption of innocence and the presumption of sanity are rebuttable. Over the course of a trial, a defendant can be shown to be otherwise – shown to be guilty, or shown to be insane. The second, and much rarer, is 'conclusive' (or irrebuttable).

Section 76 is irrebuttable.

If a deception described in the provisions is demonstrated, the defence is prevented from making its case: there is no way to counter, no way to push back. The last two elements of the offence – the consent parts, usually the hardest to demonstrate – will be conclusively presumed.

And that's conclusively that: no matter what, the defence cannot argue that sex was consensual. If these deceptions are present, the law says that consent is inconceivable.

THE BED TRICK

It's summer 2013. In a well-kept village, not far outside a city, a doorbell rings. It's 10.50 a.m. Two police officers ask for Gayle Newland. She is taken to a local police station and put in a custody suite, where she'll stay for about ten hours. Meanwhile, her bedroom is searched, and several objects are found that will become exhibits, including the dildo box, the love letters and a black eye mask. That evening, she is interviewed. The questions are read aloud at trial.

Have you ever had any sexual relations with a female?

Have you ever had any form of sexual contact with Miss X?

Do you own any sex toys?

Have you ever used any on anyone else?

Did you organize a hotel room to meet her in?

Did you pay?

Did you instruct her to wear a blindfold?

Did you think Miss X would consent to having you penetrate her by the strap-on penis?

Have you disposed of the strap-on penis?

Did you think she would have consented to this?

Would she have wanted to do that with a female?

Gayle stays silent. She's spoken to a solicitor. It's her right.

This right is a fundamental principle of criminal law, tied to the presumption of innocence. The right to silence means that a defendant does not have to prove or disprove facts during an interrogation and later, at a trial. They are not required to answer any questions, confirm any statement – nor testify at trial at all. They are presumed innocent until proven guilty.

Eventually Gayle is sent home, but the police decide the complaint merits an investigation. She is 'released under investigation' and Operation Imperia begins.

This means the police start to make enquiries and compile evidence. First, the digital strip search. Miss X has one phone, Gayle has two. Gayle's devices were seized during her arrest. Three laptops were found in her bedroom, along with the two phones: a pink Nokia and a Blackberry – hers, and Kye's. Miss X hangs onto her phone for a little while longer, eventually giving it up a month later. She keeps her laptop for nearly two years – a fact that becomes a point of contention for the defence. (An expert statement, presented by Power, suggests continued use had 'degraded' the ability to recover evidence: 'The effect is akin to the tide washing away footprints in the sand,' the expert explained.)

Examining the phones and laptops, emails and social media accounts, the investigation homed in on Gayle and Miss X, but also a third party: Kye. As the police looked for evidence to support Miss X's allegations, investigators reached back in time, digging up Kye's communications with Miss X, which had been going on for two years. The police entered Kye's online world, contacting his friends, extracting his messages from Facebook and taking screenshots of his posts. But investigators also tried to reconstruct what happened that night, and in the days running up to Miss X's complaint, gathering records of the 999 call, the CCTV footage and witnesses to the aftermath of Gayle's jump. And a log of text messages between Gayle and Miss X, sent that evening and in the days after.

That night is important because it is closer in time to the investigation. Sex is a private act, and it can be hard to compile evidence, beyond what each person says. But the fight, and what happened after, is more public. Miss X went home and tried to carry on like nothing happened. But it was different for Gayle. So much happened in the hours and days that followed. There are lots of records presented at trial; most of them concern Gayle.

The transcripts are perplexing to read in more ways than one. They don't lay out the story from beginning to end. Due to the nature of the trial, accounts are built up, only to be whittled down. As one narrative gets going, another is cut short, abandoned.

After meandering through the transcripts, I begin to piece together Gayle's narrative of the hours after the fight, and the days leading up to her arrest.

*

Gayle is not in a good way after the fight, when Miss X had 'switched, like *switched*', when they said terrible things to each other in the road outside.

In court, her memory of the evening is blurred. She remembers feeling confused and scared, getting in her car, driving around. Her thoughts are spiralling. She is so anxious that it's painful. Her best friend, the person that she's shared everything with, her shame, her deepest secrets, the only person she's ever had sex with, is calling her a liar, a freak. Something is horribly broken. And it's because she wants to come out to her parents. For the first time, she's going to tell someone other than Miss X that she's gay and that she's Kye. The secret has been eating her up. But now the fight. Now the fallout. Now the world is closing in.

She thinks she'll do anything to make it stop. She begins to have thoughts of self-annihilation. She thinks of a bridge near her old school. There's a road beneath it. She imagines jumping into the traffic and ending it, but she's scared.

Miss X texts her. Gayle doesn't say when she reads these messages, which say terrible things. ('You are sick', 'You ruined my life'.)

All Gayle remembers is that she hates herself and wants to die. She hates being in the closet. She hates being Kye. And now Miss X hates her too. She wants it all to be over. Now she's thinking, compulsively: I need to kill myself, I need to kill myself, I need to find somewhere I can kill myself.

At some point, there's a canal. She's driving and it's just there. She doesn't know where she is, although later she'll realize she is trying to drive home. She's just been driving, on and on. There's a layby and she quickly, suddenly, pulls in. She pauses, even as she decides, and tries to call her mum. She tries to call Miss X. But nobody picks up.

It's still light outside. There are cars going by, fast, although they slow down at the bridge, which is narrow and bumped. She stands there, looking down at the dark water. Then she climbs onto the ledge, and jumps.

It hurts.

And somebody sees.

She is found – wet, shaking, hypothermic.

Gayle remembers a policewoman. She remembers pulling herself out. Her ankle is injured because the canal wasn't deep. She is soaked through and shaking. She is mumbling, crying. An ambulance is coming. She remembers sitting on the canal bank. There are other people there too, strangers; someone tries to calm her down, but it doesn't work. Then the ambulance arrives, and she's bundled in, taken to a hospital nearby. There, in the ward, the policewoman asks her questions, and Gayle says that she's done something bad, and that her friend will not forgive her.

Documents tracking these hours become part of the prosecution's bundle. The policewoman will give a statement, repeating Gayle's words to the court.

The next day, Gayle is at home with her family. She doesn't say how she got there. She doesn't describe her parents getting a call in the night. She doesn't describe them coming to her bedside at the hospital. But she's home and injured. It's her ankle that's hurt, but it's her heart too. It feels smashed up, written off, beyond repair. She sits in her bedroom. It's got red walls. She's still hating herself, still crying. She hugs her dog and calls Miss X, again and again, but there's no answer.

Then they text – a run of messages, which will be transcribed by the police, read out in court.

Miss X is angry, as on the night of the fight. She tells Gayle she is 'evil', that she should be 'locked up'.

Gayle apologizes. She writes: 'I love you.' 'I'm still here.' 'It's still me.'

She writes a lot of things.

'I never wanted to hurt you.'

'I will pay for it and already am.'

'I am so sorry.'

These messages are quoted, many times, during the trial.

They appear in the opening of facts, when the first trial begins; they are read out during Gayle's cross-examination; and they appear in the closing speeches. Especially this one:

'I said lies to hide lies', Gayle writes.

'I said lies to hide lies but I didn't lie about everything and it was me and still is.'

*

Sexual trickery is a story that has fascinated humans for centuries. In a survey of bed trick literature, *The Bedtrick: Tales of Sex and Masquerade* (2000), Wendy Doniger describes the plot like this: 'You go to bed with someone you think you know, and when you wake up you discover that it was someone else – another man or another woman, or a man instead of a woman . . . or a god . . . or alien, or a complete stranger'.

In her account, Miss X is essentially saying she was the victim of a bed trick. She says she went to bed with Kye and woke up with Gayle. Instead of darkness or a fairy potion, there was a blindfold. She explains she was devastatingly tricked for months on end.

The plot appears across Greek mythology (in stories of Zeus), in the Old Testament (the story of Jacob and Leah), and in medieval Romance (in tales of King Arthur). But it was Shakespeare who made the bed trick famous; the term arose out of his plays. The plot became a popular theatrical device in Renaissance England, appearing in over forty dramas. Playwrights of this period were fixated on outdoing each other in increasingly tangled and ingenious plots. The bed trick was part of a collection of stage tricks, which included the 'cradle trick' (a switched baby) and the 'head trick' (a misidentified face, following a beheading). Turning on misrecognition, these devices provided dramatists with the opportunity for final-act revelations, misadventure, twists in the play. At times, the bed trick had a darker edge, appearing in Jacobean tragedies alongside treachery and murder. Indeed, Shakespeare's most prominent bed tricks surface in his 'problem plays', such as *Measure for Measure*. Set in Vienna, the play follows a corrupt deputy who enforces neglected sex laws and eventually becomes entangled in a bed trick. The genre of the play is slippery because its tragic elements (a woman robbed of her virtue; a man sentenced to death) are overturned in the course of the drama, and turn out to be tricks: the woman is still a virgin; the innocent man is alive. Later dramatists actually tried to 'improve' the play, bowdlerizing entire plot lines and inserting new characters, such as the production enjoyed by the diarist Samuel Pepys in 1662. Doniger argues that, over the next century, bed tricks lost popularity following the invention of night lights; illumination no longer depended on the moon or a candle, and the darkness necessary for a successful deception became less plausible.

By the Victorian period, *Measure for Measure* was rarely staged, in part due to the bed trick. A critic in 1858 bemoaned the 'blind submission' necessary for the device to work, and the following decades saw an increasing intolerance of the trick's lack of realism and general foolery. Yet as a crime, the bed trick gained seriousness, as it shifted genre from literature into law – entering legislation in 1861, solidifying in 1888, and eventually becoming Section 76 in 2003, the extraordinary sexual fraud provisions that make consent inconceivable.

GAYLE NEWLAND ON THE STAND: DECEPTION

Whom did policy makers imagine these new provisions would punish so conclusively? Was it the cunning men of old? Who would have imagined it would be applied to a case like this one – featuring two women, two students, neither in positions of power?

*

Gayle's cross-examination is long and exhausting, unfolding over two days.

Under attack from the Crown, she pushes back against allegations that she calls 'impossible', in particular the constantly worn blindfold.

'Really? Really? Really?' she asks Corbett-Jones, when he accuses her of duping Miss X with the mask. 'A blindfold the whole time . . . that's what people do? . . . Cos, cos I've never heard of that . . . I'm not the most normal of people but I have never heard of that.'

But asked about the messages sent to Miss X, and about Kye, she starts crying. Words elude her. Once, she has a panic attack. Her father, speaking from the gallery, pleads with the examiner, the judge, to stop.

And finally it's over.

Time to discuss matters of law and Section 76. The jury leaves the room, while the judge and barristers have a private tête-à-tête. Dutton identifies subsection 'a' – under which consent is destroyed if a defendant 'intentionally deceived' a complainant about 'the nature' of the sexual act (the legacy of 'fraud in the factum', the cunning doctors).

The barristers agree it's relevant. This is a pivotal moment. When the jury is called back into the room, the rules have officially changed, and the first trial moves into its final act.

Closing speeches are often a little zealous. The barristers will present arguments, not facts, in a final pitch for the jury's vote. Over the next hour, Corbett-Jones and Power will take the floor. Each will claim that their witness or client is telling the truth, and the other side has been lying.

Corbett-Jones, who goes first, starts by identifying the type of deception Gayle is accused of. 'If somebody is deceived about the nature of the penetration that is taking place then there cannot be consent,' he begins, laying out the law. The central question is, he now informs the jury, one of 'intentional deception', and whether or not 'Miss X was deceived as to the nature of the penetration'. By 'nature', he is referring to the dildo, and how it is a prosthesis made of pink rubber rather than flesh, and 'her tongue', different in nature because it was Gayle's tongue, not Kye's. He explains that consent and deception are 'inextricably linked', and if Miss X was intentionally deceived by Gayle's dildo, Gayle's tongue, then that's that. There's no consent. 'Miss X cannot have consented and this defendant cannot reasonably have believed that she was consenting,' he clarifies.

Never before at a trial had this strain of sexual fraud law, rooted in the 1880s, been applied to queer acts or to a dildo – to two students of the same age, adults of sound mind, legally women, formerly best friends.

Corbett-Jones now begins to tie Gayle's and Miss X's story to the history of 'fraud in the factum' – the cases of quack doctors offering fake medical procedures. Only in this case, the fake procedure is a dildo not a penis, a homosexual act rather than a heterosexual one. Miss X, he begins to argue, is a 'gullible and naive girl', who Gayle 'deliberately targeted'. Naivety is emphasized to explain the blindfold that Miss X says she wore, time and time again, whenever they met up. 'This defendant targeted her,' he continues, 'and exploited those vulnerabilities.' She manipulated and isolated Miss X over many months, he says.

'Fraud in the factum' only works in extremis: one person fantastically innocent, the other uniquely deceptive. 'Bizarre as it may seem,' he tells the jury, 'she trusted that person,' referring to Kye. These characterizations go right back to Corbett-Jones's opening speech, when he introduced the case to the jury for the first time. 'One of the issues in this case that you are going to have to consider as you go through the evidence, is just how gullible and naive you consider the complainant, Miss X, to be,' he notified the jury then, alluding to the blindfold. It's one of the hurdles he knows the prosecution will have to overcome – an imaginative hurdle. 'Such people do exist,' he says – gullible, credulous people. Ironically, he's asking for the jury's credulity too, inviting them to be gullible and credulous – to believe a story that he describes at the outset as 'extraordinary', just as Miss X once did.

For this story to work, Gayle must also fit another extreme – a uniquely deceptive defendant. Victorian cases were populated by cunning men able to deceive young women with power, knowledge and specialism. Gayle, too, in Corbett-Jones's telling, becomes a kind of specialist imbued with powers. That specialism is creative writing. He reminds the jury of Gayle's degree. 'Well, in my submission, she has clearly deployed that to good effect,' he says.

But he now contends it's more sinister still. Gayle controlled Miss X with her seductive plots to the point she took over Miss X's mind entirely, Corbett-Jones argues, 'able to manipulate and control Miss X's, literally, every thought'. It's an extreme story, in which Gayle's creative powers are so good, so skilful, that she 'created in essence, a whole different life', Corbett-Jones says. Gayle tricked her into thinking Kye was real, he submits. She took over her body and her mind, to the point where a dildo felt like a real penis, Kye's penis. And her tongue felt like Kye's tongue. In this way, she deceived Miss X about the 'nature of the act'. But also, he seems to suggest, the nature of reality itself.

The allegations describe a long-running deception. Since there were so many meetings, the indictment lays out a selection of charges: four dildo counts and one tongue count, in different locations over five months in 2013. The exact number of encounters is unknown, perhaps twenty. (Miss X says at the second trial, 'I wasn't counting.') The multiple counts are there to reflect serial behaviour, a pattern of offending: in effect, serial rape.

When it's Power's turn to make his closing speech, he relies on inspiring the very opposite feeling in the jury: incredulity. The specifics of the deception are impossible, he declares, describing Miss X as 'a university-educated, bright woman ... mature and sexually experienced', who could simply not have been deceived in the way she alleges. Any sensible person would have known their boyfriend and best friend were one, Power contends, as he reels off the similarities between Gayle and Kye – the same birthday, the same school, the same course at university, 'the same voice – come on – they had the same voice'. He proposes the complaint is 'literally incredible. It is incapable of belief.' How could they spend days together, and have sex with each other, without Miss X removing the blindfold even once? Simply not plausible! An undetected dildo? *An undetected best friend? Impossible!*

In those final speeches, as Corbett-Jones tries to release the jury's imagination, Power tries to restrain it, each attempting to capture the jury's vote with one story or another.

*

'Well, where does the truth lie?' Judge Dutton asks the jury. 'You are the ones who have to decide.'

It's Monday afternoon, the trial's second week. The jurors are given legal directions by Dutton and a summary of evidence before they are sent to retire. The twelve jurors are taken to a private room by a jury keeper, who is sworn to make sure nobody interrupts the deliberations. They must decide: was Gayle a storyteller, a crafty plotter, hiding in plain sight? Was she a deceptive friend, targeting Miss X, masterminding for months on end the constant blindfold, the secret dildo? Or is this allegation too rare, too extraordinary, a bed trick beyond belief? It all comes down to deception. And it all comes down to imagination.

The jury spends around six hours deliberating, announcing it is ready to deliver verdicts the following afternoon. A foreperson, chosen from among the jurors, stands to read the verdict, and Gayle is brought back into the dock.

It turns out, the jury's imagination has been released.

'Guilty,' the foreperson announces, before delivering further guilty verdicts: 'Guilty,' 'Guilty.'

All are majority verdicts (rather than unanimous verdicts), which means that at least ten jurors agreed and no more than two dissented. The foreperson confirms the ratio was 10–2, which is the legal limit for disagreement with the verdict still passing.

Gayle, who is in the dock, begins to sob.

'How can you send me down for something I haven't done?' she asks.

The court clerk calls for silence. Gayle's part is over. She is not meant to speak.

'How can you send me down for something I haven't done?' Gayle repeats. 'How? How? How? How? How? How can you send me down for something I haven't done? How could – How can you all?'

It's 3 p.m. on 15 September 2015.

Moments after the verdict is announced news items begin to appear online.

3.05 p.m. (*Daily Mail*). 'Woman, 25, who pretended to be a man to dupe female friend into sex is found GUILTY'.

3.07 p.m. (Sky News). 'Convicted After Duping Friend Into Sex. Gayle Newland, 25, cries and shouts in court'.

3.27 p.m. (*Liverpool Echo*). 'Fake penis trial verdict – Gayle Newland found GUILTY'.

Her face, her name, is everywhere.

A month later she is back in the dock to hear Dutton deliver her sentence: eight years. She will go straight to jail. 'These offences are so serious that only an immediate custodial sentence would in any way properly reflect the serious nature of your conduct,' the judge says. Dutton tells her she's getting off lightly; given what she's guilty of, the sentence could be as long as thirteen years. She is now a convicted sex offender. She will be sent to a maximum-security prison and, Dutton explains, be placed on the Sex Offender Register 'indefinitely'.

4

The Closet on the Stand: Sexuality

'Rapists who end up being convicted in a court of law must regard themselves as exceptionally unlucky,' Joanna Bourke writes in *Rape: A History*. From this view, Gayle is an exceptionally unlucky defendant, found guilty twice. From jail, she appeals. Two years later she's granted a retrial. But it's the same outcome: on 29 June 2017, she's found guilty again.

*

At both trials, Gayle tells a story about the closet, about hiding her sexuality for years, while speaking as Kye. She admits she told 'lies' about her sexuality. She says before meeting Miss X that nobody knew she was a lesbian. And nobody knew that she was living online as Kye.

This defence puts Gayle in a tricky position. These are, after all, sexual fraud trials, which means they are an especially dangerous context in which to present yourself as a deceptive person.

The closet has always been seen as a secret place, a place of hiding and withholding, associated with concealment and safety. At the beginning of *Epistemology of the Closet* (1990), a seminal work of queer theory, Eve Kosofsky Sedgwick copies an entry from the Oxford English Dictionary on the word 'closet'. As the entry shows, 'closet' has long signified a private room, 'for privacy or retirement', 'an inner chamber', often a place of 'secluded speculation'.

But as well as a private room, the closet is also a secret room. Quoting a usage from 1586, the entry reads, 'We doe call the most secret place in the house appropriate unto our owne private studies . . . a Closet'. Here, the closet is also a hidden place, perhaps concealing a trouble (as in, 'a skeleton in the closet'), or else, a place to retreat to and hide in – 'a den or lair', where a 'beast' takes refuge.

In her book, Sedgwick examined the origin of the gay closet, describing it as 'the defining structure of gay oppression in this century'. The closet was once a condition of being gay. Secrecy was necessary. In the UK, specific homosexual acts were criminalized up until 1967 in England and Wales, and 1980 in Scotland. In this context, to come out was to self-incriminate. Gay people had no choice but to hide and to remain silent; illegality, in turn, inspired shame, as homosexuality was figured as morally wrong.

This silencing had been written into gay existence in the nineteenth century, when homosexuality was pathologized and carefully outlawed, becoming, as in Lord Alfred Douglas's famous poem of 1894, 'the love that dare not speak its name'.

In these years, the legal focus was on sex between men. Meanwhile, politicians and legislators resisted defining sex between women, in part as a form of cultural silencing. Lesbian acts were figured as unspeakable but also unthinkable.

This refusal can be seen as evidence of a wider dismissal of lesbian sex, where sex without a penis wasn't, strictly speaking, real sex – it was mutual masturbation.

As Sedgwick elucidates, the closet was not vanquished after decriminalization. Indeed, 'For many gay people it is still the fundamental feature of social life,' she wrote in 1990. And it persists into this century, through shame and stigma, alongside the threat of serious injury. On top of this, containing and repressing homosexuality was until very recently a matter of public, state concern. In the UK, up until 2003, there was a government ban on openly talking about homosexuality in schools.

Gayle's defence turns on a life of secret sexuality. But, crucially, she says that Miss X was in the closet with her too. She explains their friendship was encoded, a cover for their hidden sexuality and a feature of the closet.

The line between friendship and romance has long provoked anxiety. As far back as Ancient Greece, the boundary was understood to be slippery. It was the subject of Plato's *Lysis*, a dialogue that considered the way 'eros' (love) can intrude on 'philia' (friendship), making friendship between men unstable.

For centuries, the concern about intimate friendships also centred on men. But in the nineteenth century, attention turned to female friendship. In this era, new fragments of erotic poetry by Sappho of Lesbos were circulating in Victorian England. The Ancient Greek poet had a close circle of intimate female friends and, it was observed, many of her erotic poems were addressed to them. A new unspeakable worry was in the air: was 'philia' riddled with 'eros' prevalent between women?

Were Gayle and Miss X friends or lesbians? This is one of the major questions of the trials.

Miss X says they were just friends, nothing more. She says she never knew that Gayle was gay, or that Gayle was Kye, until that final evening together in 2013. But Gayle tells a different story. She says they were secret lovers, secret lesbians. The evidence and accounts are complicated by the closet, and the entanglement of sexuality, secrecy and friendship. Both evoke the friendship during the trials, describing the concerts they went to, the sports they played together and the pet they shared. In order to protect Miss X's anonymity, I will not describe these activities in any detail. When it comes to complainants in sexual offences, legislation identifies facts that are mandatory to avoid (name, age, address, etc.). Beyond this, reporting guidance also advises careful footwork around facts that relate to the relationship between a defendant and complainant (were they married, colleagues, kin? – the type of information that could lead to identification). The fact that Gayle and Miss X were 'best friends' was widely reported in the media. There is no guidance on friendship; this uncertain bond is slippery in law too, and often outside of the legal remit. In these pages, I have decided not to name the city they lived in, or the university they attended, and to withhold specific details about their friendship.

While the friendship is agreed upon, sexuality is not. During her examinations, Miss X is asked directly about her sexuality. 'I'm heterosexual,' she says at the first trial. It's always been that way: 'I've been heterosexual since [I was] a little girl,' she says. At the second trial, she's also direct.

'I'm not a lesbian,' she says, 'I've been straight since the day I was born.'

This is her testimony. But the defence attempts to prove otherwise. In order to demonstrate Gayle's version of events, Power tries to show – against Miss X's own words – that in the summer of 2011 and up to 2013 Miss X was a lesbian, like Gayle says.

Lesbian acts entered the UK legislature only in 2003. The creation of a new offence, assault by penetration, clearly regulated penetrating tongues, hands and objects for the first time. Gayle is charged at both trials with multiple counts of assault by penetration, the majority describing rape with a dildo, and one count describing rape with a tongue. In these counts, the dildo is on the stand, and Gayle's tongue is on the stand. The last count describes deceptive cunnilingus, Gayle assaulting Miss X with 'a part of her body, namely her tongue'. Like the dildo counts, it turns on autonomy, true choice. Miss X says she did not consent to Gayle's tongue, a lesbian act (only to a male one).

Power's cross-examinations often move away from a narrow focus on sexual acts. After all, when it comes to the sex they had, or thought they had, there is a vacuum of evidence, beyond what each of them says. He therefore opens out onto the friendship – the two years in which the pair became best friends. It's in the haphazard records of this friendship that Power tries to look for clues.

He asks Miss X to open the evidence bundle and turn to the many photographs that document the friendship, which have been taken from their Facebook profiles, their laptops. There are pages of images – malleable evidence, some useful to the prosecution, others to the defence. Power homes in on a few with a common theme, pictures that show the friends with their tongues out. In some photos, the friends lick each other's faces. In others, they turn to each other, and their tongues touch, tip to tip.

I imagine the defence team whooped when it saw these images.

'What's the business with the tongues?' Power asks Miss X, pointing to them. It's the first trial, early into Miss X's cross-examination; Power hasn't shown her the dildo yet. 'Is that just a, a friendly kiss?' he asks.

He tries to suggest these images are clues, photographs that reveal their secret lesbianism, and by extension, the consensual tongue, that Miss X understood.

But Miss X shrugs off the insinuation that licking reveals the secret spilling over the bounds of friendship. Yes, they did this 'often', she replies. But it was 'just a trend'. 'For some reason when I went to uni it was cool to stick your tongue out to each other,' she says. 'It's just a joke.'

Power's excitement about the tongue as a lesbian symbol feels simplified, suspect. Touching tongues with someone, licking their face – what's that evidence of, really? It only denotes temporary intimacy, and it's not necessarily a sign of anything further. Even if there were photos alluding more explicitly to lesbian acts – Gayle and Miss X sticking their tongues between their fingers in an imitation of oral sex, say – that wouldn't be evidence that they were lesbians, would it? Signs have pliable meanings, and they're different to thought, action and identity. Miss X says it was public anyway. ('We were doing it walking round shopping centres,' she tells Power.) There was nothing secret about it; it was a public thing, a friendship thing.

THE CLOSET ON THE STAND: SEXUALITY

How are jokes to be read and interpreted? Their status as evidence is complex. For Sigmund Freud, writing in 1905, jokes held repressed sexual desires or hostilities; making a joke was a form of release. Freud saw the joke as a positive form of expression – a way to bypass our internal censor, to release inhibitions and give vent to the libido. In this view, jokes rise up from the unconscious, which is precisely why they are so ambiguous. They are encoded, their intentions often not fully known to the joker. From a legal view, jokes are a tricky, contestable form of evidence, often ridiculed when employed (an example being the public mockery in 2012 following the 'Twitter Joke Trial').

Intimacy between young women can have many meanings. Licking, actually kissing or other intimacies can be for fun, to titillate, or for men. As a teenager, I knew girls who would kiss in front of the boys. I wanted to do it too, and once I joined in. Years later, when I was out as queer, other meanings came into focus (was this my first lesbian kiss, an early indicator of sexuality?). But back then, my (conscious) intention was different: to get attention, to make myself popular, to shock.

As well as the licking photos, which Miss X says are just jokes, Power reads out Facebook messages sent between Miss X and Gayle, plucked from their constant stream of communication. 'Gayle, you look beautiful. Fuck those who don't know how to treat you, babe. Their fucking loss... My gain. They'd only be wasting the time I could be having with you,' one message reads. There's something menacing in trying to ferret out lesbianism in these messages. I've sent these kinds of messages to women friends – exuberant, a bit gushy. Miss X's words can equally be read as evidence of being a supportive friend, boosting Gayle's confidence with a bubbling display of affection and love.

*

Trying to evidence sexuality, against what a person says, is a difficult (and ugly) enterprise.

The term 'sexuality' came into being in the 1870s with the advent of sexology (the scientific study of sex), to mean 'sexual feeling'. The next decade saw a mania of sexual taxonomies and diagnoses, famously compiled by the German sexologist Richard von Krafft-Ebing in his 1886 manual of disorders, *Psychopathia Sexualis*. These theories of sexuality were positioned on a spectrum of natural to perverse, on which a normal, healthy sexuality was established (what would become known as heterosexuality), against abnormal, unnatural ones. 'Contrary sexual sensation' was an early description of same-sex attraction, arising in the 1870s. Other descriptions included 'sexual inversion', 'Uranian love', 'the homosexualist' and 'frauds against nature'. Important to sexology was the idea of normal sexuality as procreative and abnormal sexualities as sterile, alien, cheats.

The term 'lesbian' also emerged in the 1870s, competing with 'sapphism' (both literary, derived from Sappho of Lesbos), to describe female homosexuality specifically. What had, before, been illicit acts (as Michel Foucault argued in *The History of Sexuality*) now became an identity, a person, a case.

Questions proliferated. What caused these contrary sexual sensations? Were they innate? Or were they developmental – to do with a certain childhood, a certain life experience? And, importantly, how could these aberrations be detected? Could they be seen and measured? Some sexologists believed that, yes, they could – that sexuality was actually written on the body.

The theory of sexual inversion, popularized in the early twentieth century by the British sexologist Havelock Ellis, came to be affiliated with homosexuality in women. Female inverts, Ellis argued, actually *looked* masculine; they dressed like men, had 'irregular' postures and even suspicious folds in their vulvas. They were, in one thesis, actually men's souls trapped in women's bodies.

But that diagnosis was unreliable. Sexuality remained elusive. It seemed to escape detection as scientists struggled to prove their assertions. And across the twentieth century, a new concern was in the air, especially when it came to lesbian sexuality. The concern was that it might not be visible at all. In fact, it might look, from the outside, just like *friendship*.

These anxieties came to a head in the early 1920s, when a spectacular murder trial drew international attention. The trial took place in Berlin in March 1923. The defendants were Ella Klein and Margarete Nebbe, two married women in their twenties, and close friends. Ella and Margarete were charged with the murder of one of their husbands, and the attempted murder of the other. The trial revealed the friends to have been in a secret lesbian relationship. They had exchanged nearly six hundred letters, many of which were read out at trial. These were racy, intense letters of passion in which the two women plotted to kill their husbands so that they could be together. The trial grappled with female homosexuality and included testimonies from sexologists. Was it a sickness? Were Ella and Margarete even sane? The reporting was sensational, with many of the letters reproduced in the press. But also, part of the fascination of the trial was that Ella and Margarete were married women. They were normal. They'd appeared to be just close friends. Nobody had suspected their secret life.

Throughout the century, worries about female friendship continued to grow. An old anxiety about unstable friendships between men had morphed into unease about intimate female bonds. Sexologists wrote of 'hysterical friendships', 'morbid' friendships – bonds that might spill over into 'unhealthy' passion. As female friendship was assessed and medicalized, 'morbid' was a favoured term, describing a diseased state – 'morbid' friendships could lead to 'morbid impulses' and 'morbid cravings' (euphemisms for masturbation and sexual inversion). Sexologists perceived homosexuality as abnormal, and lesbians like Ella and Margarete as ill. This view persisted well into the twentieth century – the psychiatry bible, the DSM (officially the *Diagnostic Statistical Manual of Mental Disorders*), classified homosexuality as an illness until 1973. Records from North Manchester General Hospital show some lesbians found life so unbearable that they volunteered for aversion therapy, in which they were administered electric shocks while viewing erotic photographs of women – a 'cure' available until the early 1970s. If once law produced shame, now sexology and psychiatry did, figuring homosexuality as a disorder.

When it came to 'hysterical friendships', sexologists such as Ellis noted that 'ignorance' usually stopped them from becoming sexual. And indeed, the law's cultivation of ignorance by refusing to define lesbian acts became a tactic. It's one reason, as Caroline Derry argues in her recent study *Lesbianism and the Criminal Law* (2020), that lesbian sex was never officially criminalized before 2003. Silencing was considered the most effective form of regulation. When the lesbian 'vice' was debated in Parliament in the 1920s, lesbian knowledge was seen to be contagious. The very subject was 'polluting', the Earl of Malmesbury reasoned, when a bill proposing a new crime for indecency between women reached the House of Lords; naming the acts would only 'advertise' them, he warned. Another earl spoke of 'young women' who were particularly susceptible to pollution. British sexologists had long seen all-girls' schools as potential hotbeds, where lesbian knowledge – if acquired – could become especially infectious. Finally, the House struck down the bill, to conceal the 'disgusting' offence from young women who, as the earls argued, 'have never heard of it, never thought of it, never dreamed of it'. Thus, the female imagination was contained.

*

In her testimony, Gayle describes always being in the closet. She says she knew in primary school that she was different. But her attraction to girls always felt shameful, secret and wrong. It got worse as a teenager. At her all-girls' private secondary school, the word 'lesbian' was a slur. She remembers the solitude and the silence. Coming out was unimaginable. 'I'd never spoken to any gay people,' she explains. 'It's not something I knew how to be.' But with Miss X it was different. 'She knew me,' Gayle says. They had a special knowledge of each other. From the beginning, Gayle says, Miss X knew she was gay.

These trials often hang on two reports, two contrary stories. 'One of them has to be lying. They cannot both be telling the truth,' Corbett-Jones tells the jury at the end of the first trial. The beginning of the friendship, and the way Gayle and Miss X met, is one of the crucial yet conflicting accounts. Both stories start in the summer of 2011. But from there they diverge.

Reporting guidance advises careful handling around facts that relate to the first meeting. Will specificity (a date, a location) give too much away, and allow someone to identify Miss X? I've thought about this a lot, choosing to blur details and leave out certain facts.

And yet, when it comes to the first meeting, there is no single story, no clear setting or date; indeed, Miss X and Gayle tell totally different stories, and deny each other's accounts. All that their tales have in common is a year, a season and the actors, Gayle, Miss X and Kye.

Gayle says she met Miss X at a 'gay night'. It ran every Tuesday in the city where they lived. Gayle describes plucking up the courage to go with a gay male friend. She was still in the closet, and explains that she was accompanying her friend, but he didn't know she was gay. She went a few times that summer, and one night she ordered a drink, sparking a conversation with a woman: Miss X. Later that night, they talked on the dance floor. That's when Miss X asked Gayle, upfront, if she was gay. Gayle remembers it was the first time she'd been asked, ever, and she remembers saying, quietly, yes.

From there, a relationship emerged. They met at the same gay night a week later, this time chatting in the toilets, their inhibitions loosened by a few drinks, sharing the secrets that defined them. 'I opened up to her quite quickly,' Gayle recalls. They bonded over their shared experience of hiding their sexuality and finding themselves in the closet.

THE CLOSET ON THE STAND: SEXUALITY

Miss X talked about her shame, her struggles to accept her sexuality. And Gayle told her about Kye. They became, Gayle says, 'girlfriend and girlfriend'. But they weren't yet living openly. They were out to each other, but not to their friends. 'No one knew about her sexuality, no one knew about my sexuality,' Gayle explains. They hid their romance – and it worked. They were so good at it, nobody suspected a thing. To everyone else, they passed as friends.

Miss X tells a different origin story. It also starts in the summer of 2011, but not at the gay night. She says she never spoke to Gayle on the dance floor, never spoke to her in the toilets, and she never told Gayle about the closet – because she's not in one. She's straight.

Softening the gap between their accounts, Miss X does confirm going 'frequently' to the gay night, also with a gay male friend. But that's not how she met Gayle; according to Miss X, they first met in a library.

And, according to Miss X, it was *Kye* she first met that summer – not Gayle. In this account, the whole relationship and everything that followed began online with a friend request on Facebook, when a handsome guy, also a student, contacted her out of the blue. She says she met Gayle later. In fact, *Kye* introduced them; he told her Gayle was an old childhood friend. From there, her friendship with Gayle developed. Importantly, they had one big thing in common – Kye.

*

Did they first meet in a library or a gay bar? How did it start – with a Facebook request, or a confession in a toilet cubicle? The accounts are so different, but at the centre of both is Kye.

The trials try to decipher him. The Crown suggests Kye's profile was deceptive, part of Gayle's creative writing practice, her cunning skill. But Gayle describes the messages as 'role play', explaining it was part of the closet, a way to be together as boy and girl.

In the 1950s, a spectacular murder trial caught the eye of the world, with best friends enacting a fiction at its centre. The defendants, Pauline Parker and Juliet Hulme, were New Zealand schoolgirls accused of murdering Pauline's mother one summer. The friends had met at the respectable Christchurch Girls' High School and the investigation revealed an intense friendship between the two – a thrilling friendship that had, evidence suggested, gone beyond the bounds of a 'healthy' bond. Pauline and Juliet were both aspiring writers. They wrote plays and novels together, developing a rich fantasy life. In their letters and diary entries, picked over by detectives, they created a cast of characters, combining imaginary villains and 'Saints' with Hollywood stars. They had many names and aliases, writing to each other as Nigel and Philip, Charles and Lance, Deborah and Gina.

As a tale of teenage matricide, to which the defendants eventually confessed, the case was already spectacular. But the media titillation was compounded by a rumour, thickening at trial. The girls had been in a secret lesbian affair; like Ella and Margarete, a few decades before, nobody had suspected it. Pauline's diary, analysed by psychiatrists, described a night-time game in which the friends 'enacted how each Saint would make love in bed'. No one was quite sure what these scenes, in role, meant. Had the friends overcome the enforced ignorance and somehow discovered these 'morbid' acts – even as they were in role? Or was this just a fiction?

Foreshadowing the records of Kye and the messages between the two friends, it was hard to tell what was real, what was fiction, what was a joke. All anyone could be sure of was that, real or imaginary, these night-time scenes pointed to something dangerous, sick, foul. At trial, the prosecution described the defendants as 'dirty-minded little girls', while the defence put forward the only viable rebuttal – these girls were insane.

*

Are all close friendships and intimacies in some sense encrypted? At these trials, Miss X talks of 'jokes', Gayle of 'role play'. The defence barrister, interrogating their bond, grapples with female friendship, just as the lawyers in the Parker–Hulme trial did, and with its private expressions and codes.

At one point during the cross-examination, Power and Miss X debate the terms of the friendship. Miss X says she was Gayle's 'bestie', but also that she didn't know her friend's secret. For Power, she can't have it both ways. If they were 'best friends', she must have known Gayle better. Why didn't she ask Gayle about her sexuality? It was her 'business' to know, he says. Power seems to be reaching for a standard around friendship, in particular female friendship. Should friends – best friends, female friends – talk about their sexuality? Was it Miss X's 'business' to know? Who's to say what the rules of a friendship are? There's no Friendship Act, no Highway Code. But Miss X says no, sexuality was never discussed. 'We would never talk about things like that,' she tells Power. 'It wasn't something that came up.'

THE BED TRICK

The friends would sometimes leave the city at weekends, to go to Gayle's parents' house, located in a picturesque village nearby. Miss X remembers the Newlands had a 'big house' with a little driveway, cream sofas and a garden. Gayle's middle-class upbringing contrasted with her friend's. Indeed, Miss X was estranged from her religious family. It was Gayle who had the welcoming parents, the allowance and the car.

Both remember walks with Gayle's family dog, Gypsy, and visiting Gayle's nan. Power asks Miss X about these trips and rituals. He's trying to interpret the friendship – the lingo that emerged, the private terms. He's also trying to hunt down the secret sexuality to show, behind it all, that the besties licking each other's faces were lesbians, as Gayle says.

At one point, a nickname emerges. Power is reading out a Facebook message, written by Miss X. She's commenting on a photo. 'Beautiful inside and most certainly out. That is why I love my Gayle lick.'

That nickname, 'Gayle lick'. It runs through their private exchanges, becoming 'gay lick'. One message begins, 'Gay lick time'. In another Miss X writes, 'Don't be shy, Gay lick'.

'Gay lick' – it's the kind of detail that it's possible to fixate on. A nickname that also describes a queer act. Gay licking? Could Miss X have missed its significance? Is it a clue?

Miss X explains it away as just another joke, 'Gay' for Gayle, nothing more; 'lick' for the trend. In this description, the gay undertones are minor, insignificant in comparison to the things she was referencing: Gayle's name; the jokey licking everyone did on nights out for the camera, just a pose. 'So Gayle lick, licker face Gayle,' Miss X clarifies. 'A nickname, erm, that I gave to her'. Perhaps... The logic is there. But questions linger, as the problem of a private code persists. How can you tell a nickname from an identity, a real act from a pose? Should we even try?

Next, Power turns to another exchange, this one containing a sex joke. More messages on Facebook between the friends, sent after a day spent together, visiting Gayle's family and walking along a beach. When the day is over, Gayle writes to Miss X. 'You've met the fam, our relationship is getting pretty serious. Lol.' They're joking around. Miss X replies, 'I know. I think it's about time you gave it up. By that I mean give me some. Took you on enough dates now. La ha ha.'

I've read that exchange many times, wondering, like Power, is it a clue? They're joking about being in a relationship, being more than just friends. Gayle starts it. Miss X responds, and moves the joke from dating to sex.

I have plenty of female friends. I've sent them gushing texts, telling them they're beautiful, inside and out, that were purely platonic. I've made up nicknames and been given many myself, some with sexual hints. I talk with my friends about sex, sexuality, pleasure. All of this could be used in a court, I suppose, to suggest this was more than friendship. I'd have to defend my code. But I don't joke about having sex with my friends. For me, this crosses a line. When I read Miss X's words, as she continues the joke – 'by that I mean, give me some' – I think, I wouldn't send that message. But what does that tell me really? Perhaps my sense of humour is different. Perhaps my code is built from a place of knowing; I'm older than Miss X when she writes this, I'm out. Perhaps I protect the line because I know about crossing it.

*

THE BED TRICK

When Power has Miss X on the stand, he keeps drilling her on the friendship. He wants to know how Gayle's sexuality could have eluded her. As best friends, he suggests, the omission is unlikely – implausible. 'I always just presumed that she was heterosexual, like me,' Miss X eventually says.

The presumption of straightness is not a legal presumption, like innocence or sanity, but a social one. It means being presumed straight until confirmed otherwise – and even then, the closet returns; 'every encounter with a new classful of students, to say nothing of a new boss, social worker, loan officer, landlord, doctor, erects new closets', Sedgwick observed.

And this is Gayle's experience too, for most of her life. The presumption of straightness determined how she was read. No one ever supposed otherwise. That is, until she met Miss X, until that particular gay night. In Gayle's story, Miss X read her as gay right away – or at least asked her if she was gay – allowing for the possibility of disclosure.

'A gay bar,' writes Jeremy Atherton Lin in his 2021 memoir *Gay Bar: Why We Went Out*, 'affords refuge ... We go out to be gay.' Lin's words reveal the way gay spaces might be places where the presumption of straightness is reversed. After all, gay bars were once one of the few places that gay people could be presumed gay (and even *become* gay). The rest of the world was (and is) more hostile, often requiring a constant coming out. And if you're not out, you're hiding by default – you're 'in' the closet, the secret lair, as homosexuality and deception are forced together.

But Miss X says something different. She tells Power that she went to the gay night so frequently, not because she was gay, but because she felt safe there as a straight woman. For her, the gay night offered a different kind of refuge; she says she wouldn't get hit on, because gay men are not predatory towards women.

This attitude is pretty common. A lot of straight women go to gay nights for this very reason. But it vexes me, and as I read Miss X's words, I feel frustration. Aren't gay nights for gay women too? The very idea that women at gay nights are gay, and that women hit on women, is occluded.

The problem is, lesbian sexuality in this time (2011) and in this place (a city in northern England) is obscured. This obfuscation lingers in the vocabulary they both use at the first trial. Both talk about the 'gay night'. The word 'gay' has always been an umbrella term, explicitly used since the 1920s to broadly describe homosexuality. Even so, it also often describes male homosexuality specifically. Gayle says in her own testimony that she could frequent the club night with her male gay friend without suspicion. We cannot know what this friend actually thought. But, in the club, to everyone except Miss X – or, following Miss X's account, to everyone including her – Gayle remained in the closet. Despite the context, the refuge, she didn't feel the burden of her secret dissipate.

What a lonely time to be a lesbian, I think, what a lonely place.

*

At one point, in the middle of Miss X's cross-examination, Power brings up something she said to police during the complaint process – that she would rather have been raped by a man.

It's a shocking claim. Miss X said these words at the

police station, at the very beginning of the process of making a complaint, just days after she says she discovered the truth about Kye. Now, two years later, Power challenges her on it. Miss X searches for an answer, stumbling a little. She seems to understand it's an alarming thing to have declared. Rape by a man, a penis, better than rape by a woman, a dildo? Heterosexual rape better than homosexual rape? How can there be a hierarchy?

'I know I shouldn't say this, especially being a woman I just . . . it would have been a guy who's, you know, taken something from me. But this whole aspect of it, it being a woman . . .' They spar a little. 'It's just, that's just how I feel,' she eventually says.

How a person responds to sexual assault is not rational or reasonable. Nigel Power dredges up her remarks because he's looking for evidence of the closet, aversion. He suggests these words point to internalized homophobia and a loathing of lesbian acts. This horror is articulated by Miss X many times in the transcripts. 'I just cannot . . . I cannot believe that I was sleeping with a woman this whole time. I just can't,' she says. 'It makes me feel sick.'

Self-loathing, a disgust and despair at not being 'normal', has been, and still can be, a reality for many lesbians. Could this be what Miss X's words, and her preference for heterosexual rape, signal? Equally, Miss X's reaction could be a response to the intense betrayal she describes – the years of trickery by a friend who blindsided her, she explains, *because* she was a woman.

'As a woman,' Miss X says, Gayle was beyond her suspicion.

But, surely, she means as a *friend*?

THE CLOSET ON THE STAND: SEXUALITY

*

Miss X's story turns on unwanted advances – by a friend, a woman who she says tricked her into disgusting acts. Making this allegation more painful and uneven is the fact that the courts once found such disgust legible, even reasonable, when it came to defending violent acts against gay men. The 'gay panic defence', once widespread, was a strategy of criminal defence employed in cases of assault or murder, used to justify the violent acts. A defendant would claim a temporary loss of control brought on by an offensive sexual pass. The 'Portsmouth defence', as it was known, deriving from seaports where violence and homosexuality were rife, turned on the implicit assumption that gay men often made predatory advances on strangers. It was against those disgusting sexual approaches that violence was seen as reasonable, justified. Famously, at a trial in 1960s London, a defendant was absolved of murdering a gay man, whom he killed with a glass decanter, in what the judge called a 'clear . . . case of provocation'. Violence was seen to be justifiable on these grounds, and the defence, in effect, legitimized homophobia as a socially sanctioned prejudice.

Then came 1967, and the decriminalization of homosexual acts in England and Wales. The Portsmouth defence lingered, but it was slowly delegitimized as the UK entered an era of tolerance. An emphasis was placed on gays being discreet, keeping it private. The 'good homosexual', notes the legal scholar Carl Stychin in his book on legal history, *Governing Sexuality* (2003), was expected to be 'a law abiding, disease free, self-closeting homosexual figure' who knew his place on the secret fringes of society.

But on the heels of (full) decriminalization came the

1980s AIDS epidemic – re-exacerbating panic and disgust. An old conservative anxiety was afloat once again: gay contagion. And not just literally (the AIDS stigma), but also a return of the fear of homosexuality as a dangerously catching idea. The state was no longer policing sex between consenting adults; the new fear was contagion among youth, teenagers, *children*. Reflecting this anxiety, in 1988 the Conservative government implemented Section 28, prohibiting the 'promotion of homosexuality' in schools – a form of educational silencing, which remained in place until 2003.

So much of the law, the policing and the debates focused on gay men. Meanwhile, lesbian acts were left alone and repressed through silence. That 1920s fear, that women were especially vulnerable to contagion, proved incredibly persistent. Lesbian sex was legally invisible up until 2003; when it did surface in medical textbooks or films it was often figured as disordered and dangerous. Girls' schools remained a focal point of fear (and fantasy) about lesbian activity. At my all-girls' school in the 2000s, I had little inkling about lesbian sexuality beyond monstrous stereotypes. When I finally went to university, meeting lesbians who were my age was a revelation.

Trials are moments of exposure; transcripts can offer glimpses of self-revelation through letters or diaries read aloud, or through examination. Ella Klein and Margarete Nebbe in the 1920s, Pauline Parker and Juliet Hulme in the 1950s – these trials are part of lesbian history, repressed but coming to the surface, for good and for bad. The Parker–Hulme trial would be revisited in the 1990s, in books such as *Parker & Hulme: A Lesbian View* (1991) and the film *Heavenly Creatures* (1994). Written by lesbian academics, *Parker*

THE CLOSET ON THE STAND: SEXUALITY

and Hulme grappled with the way this trial exacerbated fears in New Zealand, making it even harder to be a lesbian (and even harder to come out), even as the news reports confirmed that girls fell in love with each other. In the same era, in the UK, lesbian historians such as Rose Collis published books unveiling lesbian lives, referencing these trials; and yet, by the time these histories were being examined, the educational gag was in force, implementing a new form of silencing on children and teenagers.

*

Gayle's trials take place in a different era. In 2002, the Portsmouth defence was discredited, following new guidance published by the CPS; the year after, Section 28 was repealed. These trials take place under the new Sexual Offences Act, in a new century.

And this is exactly what the Crown argues. The years of (unfortunate) homophobia, repression – they're over! For the Crown, the level of sexual shame Gayle describes just isn't plausible in today's world. At the first trial, Corbett-Jones references the Civil Partnership Act 2004, as evidence that 'these days', gay people now have 'the full protection of the law'. At the second trial, the new prosecution barrister, Simon Medland, makes a similar argument. 'Miss Newland,' he says, 'it is not as if we are looking back twenty, thirty or forty years.' The events on trial begin in 2011, and are part of our modern, enlightened era – an era of gay rights. During this period, says Medland, 'It was against the law to discriminate against gay people, yes? . . . There are pride marches in the whole period, yes? . . . There are gay clubs, yes?'

THE BED TRICK

The Crown barristers suggest, in effect, that the closet is obsolete. Gay people are no longer discriminated against. Instead of homophobia and shame, there's celebration and 'pride'. But Gayle does not concur. Her experience was different. Section 28 was repealed just after she began secondary school, but in her account, there's only silence and shame. Not only was lesbian sexuality hidden and absent at the all-girls' school she attended, she also describes the lack of education. 'You don't get educated on being gay,' she explains at the first trial. 'I didn't really know the meaning of "gay".' There were no representations of lesbian desire or any clear vocabulary. 'I didn't really even know about, like, girl on girl,' she admits at the second trial. 'I didn't really understand, like, how it was, like, possible.' She had no knowledge of lesbian culture or lesbian acts, she says.

At both trials, Gayle describes the shame spiralling inwards, through school, sixth form, the first year of university. Until she met Miss X – finding in her a best friend and secret girlfriend. But if it appears to be a triumphant story, Gayle says that it wasn't. Both women were riddled with shame; finding each other didn't fix that. They both wanted to be straight. And, over the years of their relationship, rather than getting easier, Gayle says it actually seemed to get harder. The closet remained – a new, shared one that they were both stuck in together and that, over time, seemed to amplify their self-hatred and shame.

At both trials, the Crown reads out the text exchange between Gayle and Miss X that followed the final argument – messages in which Miss X accuses and Gayle apologizes.

In many ways, the texts Miss X sent to Gayle verify her complaint. In this exchange, Miss X says almost exactly what

THE CLOSET ON THE STAND: SEXUALITY

she says to the police, and what she says on the stand. 'How could you do this to someone for two years,' she writes. 'You should be locked up for what you've done.' 'I now know that evil exists in this world.' She never changes her story, never wavers in her disgust.

Gayle, meanwhile, apologizes. She writes, 'I hate myself.' 'I said lies to hide lies'. 'You don't deserve this.' 'I will pay for it and already am.'

In some ways, Gayle's story never changes either – at least when it comes to her shame, her self-disgust.

These messages are significant evidence against Gayle. They are also especially significant in these trials, which turn on intentional deception, and whether Miss X knew what she was choosing, or if Gayle took over her mind through fantasies and lies. When she's asked about these messages, Gayle says she panicked. She struggles to answer. She says she sent those messages during some of the worst days of her life, after the suicide attempt. They'd told so many lies together to stay in the closet, and her mind wasn't in the right place. She felt desperate, ashamed. Guilty. She would have written anything to get Miss X back. Giving her answer, she becomes distraught. She has to step down from the stand. She stops.

*

By the time Gayle takes the stand at the first trial, she's 'out'. She's had to be. For her, getting arrested, the police interview, becoming a suspect, all that came after, it was a massive outing. In the days before the fight, she explains, she was preparing to live an openly gay life. To finally come out to her parents. But with the complaint, a coming-out story morphed into something else: an interrogation, a criminal investigation, eventually a trial. When she takes the stand, Gayle declares, 'I'm lesbian', 'I'm gay' – to strangers in the court who have been brought there to judge her, and to the wider world, as her face and words are printed in news outlets.

When asked why Miss X made this accusation – Why is she going through with it? Why has she come to court, twice? – Gayle says she doesn't really know. The only answer that she can give is the closet. 'The girl never ever ever wants anyone to know that she's gay,' she says at the retrial. These words suggest the trials are an extension of Miss X's denial, an extension of the closet. A way to prove she's straight, to make it a legal fact.

This is the argument Power tries to make about Miss X at the end of the first trial. 'Did she protest too much?' he asks the jury in his closing speech. He's implying Miss X's insistent objections are clues that point to her aversion, her shame. 'Perhaps she has not yet found the courage to come out,' he goes on. And he takes it a step further. He begins to suggest that Miss X's anonymity package – the condition automatically granted to any complainant in a sexual offences trial – is a part of this. Her identity is forever protected, he continues, she'll never be publicly exposed. 'The press cannot print anything at all that might lead to identifying her,' Power tells the jury. 'She agreed that she knew that, before she came on.' Here, Power suggests Miss X was particularly switched on to this condition, although it's something that all sexual offences complainants are informed of, as early as possible, because it usually encourages them to follow through.

THE CLOSET ON THE STAND: SEXUALITY

This is an inversion of the Crown's 'fraud in the factum' trope – Miss X is not naive, a person who has been targeted, but rather someone who is clued up and cunning. By invoking it, Power takes us back to an old rape myth, that this is a lying complainant, a false complaint. From this view, Miss X is ingeniously using rape shield laws as a way to remain hidden, behind the curtain, because the protections mean she can make this complaint while staying safely in her closet, her name replaced with an 'X', her face blurred.

Power's final argument reveals the double bind. There is a conniving woman either way. Either a uniquely crafty defendant – a deceptive woman, mounting fake operations on her friend, disgusting homosexual acts. Or a uniquely scheming complainant and a liar, a false and manipulative victim who is abusing the legal system and misusing special measures.

5

Identity on the Stand: Fraud

The barristers scrutinize the texts, photos and Facebook posts sent between Gayle and Miss X, as the trials attempt to determine if they were friends or lesbians.

But there's a whole other set of correspondence between *Kye* and Miss X.

Kye is an elusive figure. Operation Imperia was an attempt to flush him out. As police investigated Miss X's claims, they looked for traces of Kye, a missing person. His Blackberry phone seized from Gayle's bedroom was the starting point. Investigators materialized Kye through evidence, which includes his years of correspondence: his call logs, texts, Facebook messages and photos. The resulting evidence bundle is a kind of dossier on this man, following his digital footprints, tracking him across time.

*

Gayle has never, on record, identified as trans. On the stand, at both trials, she states her name as Gayle Dawn Newland and uses 'she/her' pronouns. Kye is not represented. Gayle appears as a cis-woman, in that the gender presented (female) corresponds to the legal sex assigned at birth (woman).

IDENTITY ON THE STAND: FRAUD

In the bundle, and in court, Kye was treated as a separate entity. He had his own phone number and social media profiles dating back several years. Photographs of Kye showed a half-Asian man. The evidence bundle revealed his world of friends – some, collaborators (Kye was a lyricist); others, women whom Kye spoke to (both friends and girlfriends), who never met him.

'You're right, they didn't know me as Gayle,' she tells the Crown. But she insists that with Miss X it was different. They were best friends; they had a whole offline life. 'It's a totally different scenario,' she says.

Miss X tells one story about Kye. She says she was duped for two years; all that time Kye seemed like a 'real' person. But he was actually a sophisticated avatar. Behind him, a deceptive operator, Gayle, was running the accounts in secret – a false friend, tricking her into a relationship and ultimately into lesbian acts. This is a story that, from the beginning, police then prosecutors found to be convincing.

Meanwhile, Gayle says a few different things about Kye. She tells a messy story. And it is a story the court finds hard to hear. Mainly, she says Kye was a 'coping mechanism', the way she dealt with her sexuality. And, according to Gayle, Kye was a way for Miss X to cope with her sexuality too. The closet was important to Gayle, and it was important to Miss X. 'She would never say she was in a relationship with a girl,' Gayle explains. 'To friends and stuff it would always be she's going out with this guy called Kye.' Kye became a useful cover story for their lesbian relationship. Explaining Kye's excuses, why he was never around, Gayle says, 'We had to tell people that Kye was sick, we had to tell people that, well, that Kye bloody existed, to be honest.'

But, on the stand, she also says something else. She says it hesitantly. When pushed to explain how she first came to create Kye, Gayle tells a story about gender trouble. She recalls being 'a tomboy' in primary school, and then feeling isolated at her all-girls' secondary school. 'I couldn't relate,' she explains. 'I couldn't really be myself.' She says she felt anxious all the time. It was around then that she logged into an 'American chatroom'. It was 2003. There, she spoke as a boy and eventually as Kye.

Gayle struggles to find the words for how it began. 'It's hard to explain,' she says to Power, stumbling. 'It's just hard . . . I think it started as . . . The only way to explain it, erm, like an alter ego almost.'

The term 'alter ego' was introduced by the prosecution at the beginning of the first trial, when Corbett-Jones described Gayle 'posing online as her male alter-ego Kye Fortune' – but Gayle takes it up. Kye began almost as an alter ego, Gayle tells Power, but over time she and Kye became one. 'You know, the more comfortable I was, the more that these two kind of people emerge into exactly the same person,' she says.

By the time Miss X came into the picture in 2011, Gayle and Kye were doing the same course at university, and both worked at a local gym. But more than similarities, more than shared experiences, Gayle says they were the 'same' person. They had the same birthday, the same childhood, the same personality, she explains. Their likes and dislikes, their habits and anxieties were 'exactly the same', she tells Power.

Across the trials, the barristers constantly refer to the dossier. Both talk about 'the Gayle phone' and 'the Kye phone'.

IDENTITY ON THE STAND: FRAUD

Whatever Gayle says, Kye is a double; there are always two. Gayle agrees there were 'distinct' numbers, two phones. She was 'in role', sometimes as Kye, sometimes as Gayle. She calls it 'role play'. For a long time, it was on the phone or online. She was Gayle on Gayle's phone, Kye on Kye's phone. But it wasn't always so precise. She'd be *Gayle* on Kye's phone, or *Kye* on Gayle's. 'It was just kind of in-out, in-out of roles,' she says.

Her descriptions suggest a kind of motion or oscillation. They'd 'fall in and out of role play', she tells the judge at the first trial; they 'slipped in and out', she tells the Crown. She became Kye, but she was Gayle too.

Often I wonder, when reading about 'Gayle' and 'Kye' in the transcripts, is the language right? By the time of the trials, the two figures are separated out. But the logic can often feel misleading, like a simplification. As Gayle describes it in her testimony, the relationship between them was fluid, suggesting they can't be separated so easily. Other formulations and terms of identity come to mind, like 'Gayle/Kye', the pronoun 'they' and identifications like 'genderqueer' – which I could import. In these years, expressions like 'gender fluid' and 'transgender' were entering the mainstream for the first time. In 2014, for example, Facebook launched fifty-eight gender options, exciting and confusing users, some describing fluidity and transness; soon after, *TIME* magazine triumphantly pronounced the 'transgender tipping point', whereby heightened visibility was enkindling 'trans consciousness'. But Gayle doesn't use these words.

*

A police interrogation room, a lawyer's office, a Crown courtroom – these are hostile places to tell a story, especially a story about gender nonconformity, and an intimate, idiosyncratic story about a secret life.

After being held in a custody suite for ten hours, Gayle faced a bombardment of questions, some about Kye.

In relation to Kye Fortune, have you made this male up?

Have you used this male, Kye, as a way of contacting females?

It is July 2013, Gayle's first interrogation; Kye is already separated off, 'this male'. Gayle doesn't respond. She is arrested as Gayle, interviewed as Gayle. In this silence, her identity is presumed and fixed.

She says nothing at the first interview, nor at the second. But eventually, she has to speak. Sexual fraud, and the presumptions it threatens, requires a defence. Gayle must say something to a solicitor when charges are pressed. She must plead guilty or not guilty. Then she must provide a defence statement. She must turn up in court. The whole process is an intense, public and very unforgiving way to come out. Eventually, she must explain herself – the dossier, 'the Gayle phone', 'the Kye phone' – to a court.

On the stand she says, 'I'm lesbian'. But when it comes to Kye, she struggles to articulate herself. Often she is unable to provide insights. While she has found words to name her sexuality, a vocabulary to describe her sense of gender is missing. 'I can't explain,' she says, 'I just can't.'

When I first read the transcripts, I expected the trials to contain terms like 'gender identity' or 'gender nonconformity'

IDENTITY ON THE STAND: FRAUD

– despite how new this vocabulary was in 2015. But they don't, and the omission feels glaring. At the trials, there is no language in the barristers' arguments to describe gender fluidity, to describe being both, without recourse to words like 'acting', 'pretending' and 'lying' – descriptors that are unhelpful to Gayle in the context of a deception trial.

Is it surprising? The court is a cis-normative and heteronormative setting where middle-aged men debate Gayle's identity formation as a teenager. And yet, by 2015, the 'transgender tipping point' had been touted by *TIME* magazine; Facebook's fifty-eight gender options included 'gender fluid', 'gender questioning', 'genderqueer'; and celebrities such as Caitlyn Jenner had come out as transgender in highly public ways, appearing on the cover of *Vanity Fair* in the months running up to Gayle's first trial.

At times, I feel frustrated with Power. Why didn't he introduce some of this language – or indeed, any vocabulary at all about gender? I keep noticing clear opportunities to do so. The 'gay night', where Gayle says she met Miss X in 2011, was called 'Gender Blender'. It is mentioned during the examinations, but it doesn't lead anywhere. Gayle often seems alone, as Power struggles to form his questions. He turns to the bundle.

'If we look at the messages, Kye appears as a, a real person,' he says. 'Was this some sort of role play or fantasy or . . . or what was it?'

'Both,' Gayle replies.

During the examination, Power keeps simplifying, imposing order on Gayle's 'both'. 'I'm going to say "Kye" so we're clear who's who,' he tells Gayle, as they discuss the similarities between them.

After Gayle explains Kye began almost as an alter ego, but became something else – 'the same person' – Power seems to think the picture is as clear as it will ever be. 'All right. Well I'm going to move on,' he says, continuing to refer to 'Gayle' and 'Kye' as separate entities.

*

When Gayle was found guilty in 2015, it turned out that her case was not isolated. The state was, in fact, very interested in this type of fraud.

As publicity around Gayle's case mounted, the conviction was revealed to be the latest in a series of cases, accelerating since 2012 – the fifth in a sequence. All suspects were accused of falsely presenting as men; some identified as trans, others as lesbians. And all the complainants, who were cis-women, alleged that they were tricked into sex they otherwise would not have consented to. They chose penises, legal men, heterosexual sex, they said. One activist and lawyer, Alex Sharpe, declared the pattern had shape and showed the emergence of a new strain of sexual fraud – she called it 'gender identity fraud' (also known as 'gender fraud'). According to Sharpe, gender was being singled out as a deception and penalized like no other part of identity.

Gayle appealed her first conviction and in 2016 was granted a retrial. By then she was eleven months into her prison sentence. She watched the appeal hearing from her cell via a live link. A judge, speaking at the Royal Courts of Justice in London, ruled the original verdicts were 'unsafe', a legal term that signifies a flaw in the proceedings. The judge pointed to a fault in Dutton's final speech to the jury, which is where Section 76 was outlined.

With the original verdicts overturned, Gayle was released on bail. She immediately went home. A retrial was ordered, and took place eight months later at a new Crown Court.

What exactly was wrong with Dutton's instructions? The Court of Appeal ruled that his summary of evidence was biased in favour of the prosecution. He put too much focus on intentional deception, leaving the jury 'in no doubt what... their verdicts should be'. Dutton is a very experienced trial judge, and it's as if Section 76 got the better of him. Unsurprisingly, at the retrial, the prosecution did not proceed on the basis of Section 76. Indeed the draconian conclusive presumption proved to be redundant; there was, in fact, a more direct, pure way to prosecute gender deception, a precedent known as the McNally Principle.

Of the recent cases Sharpe followed, only Gayle's had made it to trial. All the other defendants had pled guilty at pre-trial hearings. This meant no evidence was heard in court and the cases proceeded directly to sentencing; guilt was admitted, and the only question to be decided was punishment. But one teenager, Justine McNally, appealed her conviction, trying to take back her guilty plea.

In 2011, she presented as a boy called Scott; in November of that year, her girlfriend filed a complaint, claiming she didn't know Scott was a girl. After police investigated, the CPS took the case forward. Justine McNally was charged with six counts of assault by penetration (on the basis of 'fraudulent deception', posing as 'a male') and pled guilty at a pre-trial hearing in 2012. Several months later, she was sentenced to three years in jail. But from prison, Justine appealed. She now claimed she'd been encouraged to plead guilty by a lawyer when, in fact, her girlfriend had known all along that she was also Justine. They met online in 2008 and had been dating for over three years. Both were in the closet and hid the relationship from their parents; indeed, it was the complainant's mother who had lodged the first complaint at her daughter's school, after finding a dildo in Scott's rucksack.

But the appeal backfired – leading to a precedent, the McNally Principle.

Legal precedent is the process by which lower courts must follow principles set by higher courts. Those decided by the Court of Appeal are binding precedents; because Justine's case was decided by appeal, it became *the* gender fraud precedent. All Crown Courts are now obliged to follow it.

The McNally Principle, delivered by Court of Appeal judge Brian Leveson, considered whether gender deception can vitiate consent. Justine's claim that she was encouraged to plead guilty is dismissed. Instead, the judgment focuses on the scope of the law to ask: does the court (indeed the state) prohibit this type of deception, gender fraud?

It's June 2013. Leveson considers recent case law – the rare uses of Section 76. And actually, the judgment shows that, mostly, in cases since 2003, Section 76 was considered but ultimately rejected. Because it's Victorian and narrow, and because of its extraordinary power. And *another* route to prosecuting sexual fraud had been quietly emerging. A route using the very definition of consent. That definition was added in 2003, to become *the* rule, *the* standard. Here, consent was defined by way of sexual autonomy, the right to choose – to say yes, to say no – and defined by freedom, capacity and choice.

As these cases showed, sexual fraud prosecutions were starting to be made via the definition of consent. In other words, rather than bypassing consent, these prosecutions turned to consent and relied on its definition.

And that's what happens in this judgment too. Leveson, after building the argument through case law, returns to the case at hand. '[Miss A] chose to have sexual encounters with a boy,' he states, before citing the definition of consent: 'Her freedom to choose whether or not to have a sexual encounter with a girl' was 'removed by the appellant's deception', he continues.

The specific deception that had removed it – gender.

Thus, the McNally Principle was set out: 'We conclude that, depending on the circumstances, deception as to gender can vitiate consent.'

*

This principle figures a person's gender history as essential knowledge when it comes to securing consent, and information that marks the line between sex and rape.

Because there was no jury trial, the McNally case was modestly reported. Gayle's trial, as it went viral, directed significant attention onto the scope of gender fraud law for the first time. The reporting caught the attention of transgender activists. Although Gayle had not identified as trans on record, the trial and surrounding case law were steeped in questions around gender disclosure and consent. The case seemed to be suggesting that in order to give 'real' consent, partners needed to know each other's gender history. The principle singled out gender as a significant deception, even as other deceptions regarding identity were deemed trivial.

The judgment was clear: deliberate failure to disclose gender history can be prosecuted as rape. The judgment said it was common sense. Leveson stated, 'the sexual nature of the acts is, on any common sense view, different', when gender deception comes into it. He even used the word 'obviously' about other deceptions not counting (citing wealth as an example).

There were two more gender fraud convictions as Gayle awaited trial – one in December 2015, another in March 2016. Both defendants identified as transgender men; both were charged with assault by penetration, for using prosthetic devices; both eventually submitted guilty pleas. In other words, the pattern appeared to be accelerating.

Then came June 2017, Gayle's retrial.

In so many ways, the two trials are the same. But in 2017, when Gayle and Miss X take the stand again, it's not Section 76 that guides the prosecution's arguments or Power's defence. This time, the fraud relates explicitly to gender. This time, to the very definition of consent.

Gayle is on trial for gender fraud – even as gender, as a term of identity, is barely in use. The retrial vocabulary is a little more expansive – but not much. 'Gender Blender' is mentioned again, but this time the 'gay night' is now referred to as 'LGBQT'. Once again, Gayle describes herself as 'gay' and 'lesbian'; Miss X insists she's straight. The trial interrogates these terms, and leaves it at that.

The fact that Gayle does not use now-established terms to talk about gender and identity, at a gender fraud trial, makes her case harder to advocate for. A transgender defendant could argue that there was no gender deception; they might find shelter under gender recognition legislation.

IDENTITY ON THE STAND: FRAUD

Given the precedent deployed, and the place this trial has in gender fraud case law, I look for the word 'transgender' in the transcripts. During Miss X's cross-examination, the word 'transgender' is in use, briefly. Power asks Miss X about the 'T' in LGBQT; she doesn't know what it stands for.

It is unclear if Gayle has anything to say about the acronym, because she's never asked. In the transcripts, she uses the word 'transgender' just once. It's the fourth day of the retrial, and she is being examined again by Power. Describing Kye's online profile, and the early years of social media, she says, 'It went along from Bebo and Myspace to Facebook. It just kind of transgendered through that.' The only time she uses the word, it's a malapropism – a slip. She's describing the way users migrated, or transitioned, from one platform to another – but she says 'transgendered'. The adjective 'transgender', to describe a sense of identity and a gender that does not correspond to the one ascribed at birth, is not the story Gayle wants, or is able, to tell. She spends her hours on the stand talking about sexuality, not gender. Of being lesbian, not trans.

*

The dossier establishes the logic of two people, Gayle and Kye. There are two phone numbers, and also two faces. Kye is seen in a selection of photographs taken from his social media pages. Gayle admits to taking images from a real person she came across on Myspace as a teenager. Carlo – his surname unknown – is described as Asian-American or Filipino-American. He was around Gayle's age and lived in the US. Gayle took photos from his account for many years. The photos show a person changing over time, ageing. Carlo wears different clothes, gets various haircuts. He often appears with his family and friends. The fact that Kye's images belonged to somebody else is troubling – a real person who did not consent to his photos being used.

Adding complexity and discomfort to Gayle's account of Kye is the racial divergence. Gayle, who is white, describes Kye as 'someone that's Asian'. When she chose to represent Kye online, why did she choose Carlo's face, Carlo's images?

Neither barrister, at either trial, asks Gayle any questions about Kye's race, and how it relates to the various accounts of Kye that she gives – whether describing Kye as a cover story, a form of role play, or her sense of being 'exactly the same' as Kye. Because these questions are not asked, I don't know what Carlo's images meant to Gayle. What was it about his images that she identified with? Why an Asian guy? Why *him*? (Was it because he lived far away? Because he was cute? Did his race enable the fantasy of being other than herself? Or something more?)

At trial, Miss X clearly says that she chose 'a half-Asian guy', 'a Filipino man'. But when Gayle is quizzed about Kye's profiles, racial divergence is not discussed. The silence on this aspect of deception suggests the Crown can't quite put its finger on why this might be wrong, and doesn't want to go there. Race is not the subject of these trials, gender is.

The very idea of 'racial fraud' is unnerving. But not so long ago, race was carefully regulated by states. In *Deadly and Slick: Sexual Modernity and the Making of Race* (2023), Sita Balani considers 'the trickery of race'. Today, race is understood by critical race scholars as a historical construction, which derives from colonialism. Yet, Balani writes, 'race persists despite its fictive quality' and 'its categories have the cast of common sense'.

The making and management of race can be studied in case law. This is where the regulation of 'racial deception' appears. In early twentieth-century America, one race was guarded and regulated like no other: the white race. Historically, the path to whiteness was very narrow. In many states, 'one drop' of non-white ancestry was enough to deny somebody the legal status of a white person. These laws emerged alongside a cultural anxiety, rife at the time, that a person might look white, pass as white, but not 'really' be white. These anxieties crystallized around one panic in particular, that a person of colour could dupe a white person into marriage by passing as white.

In her 2019 study *Intimate Lies and the Law*, the legal scholar Jill Hasday unearthed a score of American lawsuits from this era, centring on claims of racial deception. The lawsuits were against women, and occasionally men, who had 'deceived' white people into marriage. Numerous husbands claimed they did not know the 'true' racial status of their wives. Marriages were nullified on the basis of premarital 'fraud' at a time when annulments were difficult to obtain. In one example from 1936, a Filipino husband was sued by his wife. She believed he was 'of Spanish Catalan descent', and had married him on that basis.

These claims relied on a commitment to racial purity, and on the authorities explicitly protecting and promoting white supremacy. Hasday considers the 'changing norms' when it comes to intimate deception and notes that, in the US today, racial deception claims have 'virtually disappeared'. That's not to say racial hierarchies have vanished, but biological racism is outmoded and restricted. Hierarchies are upheld in other, insidious ways.

At Gayle's trials, race is not a focus of the prosecution or the deception on which the case turns. But could it be? Could rape be prosecuted on the basis of 'deception as to race'?

The answer is yes – a legal framework does exist, the very same framework that justifies the McNally Principle, relying on the definition of consent.

The pure view, put forward by Jonathan Herring, is that no deception is too trivial or too uncomfortable, as long as it is meaningful to a complainant, and as long as it's an active lie. Herring doesn't use the example of race specifically, but other scholars have, arguing that racial deception should count, alongside other identity lies, such as those about occupation, nationality, religious views, education, age and health.

Following this logic, if a complainant chose somebody of a certain race or ethnicity, if that was their sexual preference and they were deceived on that basis, then it's an autonomy deficit. Their choice was distorted. It changes the act; it's not sex, it's rape. (As one philosopher of the pure view remarked, 'we must respect other people's wills as they actually are, not as they ought to be'.) By this reasoning, deception as to race can vitiate consent. Racial fraud could accompany gender fraud – and indeed many other identity deceptions.

This is the framework, but in practice it's different. At the time of Gayle's retrial, UK case law was limited. Conditions that can vitiate consent were restricted to deceptions that were connected to the sexual act, and specifically to lies about condoms, ejaculation and gender.

IDENTITY ON THE STAND: FRAUD

Even so, other jurisdictions around the world reveal the mutability of deception law, and the way new factors can emerge in precedents – including racial deception. In Australia, for example, a prosecution for sexual fraud on the basis of race took place in 2015. Several months before Gayle's first trial, a man was convicted of 'procuring sexual penetration by fraud', after tricking a woman into believing he was white. The complainant said she chose to have sex with a blond-haired Caucasian man called Jamie, whom she met online. She claimed she kept her eyes closed during the encounter at his request, and only realized afterwards that Jamie was of Indian descent when they got in the shower together and she saw his hand. Soon after, she reported him to the police. The man, whose legal name was Deepak Dhankar, eventually pled guilty. At his sentencing, the judge reportedly said that if Dhankar hadn't shown contrition and pled guilty, she would have incarcerated him.

As this case shows, it's entirely possible to prosecute racial deception.

There were other examples of factors emerging too. In another variation, this time from Israel, a man was convicted of rape by deception, on the basis of ethno-religious fraud. The complainant was a Jewish woman, who said she believed the man was a Jewish bachelor and that she consented on that basis. Later she discovered he was Muslim and married; he was also Palestinian. The conviction, which took place in 2010, highlighted the malleability of deception law, and the way factors could be crafted by the anxieties of a time and place.

When it comes to the UK, deceptions relating to identity don't tend to count. Few have been tested beyond gender.

There is another barrier, which is part of the CPS's 'Full Code Test'. These are the rules that determine if a suspect is charged, and includes a (somewhat mysterious) step called the 'public interest stage'.

The CPS is effectively a 'gatekeeper'. The service was set up in the 1980s as an independent body, answerable to Parliament, which decides what cases go forward to be prosecuted at public expense. In the final part of the CPS charging test, prosecutors must ask: 'Is it in the public interest to prosecute?'

But what does public interest mean? How is it measured?

The list of considerations outlined in the CPS code include community impact, harm caused and the culpability of suspects. The step is generally understood to be there to weed out complaints that are trifling, unbalanced or uneven, particularly those relating to vulnerable suspects, or young, immature suspects. (As I read the guidance, I think, suspects like Justine McNally, who was seventeen years old at the time, and presenting as a man, queer?)

Gender deception is complicated by the way it relates both to identity and to sex. Is this why it is seen as more reprehensible than other identity deceptions? Or is there something else at play?

In her recent book *The Transgender Issue: An Argument for Justice* (2021), Shon Faye tracks the way transgender rights became a culture war 'issue' in the 2010s, reduced to a 'talking point' and chewed over as a 'toxic debate'. An increase in 'trans consciousness' turned out to be a double-edged sword. The optimistic 'tipping point' of 2014 soon morphed into a gloomy 'transgender dipping point' of 2017, as awareness resulted not in liberation and rights but

IDENTITY ON THE STAND: FRAUD

heightened vulnerability. In the UK, as trans people gained visibility, the question of transgender authenticity became *the* flashpoint. 'Perhaps no topic – other than Brexit and, latterly, the coronavirus pandemic – has received such a consistently high and recurring level of popular media coverage', Faye writes.

Popular and often violent and harsh, as the coverage and debates became expressions of fear, panic and hate. Faye describes the amplification of anti-trans campaigners in the UK and beyond, who contended that trans people (or indeed, any genderqueer people) are mistaken, deluded or deceptive about their identity. Across the 2020s, this campaign has only grown.

The case tracks Gayle over a long period, a considerable part of her lifetime. But as the trials take place in the 2010s, the case is caught up in a heated context – part of the pattern of cases, accelerating since 2012, surfacing at a time when gender, identity and deception were very much in the public eye, and when transgender people were increasingly being depicted as dangerous, predatory frauds. During this period too, the very definition of gender and its relationship to sex was beginning to be viciously debated. For some, gender could not be reduced to genitals. For others, this was exactly what gender – and indeed gender fraud – was all about.

*

On the stand, Gayle is 'out' as a lesbian. She talks about her struggles with anxiety, depression, OCD and suicidal thoughts. She roots these issues back to her sexuality and the closet. But when it comes to gender, identity, Kye – it's hard for her to find the words.

Her testimonies are freeze-frames in time, accounts she gives on the record in hostile environments. In these fragments, she tells varying stories about Kye. Her story is messy, fluid. It does not conform to a standardized narrative – specifically, the legal narrative about gender recognition. In the UK, the Gender Recognition Act sets out a narrative in which 'real' (authentic) gender is understood in ways that are stereotyped, binary, medicalized. The Act outlines the way gender identity can be legally affirmed by the state: if it is continuously presented; if it is one or the other (male or female); and if the applicant supplies (specific) medical notes.

The fact that Gayle does not conform to recognized ideas about gender, cis or trans, makes her case harder to advocate for – and harder for me to tell.

Often, in the process of researching this book, I have thought about closets within closets. As I write, I consider motivations for keeping quiet and what it means to not know. I think of Gayle's malapropism and her words 'in and out'. Repeatedly, I wonder if Gayle is gender fluid, but has not found the words. And yet any label is a kind of imposition. It comes from the future, and from the outside. I'm trying to give it language, but I'm hesitant too.

*

I've been listening to what Gayle does not say, what slips through.

But I've also got to listen to what Gayle *does* say, to her specific account of Kye – which she describes as a temporary identity; a half-Asian man she spoke as, and then lived as; a role from which she moved 'in and out'; her way to be a

IDENTITY ON THE STAND: FRAUD

lesbian, a boy – both. And, importantly, by the time of the trials, an identity in the past, no longer there.

Kye is a central focus of the trials, which are preoccupied by the question: who, or what, was he? He is materialized via the dossier, the exhibits and through Gayle and Miss X's testimony – which give him, in a sense, *locus standi* or 'place to stand', which refers to the right to be heard in court.

During these trials, Kye – though he lacks a body – seems to take the stand too.

6

Kye Fortune on the Stand: Avatars

By the time Miss X filed her complaint, Kye was gone. She spent two years texting him, five months meeting up with him, but she says she didn't know who he really was. She says, seeing him at her flat that last Sunday, for the first time, changed Kye. He vanished, became strange, lost his personhood, expired.

'I felt like on Sunday Kye had died,' she explained to the police when she made her statement. 'I was in shock. I *am* in shock.'

As police investigated Miss X's claims, they looked for traces of Kye. In so many ways, he was a non-person: he had no rights and lacked a body. But over the course of Operation Imperia, pieces of his life preserved online were amassed in the dossier. The exhibits found in Gayle's bedroom also provided traces, clues as to the history and whereabouts, shape and form, of this missing person, an absentee. His possessions included a phone, a dildo, two love letters, a ring.

*

Gayle describes logging into 'American' chatrooms at thirteen. Through years of online role play, Kye progressed from a username to an avatar as a digital identity was built.

In her manifesto *Glitch Feminism* (2020), Legacy Russell explores the creative potential of online forums. She recalls logging into chatrooms as an adolescent girl growing up in 1990s New York. Her username was LuvPunk12. 'Online I could be whoever I wanted, and so my twelve-year-old self became sixteen, became twenty, became seventy,' she writes. The World Wide Web had recently launched; in this era, it was a kind of playground, characterized by freedom and potential for experiment. For Russell, this allowed for marginalized bodies to take up space, to refuse to perform their assigned roles, to (as she has it) 'glitch'. 'My "female" transmogrified, I set out to explore "man" to expand "woman",' Russell continues. 'I toyed with power dynamics, exchanged with other faceless strangers, empowered by creating new selves, slipping in and out of digital skins, celebrating the new rituals of cybersex.'

When Gayle went online in the early 2000s, she also used chatrooms to create a persona, to experiment – entering anonymous rooms, as Russell did, adopting a username and chatting to other strangers. Speaking online as Kye was a 'mechanism', Gayle explains at trial, to escape from life as an unhappy teenager, and from her single-sex secondary school where it seemed as if there were only straight people, where the word 'lesbian' was a slur.

But Kye soon moved beyond chatrooms. If these rooms were the fertilizer, Kye took root and grew as he migrated to other platforms – first to instant messengers and blogs, and then to new social media sites that were being launched just at that time: Myspace, Facebook, YouTube. These were no longer anonymous, faceless chatrooms, but networks of profiles – places to post, find friends and build an identity. To migrate here, Kye needed a form, a body – a digital skin.

Gayle took photos from Carlo, a Filipino-American man she came across on Myspace. The man in these pictures is described as 'athletic'. He had a muscly torso and boy-band good looks. He often appeared with friends and liked to sing and dance. Gayle reposted these photos on Kye's Facebook page, which she set up in 2005 – assigning Carlo's photos to a new name, a new identity. There were videos too, which she reposted on Kye's YouTube channel, under the name KyeDanceaholic. The videos showed Carlo – and now Kye – dancing in the park with his friends, lip-syncing to the Backstreet Boys, playing Katy Perry songs at a piano.

Those were the images, the videos, but Kye was also a character. While Carlo lived in the US, Kye Fortune was from a peninsula in England, where Gayle had also grown up. He kept a Blogger page, titled 'Inside the Mind of Kye Fortune', set up in 2008. He was a romantic, 'into poetry', posting ballads and lyrics.

Gayle explains that, in role as Kye, she could be herself. Over time, their identities merged. Both were aspiring writers and lyricists, who liked 'chick flicks' and love songs. Gayle describes finding friends online as Kye, as well as collaborators. By 2010, Kye was also studying Creative Writing and Marketing at the same university as Gayle. Outside of his studies he wrote song lyrics under the name Kye4Tune, and during these years he collaborated with real musicians whom he met online. As his lyrics attest, he was a die-hard romantic; for the power ballad 'Valentine', released

KYE FORTUNE ON THE STAND: AVATARS

by Wild Pack Records in 2011, Kye4Tune wrote the lyrics, 'More than a single dream came true/Hope I'll still be next to you/Don't need a rose to keep us together/Because you'll be my Valentine from today 'til forever'. This was all under Kye's belt when he began writing to Miss X in 2011.

Miss X says she believed he was a 'real person', while Gayle insists she knew Kye was an avatar, a digital skin.

In the late 2000s, just around the time that Kye and Miss X began corresponding, a new legal field emerged: virtual law. A spate of books published by lawyers and cyber scholars outlined the field and its concerns. New virtual worlds such as Second Life and Habbo, which launched in the early 2000s, were at the centre of this field. In particular, the law focused on a new species inhabiting them: avatars. These humanoid forms offered a new kind of digital embodiment. During this period, users were beginning to live in these new, digital worlds via their avatars, spending huge amounts of time online and living out a kind of alternative or parallel life, as the name 'Second Life' suggests. Alongside this immersion in virtual space, legal questions were surfacing about the relationship between online and offline worlds. A traditional logic whereby play was seen as separate from life was being disrupted. The 'magic circle' theory, rooted in the 1930s, had proposed a clear dividing line between game and reality, a boundary that shielded play spaces from legal consequences. But now that boundary was being challenged. Avatars in particular – as humanoid virtual 'persons' – seemed to challenge the dividing line.

In 2000, the game designer Raph Koster published a 'Declaration of the Rights of Avatars'. Based on the US Bill of Rights, he argued that avatars should be treated as 'actual people in an online medium' not 'soulless puppets'. A new vocabulary was emerging, as users formed intense emotional connections with avatars, leading to an identity overlap termed 'character attachment' or 'bleed'. New analogies were emerging too. Greg Lastowka, in his book on virtual law, *Virtual Justice: The New Law of Online Worlds* (2011), wrote that 'chess piece' or 'marionette' felt inadequate as descriptors, because avatars were more than pawns or puppets. 'Perhaps the most apt candidate for an avatar-like object is the prosthetic limb,' Lastowka wrote. Here, the avatar is figured as an extension of the self.

There were even some suggestions by scholars in this period that it might make sense to treat avatars as 'legal persons' entitled to legal protections. After all, the model already existed in law; in many jurisdictions corporations are, by statute, legal persons, entitled to certain rights (albeit for limited purposes, most commonly for making contracts).

Virtual law emerged in response to the growth and popularity of virtual worlds, and crucially in response to avatar complaints. For all the freedom that Legacy Russell found in online forums – logging on as LuvPunk12, toying with power dynamics, discovering cybersex – there was always the complication of other users, their autonomy and consent. A decade on, those faceless strangers and personas were now avatars. Some avatars were experimenting, playing and transgressing, pushing the boundaries of the 'game'; others were feeling harmed, coming forward and making complaints.

Avatars were at the centre of these early lawsuits, as lawyers fumbled towards the idea of legal consequences for virtual actions, a concept that was still very new. Most viable complaints followed by Lastowka and other scholars in these years centred on an avatar experiencing some kind of financial loss. These complaints were recognizable; both the avatar and user had lost money, making the 'real-world' consequences clear.

But other cases were more ambiguous. Take a 2007 UK divorce case; the couple were married in Second Life, as well as in real life. When the wife found her husband's avatar having an affair, she sued for a real-world divorce. Capturing legal (and media) attention, the case seemed to be based on a new allegation – avatar infidelity. As well as civil law there were also questions emerging in the field of crime – questions that had been building since the 1990s, specifically concerning another novel accusation: avatar rape.

In 1993, a journalist in an early virtual world witnessed a rape; he subsequently wrote an article entitled 'A Rape in Cyberspace'. At the time, it inspired heated debates: was this a crime? If so, what kind? The fundamental basis of rape is rooted in the idea of bodily harm and requires physical contact: penetration without consent. But this crime was virtual. Was the harm, then, a rape of the mind, emotional distress?

These debates returned with force in 2007, when Belgian Federal Police investigated a virtual rape that had allegedly taken place in Second Life. Think pieces circulated online, with titles like 'Virtual Rape . . . Is It a Crime?' The old questions returned: what was an act of rape, exactly? In virtual contexts, was the user injured? Or was it the avatar – as a prosthesis, an extension of the self – that was, in some way, harmed? In the very same era, sexual fraud complaints were emerging too. So many of the stories – in particular, the gender fraud stories – start online. Some, in immersive online worlds.

*

The case that set the gender fraud precedent, the McNally Principle, on which Gayle was finally convicted, began with avatars in a cyber romance. The defendant, Justine, lived in Glasgow; the complainant, Miss A, in London. In 2008, they met in a virtual world, Habbo. Justine was thirteen years old and Miss A was twelve.

Habbo is an online world aimed at teenagers. Users create an avatar and enter a 'hotel', which has rooms teeming with avatars, making up a kind of city. 'Public rooms' include restaurants, beauty salons, a beach, libraries and cafes. Avatars can teleport around the hotel and go to the most popular rooms. They can also enter 'guest rooms' built by users for role play; there are police departments and hospitals. To take part in the role play, avatars enter the room and look at a board full of Post-it notes to see jobs available. The hospital features cubicles with beds, mint-green sheets and machinery for role play.

Justine's avatar was Scott, a goth, and Miss A's avatar was a girl. They began chatting and role-playing, eventually dating, becoming boyfriend and girlfriend. As a world teeming with role-playing avatars, Habbo is also a site for teen romance, offering a range of bespoke 'furni' for virtual daters, features such as giving each other roses, teddy bears or giant hearts. Seasonal Valentine's Day furni includes 'love locks', pink padlocks that avatars can bolt to each other, their names and the date preserved like etching initials onto a tree. Other romantic activities include movie nights, watching 'iconic rom-coms' together, and looking after virtual pets.

Scott and Miss A's cyber romance played out over three years. Their avatars would meet in public rooms – at the beach, in the cafe, going on dates and role-playing. But they also took it beyond Habbo – chatting on MSN Messenger, then swapping numbers and texting, sometimes speaking on a webcam over Skype. They moved from the virtual world to the real world, eventually meeting in person in 2011.

*

Justine used Habbo to speak as a boy, to experiment with Scott as a digital skin. The account suggests character attachment, a digital alter ego, bleed.

In his 2013 book *The Psychodynamics of Social Networking*, the writer and scholar Aaron Balick considered the way young people across the mid-2000s were forming identities online – exploring new virtual worlds and experimenting with identity, often through 'fantasy avatars' in 'role-playing' worlds. Balick also observed the way many teenagers were trying out alternative personas on social networks too. He noted that, whether an 'avatar self' in a game, or 'persona' on a network, both could equally feel 'psychologically real'. In the teenage years identity is in formation, he continued, not yet settled and many young people in this new, online era were living 'hybrid lives', part online and part offline. Scott appears as an expression of this; Kye, too, as a digital ego and persona that seemed to become psychologically real.

And yet, there are important differences when it comes to behaviour and expectations in these two forums. Worlds like Habbo and Second Life are built as games. They may be immersive, but the foundation is a role-playing world, an alternative reality, a play space and a game. In virtual worlds, avatars aren't expected to correspond to real life. They are customizable, a setting that encourages users to play with appearance. While base avatars typically have humanoid form, the avatar's body shape, skin tone, age, gender and other aspects of appearance are selected. Traditions of 'avatar drag' are customary (a practice also known as 'gender-bending'). In Habbo, avatars take cartoon-style humanoid forms. In Second Life, avatars are generally humanoid, but there are options for post-human possibility too, avatars that are blue-skinned aliens or cyborgs.

On social media, it's different. There are degrees of editing and self-sculpting, but it is not built as a game. Rather, these networks are rooted in real life. The base materials are photographs, which are indexical documents and primarily signify identity. Unlike Scott, Kye did not begin in a role-playing world. He emerged in a different context, migrating from faceless chatrooms to Facebook, eventually living on social media as a profile. Gayle admits taking images from Carlo's online presence.

'Gayle must have followed somebody,' Miss X hypothesized in her statement to the police, 'like, copy-catting their life.'

Repurposing photos that are not your own to create a social media profile – this is generally considered online impersonation. This is not a crime in itself in the UK (although it is in other jurisdictions such as France). To be prosecuted, online impersonation must intersect with other crimes, such as fraud or theft. Gayle says she didn't steal

Carlo's *identity* exactly. She didn't want to become Carlo, or live out a version of his actual life. His pictures were the raw material, but his body was assembled from other images. To Kye's profiles, Gayle added other pictures of 'just random guys' found online, she explains. An image of a man's torso became Kye's body; when Kye was sick, an image of a man's arm with a cannula in it became Kye's. His body was pieced together with globalized, miscellaneous images, literally stock.

A profile pieced together from found images and Carlo's pictures – there's little doubt this was a deceptive account. Gayle never denies this – she agrees, when it came to most people Kye wrote to, that it *was* deceptive. At trial, three of Kye's correspondents, all women, are named, including an ex-girlfriend, who, in a statement read out in court, describes falling in love with Kye online before eventually busting him after doing a little internet sleuthing. But Gayle explains that with Miss X it was different. They were best friends, and she insists that Miss X knew that Kye was an avatar and took part in the story – *as if* they were in another reality, a role-playing game.

Around this time in the late 2000s, a huge number of 'fake' accounts were being identified – social media avatars passing as real, as human. Facebook admitted that 83 million profiles were fakes or dupes in these years – almost 9 per cent. These networks, after all, were new and unregulated; it was easy to create a profile at the click of a mouse. And as Balick noted, teenagers among other groups were experimenting on these platforms, creating alternative personas and living through these accounts. Of all aspects of online life, deception was manifesting in one area in particular, romance. The phenomenon was given a term in 2010, newly coined: catfishing.

Catfishing was first exposed and named by a documentary. *Catfish* (2010) followed Nev Schulman, a photographer in New York, who was embroiled in an online romance with Megan, a beautiful, blonde woman living in another state. Megan was revealed to be a deceptive catfish profile, one of a dozen fake accounts run by an older woman in Michigan who was repurposing photos of a fashion model to create Megan's Facebook page.

The documentary opened a dam; Schulman explained that in the aftermath of its release (and in the same years that Miss X and Gayle were corresponding, 2011–2013) hundreds of people came forward with similar tales. He went on to uncover seemingly endless cases across the US of people being catfished and falling in love with deceptive avatars.

In his subsequent book, *In Real Life: Love, Lies & Identity in the Digital Age* (2014), Schulman considered a catfisher's motives. He described these fake, lifelike profiles as 'digital human beings' and compared them to avatars. But this wasn't clear 'scam' territory. The older woman living online as Megan, and who Schulman finally met, was not a malicious, unscrupulous person trying to defraud Schulman; nor was she using Megan's images for identity theft. Rather, her motives, like other catfishers, were more ambiguous and complex. Schulman noted that catfishers rarely attempted financial extraction. Instead, the main motive appeared to be love under false pretences, reflecting the way catfishers are so often lonely people. They are isolated and insecure, occasionally in the closet, using avatars as ways to find relationships that are missing from physical life. In this reading, catfishing is seen as a kind of coping mechanism and a form of wish-fulfilment.

Schulman explored what draws in the catfished party too. He calls those on the other side of the dynamic 'hopefuls'. He suggests that these people are often struggling as well. They might be lonely, vulnerable, insecure and looking for love (as he was), and they are targeted for those insecurities. Catfish relationships can go on for a long time, sometimes years, and Schulman suggests that it's those vulnerabilities – that 'hope' – that keep the catfished party hanging on, and can mean, at some point, they begin to take part in the deception, half-knowingly.

As forms of wishful thinking, catfish profiles are born from and speak to fantasy. As Schulman observes, dream boys and dream girls are very common to catfish accounts, which often use idealized images – like his catfisher, repurposing photos of a young fashion model. Typical to a catfish profile are not just photos that aren't the user's own, but also images that show implausible people – slim, blonde women and handsome, muscly men. Dream digital skins. People out of movies and the pages of magazines.

*

Gayle and Miss X, by their own admissions, both struggled during the first year of university.

Gayle says she wasn't having a good time. She was still in the closet and still didn't have many friends. She was older now, independent, but often it felt like the big things hadn't changed. Until she met Miss X, nobody knew she was also living as Kye online. He remained a necessity – he could be popular in a way she couldn't, speak to girls in a way she couldn't.

Miss X says she was also having a hard time. She was finding university life difficult. She took jobs to support herself and wasn't very happy. She felt that nobody was attracted to her. 'No one was really asking me out at the university societies,' she says. She dreamed of living elsewhere, of getting swept off her feet.

In some ways, Gayle and Miss X appear as catfisher and hopeful, two lonely people. Reading their accounts, I think about the ways Kye fulfilled a wish for both of them. Together, their testimonies form a composite portrait. There is so much they disagree on, but when it comes to Kye, they're in tune.

As Kye, Gayle could be a boy that girls loved, a man that women adored, while Miss X could be enlisted into the part she so desperately wanted to play: the girlfriend, the chosen one. Kye offered them both an escape from lonely lives, from the monotony of university. An escape into a script, and into the rom-coms they loved to watch together – girl meets boy in its fairytale elaboration.

*

The ever-popular high-school rom-com has at its centre a timeless figure, the prom king. He's a handsome, popular jock, who in the archetypal plot, falls in love against the odds with the unexpected girl – a hidden princess. The unattainable crush gives way to a prom invitation, a first kiss, before she is finally voted his queen. In the rom-com classic *Never Been Kissed* (1999) that unseen girl is Josie. (She is actually an impostor, an undercover reporter writing an exposé on high school, and only pretending to be a teen.) Guy is as generic as his name suggests – so generic, in fact, that Josie keeps mistaking him for another prom king, the one she had a crush on when she was really seventeen. 'High school hasn't changed,' Josie writes in her final article. 'There's still that one guy, with his mysterious confidence, who seems so perfect in every way, the guy you get up and go to school for in the morning . . . High school would not have been the same without him.'

In many ways, Kye appears to be a figure from this Hollywood genre. He's *that* guy – the one you go to school for, the athletic poet, the sensitive hunk. In Gayle's and Miss X's accounts, Kye is described as 'handsome' and 'attractive'. Both recall that 'a lot of girls fancied him'. He was romantic, a ladies' man, but not like other men. 'Sensitive' gets used a lot in relation to Kye. Gayle says he loved rom-coms and poetry. Miss X liked 'his gentleman ways'. In the many months they corresponded before meeting up, both say he sent Miss X flowers, gifts – a necklace, sweets. He was sincere about Valentine's Day and was a fairytale-ending kind of guy. He wanted to talk about the future, the family they'd have, the house on the beach.

Miss X recalls, 'He'd say to me all the time, like, *"You're lucky, you know, 'cause guys don't really, you know, think the way I think. They wouldn't be able to empathise with you the way I can. I get it."'* Kye would continue: *'"But, you know, I work out, I'm still a manly man, I could look after you. You've got the best of both worlds."'*

Kye, by his own admission, had it all. The prosecution sums him up in four words: attractive, athletic, charming, sensitive. The dream guy.

THE BED TRICK

Gayle says for two years she was Kye for Miss X – texting and calling every day. She performed him, she *was* him; yet it was part-time, a role. She had always done Kye alone but now she did it with Miss X. As they began to co-author him, his story and his life evolved organically. A dialogue developed using Kye's profile. They made up stories about the people in Kye's photos – pictures that Gayle had been taking from Carlo and others for years. Kye had a brother called Marl, who lived in a nearby city with his baby Nori. There was also a cousin, Reggie, who Gayle was going out with – she needed a boyfriend too.

Doing it with Miss X felt different. It had never been so elaborate before. The picture began to grow. Kye and Miss X were the protagonists, the romantic duo. They'd go to the uni ball together and get married one day. 'It's a joint effort,' says Gayle in court. They did it 'together'.

Miss X's story is a mirror image. She's not willingly co-writing the fiction in this version. But when it comes to Kye, his character and his story – he's the same. She says that she finally found somebody to love her. She candidly explains that she had felt invisible during the first year of university and that she didn't fit in. 'I wanted to have that boyfriend fantasy that all my friends had,' she says. Other girls she knew were going out with guys 'from the rugby league'. Kye contacted her 'out of the blue' and wanted to be her boyfriend. He offered an answer to all this. 'I wanted that kind of dream life that he was promising me,' she explains.

By the start of second year, it was official. They moved off Facebook and were talking on the phone. He was the dream boyfriend, calling her in the middle of class to tell her

KYE FORTUNE ON THE STAND: AVATARS

he loved her. They were texting constantly – the evidence bundle suggests around eighty messages a day. They spent hours on the phone. 'I was able to open up to him,' she says at trial. 'He never kind of judged me.' They exchanged love letters and poems. Two of the exhibits are cards she sent to Kye. By Valentine's Day that year, they were talking about their future, saying they'd get married one day.

Miss X talks about Kye tenderly. He gave '[me] this love that I'd been searching for', she explains – she felt 'lucky'. She describes the glee of being Kye's girlfriend. 'It's my turn to be happy. It's my turn to brag and be in a relationship, like everyone that I was on my course with. It's my turn to, "*Oh, sorry, no, I've got to take this [call] I've got a boyfriend.*" It was my turn to be in a relationship.'

And yet Kye was virtual, a digital jock, an avatar who couldn't be touched. For eighteen months, the whole relationship played out online. He was never on campus and never around. In both their accounts, he was bunking off – away in Monte Carlo with a rich uncle, in another city with his brother, or dealing with the many dramas that characterized his life.

At trial, Gayle says it remained virtual for so long because she didn't yet know how to be Kye, how to embody him. 'How, how could I possibly meet as Kye?' she asks at the first trial. It didn't feel possible.

But Miss X says she thought Kye was a real person. She really believed they'd get married. She didn't meet him in a role-playing world, and when they imagined their future and discussed what their kids would look like, it wasn't a game. She was planning to spend the rest of her life with him – for real.

Both spent significant chunks of their day logging onto the library computers and texting on their phones. That's where he existed, that was his world. Speaking *to* Kye, *as* Kye – he offered them parts in the fairytale, a role in the movie where the sensitive prom king meets the hidden princess. That is the storyline of the 2004 rom-com *A Cinderella Story*, a remake of the fairytale, in which the royal ball becomes the prom, and Cinderella's slipper a lost cell phone. In the film, the sensitive prom king is the misunderstood jock, Austen Ames. He's played by Chad Michael Murray, perhaps the most generic of all teen heartthrobs with his clean baby face, spiky blond hair, button nose and sparkly blue eyes. Worshipped as the school's football star, he's popular but unhappy – secretly a poet and intellectual, who has applied to Princeton. His dreams are shared by the hidden princess, a bookworm called Samantha, played by teen idol Hilary Duff, who hopes to escape to Princeton too.

Austen and Samantha exist in different worlds at school – one popular, the other invisible. Unbeknownst to them, they've met online under aliases in a Princeton chatroom. She is Princetongirl818. He, Nomad609. They've been talking for months and are deep into a cyber relationship that is tipping into a cyber romance. Like Kye and Miss X, they text every day on their flip phones, chat at lunch on the school computers, then text before bed for five hours at a time. They send each other poetry and share secrets. Online they can open up. Nomad609 says he's living as someone he's not. None of his friends know who he really is, a poet not a jock. He wants to meet her, but she's afraid. 'You're not a guy are you?' Nomad609 asks at one point. 'Otherwise I'll kick your butt!' 'I'm absolutely not a guy!' Princetongirl818 replies.

KYE FORTUNE ON THE STAND: AVATARS

When Nomad609 and Princetongirl818 finally meet in person, the fantasy continues. As it turns out, Austen and Samantha are no different from their handles. He's still the prom king. She's revealed as a princess (aided by a secret will that transforms her fortunes). Dashing out of prom, Samantha drops her cell phone on the stairs, which Austen uses to find her. Eventually they drive off to Princeton together.

Gayle and Miss X, too, found someone online to confide in. For a while, it's like the movie. Gayle can be both Austens at once, prom king and poet. Miss X, like Samantha, can have her boyfriend fantasy, a cyber sweetheart who she hopes will eventually materialize at the Student Union ball. But the movie doesn't last. There's no fairytale ending. Taking it offline changed everything. Gayle says they were stuck in the closet. Coming out, it all went wrong. Miss X says she was duped, she didn't know Kye4Tune was a girl, was Gayle. The pair end up in a courtroom, not Princeton, their cell phones are analysed by experts, not cradled by a prince.

*

As well as logging on and writing to each other like Austen and Samantha, this pair were also constantly speaking on the phone.

Kye's Blackberry is an exhibit. His call log, which takes up many pages of the bundle, shows thousands of calls to Miss X over the years. Miss X describes spending hours on the phone to Kye every day, spending 'every morning talking to him, every night talking to him, falling asleep talking to him'. A big point of contention at the trials is Kye's voice. Miss X insists she thought there were two people, Gayle and

Kye (the Gayle phone, the Kye phone). But while photos of Kye show a different person, two faces, Kye and Gayle indisputably had one voice (a voice that Power describes as 'identical').

During the trials, Power focuses on the call logs. Miss X's log shows back-to-back calls with Kye and Gayle, as Miss X rang her boyfriend, spoke for ten minutes, then called her best friend right after. 'Never suspected that they were the same person?' Power asks sarcastically at the first trial. She must have known, he suggests, since Miss X and Gayle were also best friends in daily life. Typical online deceptions are carried out by strangers, thousands of miles away – like the catfisher behind Megan, who lived in another US state. Similarly, in the original gender fraud case, Scott and Miss A resided in different cities, Glasgow and London. Miss A didn't know Justine, and only spoke to Scott. But here, in the story on trial, Miss X knew Kye *and* Gayle. She spoke to both of them many times a day.

For the defence, Miss X's complaint is 'incapable of belief'. The blindfold makes it so, as does the identical voice. At the first trial, Power pushes the point, telling the jury, 'the same voice – come on – they had the same voice'. At the second, goading Miss X again, he asks, 'Did you not think: gosh they sound alike?'

But Miss X says, 'When I rang Kye I thought I was talking to Kye, when I rang Gayle, I thought I was talking to Gayle.' She insists there were no 'alarm bells', no suspicions, and that she was totally deceived by Kye's profiles and by Kye's voice. He seemed so real – not an avatar, a digital skin, but a profile that passed as a person with a detailed, human life. Often a stressful life.

KYE FORTUNE ON THE STAND: AVATARS

*

The paradox of Kye is that he was bland in some ways – a generic prom king, a blank canvas to project onto – and exceptional in others. 'What an extraordinary man Kye Fortune was,' observed the prosecution barrister at the retrial, describing him as a tease, a trap: a man who was 'sensitive, charming, talented, handsome' – and 'just out of reach'.

He was extraordinary, in part because of his looks – the pictures Gayle took from Carlo and random guys portraying perfect muscly bodies, dream digital skins. But it wasn't just Kye's images that were striking. His life story was pretty astonishing too. Big things, sometimes bad things, always seemed to be happening to him. There were illnesses that had shadowed Kye for years. There were accidents. Six months into the romance with Miss X, he was badly injured in a car crash. He spent a long time in hospital suffering from nerve damage to his leg. Then, while he was recovering, doctors discovered a tumour in his head – cancer. He underwent surgery and began treatment. He was often in intensive care. Pictures on his Facebook page showed Kye from the body down with a cannula in his arm, in a hospital bed.

Sickness is another common thread in catfishing stories. Schulman observed that catfish often tell the same extraordinary stories. Writing of Megan and his own experience of being deceived, Schulman recalled, 'There seemed to be no limit to her incredible stories,' listing car mishaps, hospitalizations, arrests. In the hundreds of other catfish stories he came across, Schulman identified chronic illness (usually cancer) and accidents (particularly car crashes) as most common to these tales. Being ill or in danger is such a frequent narrative trope, explained Schulman, because of its use; it explains why a catfish can never meet up.

These stories – where a love interest is unwell, or on the receiving end of something catastrophic – work, not just as excuses, but because of their emotional power. These deceptive stories insist upon their target taking a leap of faith, almost as if they are testing them, while also dialling up the emotion to the max. This is precisely how emotional manipulation works, using narratives that are intended to trap someone, to stop them leaving, because most people find it hard to abandon somebody who is sick, on death's door.

By the summer of 2012, Kye is in hospital for a 'big op', getting the tumour removed. Miss X says he had a lot of operations that year. He had bandages around his head over the operation scars. She remembers calling him first thing in the morning, last thing at night, and Kye often sounding groggy from all the meds he was taking. She was desperate to meet up with him but his sickness always got in the way.

From the prosecution's point of view, the sickness narrative is particularly damning. It is viewed as part of a manipulative pattern, where Kye's perpetual health crises are a form of controlling behaviour. The prosecution contends, time and time again, that Miss X is manipulated into caring for Kye by an emergency, by his imminent death. And Gayle is the unscrupulous wizard behind it all; as Medland puts it in the second trial, Kye's sickness was 'a way for you to control Miss X for your own ends . . . To keep her as it were dangling on a hook for twelve months or more, until you had got her into the place where you wanted her to be mentally.' In this view, Kye's illness is just one of Gayle's sinister, cynical 'mind games'.

KYE FORTUNE ON THE STAND: AVATARS

Illness fictions or scams are not new. But, across the 2000s, increasing reports began to surface featuring people found to be faking terminal cancer or other serious illnesses in online support groups. In one report, a woman joined a group on Facebook for people diagnosed with breast cancer. She posted pictures of herself bald from chemotherapy, chronicling the cancer as it spread to all her major organs and became terminal. Eventually she stopped posting, appearing to die. Later, the account was revealed to be fake.

A fictional wound can be a way to escape guilt and other lies, as it transforms a person into a victim. Sick 'roles', as in Munchausen syndrome (a behavioural condition in which somebody fabricates or induces symptoms of illness), can also express a desire to be cared for; psychiatrists would go on to describe this wave of online illnesses as 'Munchausen by internet'.

But Gayle says she didn't identify as sick. She says it was role play; it unfolded on Kye's profile, his email, his phone. Kye had been sick before, in his dialogues with other women. But she says Miss X knew he wasn't sick, because she knew Kye was Gayle. It was part of the story, part of the fantasy. It was also part of the closet too – the illness a story they told 'other people', Gayle says, an excuse they could give to family and friends.

As 2012 drew to a close, Kye was only getting sicker. He moved to a private hospital many miles away. Miss X recalls the doctors saying his cancer was terminal and he might only have 'a couple of months' to live. He began to undergo treatment and had to be connected up daily to a machine.

Romantic literature abounds with tales of unrequited love, forbidden love, doomed love. Dying lovers are a staple of opera – take the pale, sick seamstress Mimi in Giacomo Puccini's opera *La Bohème* (1895), who becomes bedridden and dies in the final act, coughing and falling into a coma as her lover watches on. In modern times, a genre known as 'terminal romance' has taken the place of opera, and features sick, dying lovers. In the formula, which gained popularity in the 2000s, a couple fall desperately in love, only for one partner to discover that they suffer from a terrible, life-threatening disease. The drama moves savagely from honeymoon to hospital bed. In *Sweet November* the female lead devastates her lover by revealing she has terminal cancer; in *P.S. I Love You* a new husband is lost to a brain tumour; in *A Little Bit of Heaven* a starlet battles terminal cancer while her lover looks on.

This genre was epitomized by *The Fault in Our Stars*, John Green's popular sick-lit novel of 2012, which went on to become a Hollywood hit. It's a love story about two teenagers who are battling cancer. Hazel has stage-four thyroid cancer that's spread to her lungs. She carries around a portable oxygen tank and wears a nasal cannula. Gus, the love interest, has lost a leg to bone cancer. The sick teenagers meet in a cancer support group and fall in love. Despite medical setbacks, they manage to have a holiday in Amsterdam. Their first kiss is, somewhat gothically, in Anne Frank's house, stolen as they wander the rooms where Anne hid for over seven hundred days, before being transported to the death camps. They lose their virginity in a nearby hotel, before Gus confesses that his cancer has returned. It's spread through his body and is now terminal. At a 'pre-funeral', organized by Gus himself, the anguished lovers profess that they would not trade their short time together for anything.

The film was so popular that it spawned an abundance of other terminal romances, featuring sick teenagers with immune disorders or allergies that mean they can't touch other people or leave the house.

Some of Kye's messages to Miss X are desperate in the extreme. 'They've put me under sedation. I was in so much pain I was screaming,' Kye writes feverishly. 'Don't leave me, baby.' In other messages, sent from Kye's phone while he was unconscious, he skims close to death and falls into a coma. It's unclear who is sending these texts in the story (his brother? Gayle? A nurse?). 'He's not well and stopped breathing,' one text reads. 'He's under intensive care now', 'Pray for him', others state.

Gayle insists it was part of the romance, the story. 'She always did, like, continued on with the role play,' she says. 'As bizarre as it sounds.' Did Kye's sickness spur them on, make it more intoxicating, where every night he escapes death, comes back from the edge? At times, Kye functions like a character in a terminal romance: beautiful, brilliant, often on the verge of death. But the messages scream of coercion too, with Miss X trapped in the drama, hooked by the catastrophic story, unable to escape.

By the end of 2012, Miss X says she was starting to despair about the future of their relationship. But then, just before Christmas, Kye sent her an eternity ring from a jeweller, a symbol of never-ending love. It was a proposal, the commitment she'd been waiting for, and she began to hope once again.

Gayle tells it differently. They were never engaged. That was Miss X getting carried away. 'She'd talk to her friends about, you know, like about plans for the wedding day and all this type of stuff,' Gayle says. It was snowballing, spinning out of control. At some point, the story does seem to run away with both of them. Miss X admits she fibbed to her friends that she'd already met Kye, making her more frantic to meet him in real life. Gayle, speaking as Kye for years, had never come so close to stepping away from the keyboard, becoming Kye offline.

And finally she did.

Kye and Miss X first met on Valentine's Day 2013. In court, the meeting is of little importance. It doesn't feature in the counts against Gayle. It was brief; they only kissed. But Gayle and Miss X both describe it in their testimonies. For them, the meeting was pivotal. After years speaking *as* Kye, *to* Kye, they decided to make it physical and put their bodies in the same room.

That Kye chose Valentine's Day feels in character – a rom-com plot point, something Kye, the dream man, was almost programmed to do. In a kind of mechanical sentimentality, Kye performs that boyfriend fantasy. I think of the sweet monotony of his song lyrics. He acts like an extension of the day's merchandise: the pre-written verses, heart-shaped sweets, the Habbo furni, the teddy bears holding 'I love you' signs.

*

To write the following scenes, I combed through thousands of pages, trawling through the barristers' arguments, the testimonies, statements and agreed facts. I gathered up all the details. The first meeting feels so important to the story, and to establishing how their relationship worked, the rituals they created, how they normalized it – whether as a deception or as role play. I listened to what they both say, seeking to understand the students, the best friends, the lovers, Kye.

For every memory, piece of evidence and event, there are always two accounts. Only one can be true, and the court is on the hunt for the liar: the cunning complainant or the cunning defendant. Against this structure, I try to write from both points of view, and to create a scenario where neither are lying, and where both stories can be true.

*

She's been waiting so long for this moment. Kye is the boyfriend she's dreamed of. They speak every day. But he's so sick and she's terrified he might die. Sometimes she can hear the beep of his hospital machinery on the phone. His sickness consumes her entirely and leaves little room in her life for much else. Since they've been dating, she's lost friends; only Gayle is left.

Then it happens – he sends her an engagement ring. It's what she's always wanted. Now she's more desperate than ever to meet him. She's going to be Mrs Fortune! She tells him she'll come to the hospital in Manchester, she'll meet at a hotel – anything just to see him. It's an 'uphill battle', she explains at trial. He doesn't want to meet, because he's embarrassed about his injuries, and he's too weak from the treatment. But finally he agrees. She's his fiancée now, he's got to trust her. They settle on a date, but she's scared he'll back out like he always does. At trial, she forgets the date they met, then remembers it – Valentine's Day. He says he'll leave the hospital to come and see her. He says the nurse thinks he shouldn't, but he's going to do it anyway. Gayle will drive him to her flat, and back again. She was helpful like that.

Miss X says, in the run up, she is mainly excited. Finally, they're moving things forward. He tells her he can only stay for a few hours, because he's so sick. And there are conditions – he has scars from all the operations under his bandages. He's self-conscious. He tells her he doesn't look like his photos but she says she doesn't care. He doesn't want her to see the scars on his chest and on his head. When he asks her to wear a blindfold, she agrees – by now, she'll do anything to meet him, she explains at trial. Her flat at this point is on a busy road and she shares it with other students. On the phone, they discuss how they're going to do it, because Kye doesn't want to meet her friends. It's too soon. But Miss X says it won't be a problem. Everyone will be in their bedrooms – it's Valentine's Day, and they're doing something special with their boyfriends too. They make a plan: Kye will text Miss X to say he's nearby. Then she'll unlatch the front door, climb back up the stairs and wait for Kye there. She'll text him to say she's ready, put on a blindfold – she'll use a silk scarf – and stand with her back to the door, waiting.

At trial, she says she hears Kye come in, climb to the fourth floor. Then she feels him as he puts his arms around her to touch her face – checking the scarf is in place. Finally, he turns her round and they embrace.

She remembers he guides her into the bedroom. She can't see anything but describes hearing a rustle, feeling wool on her face, as Kye ties something over the silk, another layer – and she realizes it's her pink woolly scarf. She remembers Kye is nervous. His hands are shaking when he ties the scarf. He's breathing heavily, and then they sit on her bed, and they lie back and kiss. 'When we cuddled his heart was going ten to the dozen,' she recalls. She assumes it's because he's on so much medication. 'We lay there for a bit,' she remembers, listening to each other's heartbeats.

He's real – she can feel his body, taste his lips, share his breaths. They kiss for a while and then he leaves. He has to go back to the hospital, back to the machines.

*

Gayle also says she's been waiting for this moment for so long. She's been speaking as Kye for almost a decade, but has never made it physical, and has still not kissed a girl.

She remembers everything with Miss X was a first. She'd come out to Miss X in the club toilets and told her she spoke as Kye – both first times. And now, she was going to meet her as Kye and take Kye offline for the first time in her life.

The year texting as Kye has been exciting and scary – the dialogue between them like an invisible force. After all the years of secrecy and shame, she can now be Kye for someone she knows, and be Gayle and Kye at once. But she says she doesn't really know what she's doing; neither of them does. They're making it up as they go along, improvising. In court, Gayle calls it 'two stupid girls really, just experimenting'. They're working it out in different ways and she's learning Miss X's way is very different to hers. When Miss X gushes over the engagement, the house on the beach, telling her friends, Gayle feels a mixture of fear and also pride. It's just getting bigger, snowballing. But she wants it so badly.

Sometimes it feels confusing: she wants to be with Miss X openly as a girlfriend – to tell their families, to come out of the closet. But she wants to be with her as Kye too. They're texting every day and speaking every day, on two phones, Gayle's and Kye's. Every morning, Miss X asks about Kye, about the hospital, about the treatment. Kye says he's so sick, he might die. Then they say they love each other. On the phone, they talk about their future. Kye gets sicker, Kye gets better. Miss X asks about the machine. Sometimes Gayle wonders if he'll have to die. She doesn't know how to meet up as him. How is it even possible? He's always at death's door, but he survives. And Miss X wants him to live so badly. She's always saying please meet me, come to my flat. Gayle has been to the flat loads of times before but it would be different if she went as Kye.

Eventually they decide to do it. Gayle wants to please her, so she lets Miss X talk her round, whittle away at the physical wall that's always divided Kye's life and hers. Miss X is her best friend and if she can do it with anyone, it's with her. They choose Valentine's Day, because Kye loves it. Last year he sent Miss X flowers. This year he'll send himself, and they'll have their first kiss. It will be Gayle's first kiss as Kye, the first time she's kissed a girl.

On Valentine's Day, Gayle drives over to Miss X's flat. She parks in the usual spot, feeling nervous, wondering if the other housemates are in. Then she walks down the busy road and buzzes Miss X's door. She's been here dozens of times, but it's different as Kye. She's brought a baseball cap with her. It's Kye's – he supports the New York Knicks. She puts it on. She's waiting. She doesn't know if she's Gayle or Kye. But she knows they're both virgins and they've never kissed a girl.

The door opens and Miss X is there.

She's Gayle and Kye – both. They follow her up the stairs and they go to Miss X's bedroom. For a second, it's weird. At trial, Gayle remembers being at the flat a few weeks before, as Gayle, helping Miss X build her new bed. They sit on it now, fall back and hug. They are in and out of role. They've never been Kye before. It's the first time they're hugging as Kye, but they're Gayle too. 'Obviously we hugged, but you know, we've hugged loads of times,' Gayle says at trial. Then they kiss. That's different. They've never kissed a girl before. 'I'm not ashamed to say I was shaking, like,' Gayle explains at trial. It feels too much. Then Miss X calls them Kye, and they know it's going to be okay.

7

The Dildo on the Stand: Bodies

Nev Schulman writes that catfish are 'doomed'. Their relationships will almost always end when the people meet in real life.

But for Miss X and Kye it was different, at least for a while. After the first meeting on Valentine's Day, they met up regularly for five months, initially at local hotels and later at Miss X's new flat.

Miss X says she remembers the first hotel in the most detail, which is why she describes it in her police statement. She says that Kye continued to be the perfect man, a Romeo. He kept making sweet gestures. She arrived in a taxi he paid for, to find rose petals on the bed, a Hello Kitty teddy waiting for her on a pillow. He'd booked the room and was waiting for her in the bathroom. The only way he'd agreed to meet: her eyes had to be closed. After the accidents, the facial disfigurement and wasted muscles, he was shy. From the bathroom, he instructed her to put on the blindfold – this time an eye mask that he'd laid out on the bed too. When he came out, they hugged, kissed and eventually took off their clothes. Miss X remembers Kye saying, 'Are you ready?'

and 'We've been waiting for ever' and 'Gosh you look beautiful'. She remembers he was shaking again, because he was nervous. He'd signed himself out of hospital to be with her.

'It was like, like . . . It was like a normal boy and girl having sex', she says.

They'd lie there for a few hours, and eventually Kye would have to leave. Usually Gayle would pick him up, driving him back to the hospital ward.

*

At trial, the dildo is held up: Exhibit 3, an Ultra CyberSkin Penis. 'CyberSkin' is made of an elastomer called SEBS (styrene-ethylene-butylene-styrene), which is a skin-like material that originates from the space industry. The product is sold as a 'strap-on flesh penis' and comes with a pair of black pants; the dildo attaches to a plug at the crotch. 'CyberSkin feels like real human skin,' the product box boasts. Elsewhere, it is described as a 'dream penis', a 'lifelike lover'. The descriptions are telling: it is at once a fantasy body part, but also graphic and exact. Somehow both a faithful representation (scale 1:1), yet also an ideal.

Exhibit 3 is a replica, because the original dildo was never located. It is neon pink, but actually Miss X says that the original was 'skin' colour. The dildo is brought to court by the defence. Power holds it up at both trials, presenting it to Miss X and then to Gayle. He is clearly uncomfortable holding it. 'So how did . . . How would you come to – I'm not holding it the right way,' he fumbles, changing his grip twice.

It's as if the facsimile penis is hard to make sense of, alone. It is shown to Miss X and Gayle, but there's another audience too, the jury. 'I'm going to hold it up so the jury can understand,' Power relays. It interests the fact finders. At both trials, jurors will ask for the rubber penis to be delivered to the deliberation room. It can be touched, held, weighed up and passed around, in a way a flesh penis never could be.

In Miss X's descriptions, the dream penis is imbued with a mysterious power: wholly deceptive, fully lifelike. As such, it appears as a guilty object.

*

In Ancient Greece, objects could be accused of committing crimes; indeed they had a court, the Prytaneion, dedicated to trials of murderous objects. In a case from the fifth century BC recorded by the chronicler Pausanias, the statue of a famed boxer, Theagenes, was put on trial. The boxer had won multiple victories at the Olympic Games, and also racked up rivals. One visited his statue, whipping it every night in a kind of posthumous revenge. ('[He] flogged the bronze image as though he were ill-treating Theagenes himself,' Pausanias wrote.) When the statue fell on the rival and killed him, the victim's son took the bronze to court. The statue was found guilty of murder and punished – thrown into the sea.

While the statue of Theagenes seemed to fight back, the dildo's transgression was to appear like flesh. According to Plato, the Prytaneion was a court where 'a thing' could be 'defeated'. In Chester and then Manchester, Power brings the CyberSkin to court, in an attempt to undo its power. His line of attack is, on the face of it, straightforward. The dildo may look lifelike, he argues, but it is not. 'The prosthetic isn't real,' he says, many times. 'While it may provide the sensation of a penis-shaped object going inside, it can't do what a penis does because it's not real.' He strives to make clear distinctions between plastic and flesh, calling on common sense about penises, average ejaculations, and at times turning to scientific literature. ('What about, this is what the scientists call it, okay, rhythmic contractions?' he asks Miss X at one point.) A real penis gets hard and goes soft; a dildo is still. This distinction makes Miss X's complaint 'incredible', Power argues. ('You knew,' he tells her.)

But Miss X says the dildo passed. It was entirely convincing. 'Like, all I know is there was a penis inside me and I thought I was making love to Kye Fortune,' she says. She insists that without being able to look at it, the prop was wholly deceptive – so convincing that she consented, over and over again.

Although the exhibit is brought to court by Power, it is actually unclear if it serves the defence. Neither side can seem to gain mastery over it, as if the object cannot be brought to heel. The exhibit doesn't neatly assist one side's account, or the other. As such, it exudes a kind of independence.

Trials of objects persisted in medieval England. The accused items, named 'deodands', were murderous, seemingly with agency, described in law as 'a thing that moved to cause death'. Legal rolls record hundreds of prosecutions across the centuries: guilty items included a vat of boiling water into which a woman fell; a maypole that crushed a person to death; a carving knife that fell into human flesh; a cart that ran over a sleeping man. The objects were held responsible – and punished – for these crimes. In one case from 1552, a piece of wood fell on a child as she played in a yard, killing her. The stick was delivered to a local jail.

The prosecution of deodands reveal the law acting upon objects in unexpected ways. A deodand was considered semi-independent, taking on a fictive personhood – the stick, the maypole, the knife, the vat, imbued with a kind of volition or free will.

Deodand laws were formally abolished in the 1840s. Nevertheless, the dildo in the dock appears as a semi-independent object. It is not murderous, like a deodand, but dangerously lifelike and treacherously deceptive. It is named in the indictment, 'a prosthetic penis', and at trial it is presented as an object that passed, almost miraculously, as flesh.

In court, both Gayle and Miss X distance themselves from the dildo. Gayle says she was a virgin with 'no sexual experience whatsoever' and that the dildo was Miss X's idea; 'I just remember her saying, well, you know, there's ways,' Gayle says.

But Miss X says the opposite. 'It was not my idea to use a strap-on because I didn't believe we needed a strap-on,' she tells Power. She thought she was having 'normal' sex with a 'real' guy and she was tricked; in Miss X's version, Gayle slipped the dildo into the scene, and into her.

Neither of them wants to be attached to the dildo – a promiscuous object, a queer object. A sly, threatening and witchy object. But the dildo was, literally, attached to Gayle – 'strapped to her waist', as Corbett-Jones puts it. The term 'strap-on' is used throughout both trials, along with 'the dildo' and 'the penis'. But it wasn't attached to Gayle's 'waist', as the Crown's description suggests, but to her crotch. It was, after all, a prosthesis, made to fit exactly in place.

*

Prostheses resist the traditional distinction between body and object. This is a difference rooted deep in law, which dates back to the Roman era. The legal body is understood as biological (blood, bones, flesh); its boundary is the skin. The body has a special status, and strong protections even from touch. Objects, meanwhile, are in a different legal category, seen as property and not protected to such a degree.

Across the twentieth century, however, this established distinction proved increasingly fraught. Border cases kept emerging – parts of the body that could change category, such as donated organs, which acquire independent legal status once detached from the body. And, in the other direction, things that can become part of the body, from cochlear implants to pacemakers and artificial joints.

Prostheses are another problem category. The term first appeared in English in eighteenth-century medical texts, where it was used to describe the replacement of a missing body part with an artificial one. In *Visceral Prosthesis* (2022), the theorist Margrit Shildrick tracks the shift in meaning of prostheses as a result of phenomenology, the twentieth-century philosophical enquiry into the nature of perception. Thinkers such as Maurice Merleau-Ponty upset a nineteenth-century confidence in the line between bodies and objects. In the 1940s, Merleau-Ponty set out a thought experiment, now famous, about a blind man with a white cane navigating a city street. As the cane became part of the blind man's perceptual apparatus, it stopped being simply an object,

Merleau-Ponty argued. The tip of the cane 'is transformed into a sensitive zone', he wrote, becoming an 'instrument of perception'. 'The world of feelable things recedes and now begins, not at the outer skin of the hand, but at the end of the stick.'

For Shildrick, all prostheses can be transformed into sensitive zones, becoming integrated into a body's perceptual apparatus, in a manner akin to the blind man's cane. She considers phantom limb pain, as experienced by prosthesis users, to contemplate the slipperiness of incorporation and embodiment. The boundary of the skin is too limited when it comes to the body and even the human, she argues; 'artificial' prostheses can be experienced as living, as self, in myriad ways.

UK law does not consider prostheses anything more than things. Strike a wheelchair, kick a prosthetic limb, and it is property damage, not assault. As such, the violent act matters less. After all, it's just an object, the logic goes. It is replaceable.

The prosthetic penis on trial is, in legal terms, 'a thing'. It is not considered a part of Gayle's or Kye's body. Even so, I think about Shildrick's idea of the visceral prosthesis and about prostheses' special relationship to the body. In an article on penile prosthetics, the theorist Chris Straayer writes of the small but flourishing industry of prosthetic products for trans men, in particular those made by a company named Transthetics. Set up in 2014, Transthetics offers a range of prostheses, including a realistic penis called the Joystick. Like the CyberSkin, its production is ultra lifelike and comes with briefs rather than straps; there are also colour choices to match a user's skin tone. Transthetics founder Alex describes the prosthetics as born from a personal need for products that would alleviate his gender dysphoria. He suggests he's able to experience the Joystick as a sensory zone. Writing of using the prosthesis, he describes the way it extends his perception: 'I can feel the Joystick penetrating my partner, can experience an orgasm inside my partner', Alex writes. Straayer goes on to argue that, for some trans men, prostheses of this kind can promote trans male embodiment. 'The trans man inhabits the prosthetic, incorporates it into his body, brings it to life', Straayer writes.

The CyberSkin – as a skin-coloured, lifelike dildo, fitting exactly in place – shares characteristics with the Joystick. Did Gayle choose a lifelike dildo, so akin to the Joystick, because she wanted to feel it, like Alex, as her own?

A month after the retrial, Gayle was diagnosed with gender dysphoria. This is a sense of distress resulting from a mismatch between gender experienced and gender assigned. It can deepen into depression, anxiety and suicidal thoughts. In some ways, the diagnosis further opens up the possibility that the lifelike dildo might have been a way for Gayle to alleviate her symptoms – just as Alex alleviated his.

At the trials, nobody argues that the CyberSkin Penis is anything more than a thing; no one suggests it was incorporated, embodied or brought to life. This is not a question that concerns the trials: consent is. Did Miss X know what was inside her, or was she deceived by Gayle? Did she consent to rubber or flesh? Often, Miss X's sensations are foregrounded. In examination and cross-examination, the dildo is evoked through her perceptions. Miss X says she couldn't see; all her memories of Kye were blind ones. Her senses take the stand (and at times, it's as if her vagina takes the stand). She insists that the function, the feel, the performance, felt 'like a guy', like Kye; the dildo felt human, felt like flesh.

But these are deception trials, and they also interrogate Gayle's decisions, her reasons and her mindset – in an attempt to evaluate her cunning. Gayle says a range of things about Kye. Often Kye is 'other', a story, an avatar with his own phone number, a separate life. But he's also Gayle; she's Kye at the keyboard, then she's Kye for Miss X.

They met many times across spring 2013. Each time, Miss X says she believed it was Kye. Each time, Gayle says she became Kye, but she was Gayle too.

At one point during the trials, Gayle is asked to describe her orgasms. Power asks, awkwardly, if Gayle orgasmed as Kye. 'When you were acting as Kye, did you act as if you were ejaculating?' he asks. Power's question surprises me. It's the closest he gets to drawing out Gayle's experience of using the prosthesis. Gayle says a few things. She says 'no', then she says 'sometimes'. She explains it was 'Gayle' who ejaculated. Then she says she isn't sure. Language seems to fail her.

For me, her answer reveals the difficulty, perhaps impossibility, of separating out Kye's feelings and perceptions from her own. They shared a body. They moved 'in and out' of role. Where does Gayle's perception end and Kye's begin? Is it possible for her to know, or even say?

For the Crown, Gayle had one intention when she chose the prosthetic penis: deception. It is nothing more than a clever tool. The fact that it is lifelike, made of CyberSkin, is seen as pure strategy – evidence of the 'lengths' Gayle went to, part of her 'semi-professional' deception, as Medland describes it at the retrial. It's an accelerating trajectory: the more real the prosthesis, the more deceptive it gets, its

THE DILDO ON THE STAND: BODIES

trickery only heightened, its guilt intensified. Together, the 'stolen' pictures of Carlo, the deceptively lifelike dildo and the mask are all parts of Gayle's cunning deception, her 'twisted' stunt.

*

Dildo anxiety is old. The artificial penis has probably been around as long as the natural one, and used as a masturbation aid by women and men alike. The Old Testament identified 'onanism', as masturbation was then named, as a sin, and by the medieval period it was officially condemned by the Catholic Church. Onanism was diabolical, a crime against nature – worse, some argued, than the so-called natural sins of fornication, incest and rape. While the Ancient Greeks made jokes about dildos and masturbation on stage – in Aristophanes' play *Lysistrata*, for example, women used 'olisbos' (leather penises) to satisfy their needs – in medieval Europe, such things were deemed wicked, especially when associated with women.

A medieval witch-hunting manual, the *Malleus Maleficarum*, describes witches' practices. One in particular struck terror into clergymen of the time: penis theft. The manual warns that witches would domesticate stolen penises, keeping them as prisoners or pets. The cases relayed in the manual seem to be a way of talking about dildos, without explicitly mentioning them. Dildos take the form of stolen penises that witches would fatten up ('with oats') and keep in a secret place (either 'in a bird's nest' or 'in a box').

Occasionally, women were prosecuted for sexual relations with other women. These unnameable acts, often silenced and ignored, were deplored if a witchy penis-substitute was involved. In a rare trial from fifteenth-century Germany, a woman named Katherina Hetzeldorfer was tried for sexual relations with women. At trial, Katherina scandalized the court by describing a home-made penis, which she fashioned with 'a wooden stick' and 'a piece of red leather'. She admitted to tying it around her waist with 'a string' and having sex with her 'wife'. The crime didn't have a name in 1477. The baffled, angry judges issued a death sentence and Katherina was drowned in the Rhine.

Anxieties took on a new form in the eighteenth century, when explicitly lifelike dildos began to be manufactured after a new material hit the marketplace: rubber. Then known as 'gum elastic', it was arriving in Europe from colonized countries, obtained from the sap of rubber trees. Lauded applications included rubber erasers, to remove marks from paper (replacing wax or bread). But there were private uses too. In his memoirs, Casanova relayed an escapade with a castrato singer named Bellino. In 1740s Venice, women were not allowed on stage, and Bellino had been 'inspected' many times to ensure that he was a boy. But Casanova revealed that, actually, Bellino was Theresa, a girl who had been fooling inquisitors with a lifelike rubber penis, which tricked the naked eye and attached to her crotch with 'glue'.

In the very same period, the so-called female husband trials began to reach courts in England. One famous case, featuring a quack doctor named Charles Hamilton, appeared in broadsheets (early newspapers), exciting public interest. His wife complained, several months after their honeymoon, that Charles was not a man. She said the marriage had been consummated and she'd been deceived. At trial in 1746, Charles was exposed as Mary, a woman. The crime provoked confusion and debate, since there was no clear legal procedure to prosecute such an offence, but eventually Mary was convicted under vagrancy laws. The punishment was very public; Mary was stripped and whipped in four towns (illustrations show a topless figure on a stage, hands in stocks, being whipped as a crowd looked on). A dildo was never mentioned at the trial, but the penny pamphlets and fictional retellings were more explicit: something 'scandalous' was found in the doctor's medical bag, something 'vile' and 'wicked' – in other words, an object that was very guilty indeed.

Legal historian Caroline Derry traces the many other 'female husband' cases in England and Wales in the nineteenth and twentieth centuries, which she reads as precursors to gender fraud. In many cases, wives complained their husbands were not men, and that they'd been duped in the bedroom. The problem was, there was no crime for such an act and the trials did not change that. No new legislation was suggested, as if the anxiety that belied the allegations was unthinkable (penis thieves having sex ... *as men*). The 'female husbands' were tried under other offences: vagrancy, perjury, breach of the peace.

By the 1990s, there was still no crime for dildo rape. But the trial of a teenager in Doncaster in 1991 became one of the first explicit UK dildo trials. The teenager had presented as a man called Jimmy and was accused of deceiving two women into sex. One described the baggy clothes Jimmy wore and the 'sharp' feel of his penis. Another described having sex six times a week, and the 'lumps' on Jimmy's chest that he'd explained were cancerous boils. Although both accounts described penetrative sex, the dildo remained legally invisible. It didn't feature in the counts, since there was no clear offence – Jimmy, legally Jennifer Saunders, was charged with 'indecent assault'. The remarks of the judge who heard the case pointed to a hierarchy of rape, if not written into law then into culture: 'I suspect both those girls would rather have been actually raped by some young man than have happened to them what you did,' Judge Crabtree said.

Miss X says, in the days before she went to the police, she spoke to Gayle on the phone. 'I spoke to my nurse, it's not a crime,' she remembers Gayle saying. Gayle denies this, but in any case, by 2013, it was a crime – assault by penetration, Section 2, equal to rape.

The streak of gender fraud cases since 2012 are almost all dildo cases. The objects are described in police and court documents as 'prosthesis', 'dildo', 'strap-on', sometimes 'unknown object', sometimes 'sex toy'. At the centre of the allegations is a new, explicit and hyper-visible dildo.

The Sexual Offences Act 2003 made rape by a prosthesis and rape by a penis parallel offences with equal punishments. But case law tells a different story. Since 2012, the prosthesis that passes has become a very guilty object. Meanwhile, deceptions in which a person has lied or obscured other parts of their identity are not prosecuted – seen most recently in the 'Spy Cop' scandal ruling of 2018.

The scandal exposed the undercover policemen who posed as activists, under elaborate false identities (known as 'legends', because they began with a seed of truth: the spies took the names of dead children to ensure birth certificates existed). Many of these undercover police officers had relationships with women, often activists themselves, some lasting years and some resulting in children. Women, coming forward since 2012, said they did not consent to sex with these 'random' actors. They had no idea they were having intimate relationships with married cops; they had consented to entirely different men.

As of 2025, more than fifty women have spoken out. One case was taken forward under the pseudonym 'Monica', and under the banner of rape by deception, but in 2018, a High Court refused the complaint. Sex with men pretending to be fictional men was not rape, the court ruled – essentially saying that, if your lover with a penis has lied to you, by pretending to be someone else, what matters is that you chose to have sex with a penis. The refusal to charge Spy Cops in 2018 and the years since contrasts sharply with the dildo trials, suggesting a willingness to prosecute the dildo over the penis. Is rape by prosthesis more credible to (regular) cops? Is the dildo more guilty – more prosecutable – than flesh?

During Gayle's trials, the Crown describes Kye as 'non-existent', an elaborate 'story' – in other words, he's a legend too. But unlike the Spy Cops, the deception counts. And the reason – the fictional penis.

The Spy Cop rulings could be read as exceptional, as a state-sanctioned deception, and a closing of ranks. But in fact, by 2020 a new ruling enhanced the Spy Cop logic. The Court of Appeal decided that a man in Scotland, who lied about a vasectomy, was not guilty of rape. The only deceptions that would be taken seriously, the court stated, must be connected to the 'performance of the sexual act'. The judgment ruled that deceptions relating to the 'outcome' of the act (i.e., a vasectomy) would not be prosecuted, while deceptions relating to the 'performance' of the act (i.e., dildos, condom stealthing) could be prosecuted.

At the trials, the defence argues against Kye's performance. The legend didn't make sense. Kye was a sick man, on death's door; he had a heart monitor implanted, and a 'nozzle' going into his heart. How did he get up the stairs on Valentine's Day? How did he perform as a lover?

In Miss X's DVD statements, she describes meeting Kye in different hotel rooms across 2013. There, they had 'normal boy and girl' sex; she conjectures that the dildo was secretly put on when Kye reached for a condom, each time. During the trials, the Crown suggests Gayle pulled off the stunt by clever manoeuvres in the bedroom. An exhibit is passed around, this time the packaging box for the Cyber-Skin, found in Gayle's bedroom; there are instructions for use on the back. At the first trial, Corbett-Jones imagines the bed trick scene. He speculates that Gayle hid the detachable penis 'down the side of the bed', or 'in a bag' nearby. In Renaissance theatre, the device was part of a collection of stage tricks, but it was rarely acted out. A 'good dramatist', noted a Shakespeare critic, does not 'flaunt' the implausibility of the bed trick; it is reported, rather than enacted. But at trial, it's different. The Crown must convincingly explain how the deception worked. Evoking the hotel scene, Corbett-Jones describes Gayle 'moving around on the bed', rolling off Miss X, reaching for the hidden penis, rolling back.

During Gayle's cross-examination, Power presents a receipt for the CyberSkin, purchased by her on 12 April, which is after the hotel dates Miss X describes.

Gayle's account of the hotel meetings is different. She agrees they met four times, but it wasn't for sex. In her account, being 'in role' as Kye didn't involve a penis, at first. It was more than sex, more than a body part. Being in role, being in the same space – it was new. According to Gayle, there was no blindfold. She would arrive first and give Kye's name at the reception; then she'd wait in the hotel room, as Kye. Miss X would arrive soon after. They'd spend the afternoon holding each other. At the first hotel, they massaged each other, kissed, ate sweets. Afterwards, Gayle gave Miss X a lift home.

The dildo receipt confuses Miss X's account. If they had sex at the hotels, like she says, what did Gayle, or Kye, use? Were there two dildos? 'Did Kye have different penises for different occasions?' Power asks, slipping into courtroom farce. (It's always close by: men in wigs, holding up the dildo, discussing how sex 'works'. Occasionally laughter is reported from the public gallery.) But Miss X won't back down. 'She must have had sex with me with something,' she replies.

Here, the prosthesis blurs into 'something', the 'unknown object' of other trials – away from a prosthesis, a part of the body, quasi-sensory, limb-like, to an alien object without a name. In other recent gender fraud cases – such as the prosecution of Carlos Delacruz in Scotland in 2018, and Blade Silvano in England in 2023 – defendants were accused of slipping an 'unknown object' into their partners' bodies. 'Unknown' opens it up to being anything, thus making it at once farcical and sinister. A wooden spoon? A bottle? A loo brush? A knife?

Gayle was found guilty at both trials, but at the retrial, there's a small shift. She's found guilty on all three dildo counts, but interestingly, not on the single tongue count.

That one slips away, seeming to demonstrate the dildo's optical power, as a prop that looks exactly like a penis, and that captures the imagination of the jury – as the stealth penis, the trick penis, the prosthesis, is figured as a very guilty object indeed.

8

The Blindfold on the Stand: Touch

As a child, I had what doctor's call a 'lazy eye'. I had to wear a patch stuck over one eye for several hours a day. I hated wearing the patch. Nobody seemed to listen to me when I explained that, with my left eye covered up, I could barely see.

Later, retinal photographs would reveal something else, a different kind of patching, this one interior. My eye wasn't 'lazy' after all. The problem was much worse, a genetic disorder called retinitis pigmentosa. The images revealed deposits of dark pigment at the back of my eyes, greater on one side, beginning around the edges and creeping inwards in a dappled ring. Retinitis pigmentosa is degenerative and there is no cure. The patches spread, causing tunnel vision, which gradually narrows into blindness.

I was diagnosed in my early twenties, when I was working in the visual arts. For a while, thoughts of the future were difficult to bear. The prickling sense of fear was almost constant. At times, it would erupt into a flow of dread.

In literature, blindness is often a punishment for sin. But it's also tied to ideals of justice and virtue. A sculpture of a blindfolded woman holding a pair of scales can be found in law courts around the world. This figure is known as Lady Justice. Her eyes are covered by a scarf or bandage; sometimes it's an eye mask. She weighs evidence without the distraction of visual judgements.

The allegory suggests that blindness is an elevated state in which to judge. If sight misleads, removing it can make assessments fairer and blind justice a purer form of judgement. And yet the first depictions of blind judgement, emerging in the fifteenth century, were satirical. In a popular woodcut from the allegorical poem *The Ship of Fools* (1494), a jester ties a scarf over the eyes of Lady Justice. She is being hoodwinked. In another woodcut from the same period, a group of judges are pictured wearing blindfolds and jester hats in an image of corruption, madness and folly. Both images bind blindness to deception. Wool is being pulled over the eyes of powerful decision-makers. Justice is compromised, robbed of her ability to see things straight and blind to simple truths. Here, blindness is not a symbol of truth and clarity, but signals vulnerability and even stupidity.

Retinitis pigmentosa first reveals itself by night. Symptoms include the dark feeling thick and impenetrable and the experience of stumbling into furniture, groping around for a light – the eyes unable to adjust. I'm always on guard. I watch out for signs. But since the patches were first tracked over a decade ago, they have not spread. I don't have tunnel vision, and my sight remains stable. Somehow, the condition is benign. The results baffle experts; the prognosis is good.

But in the periphery of my unconscious, I'm still haunted by the idea of losing my sight. After bumps in the night come illusions by day. Writers who have lived with retinitis pigmentosa, progressing down the tunnel into darkness, have described the surrealism of the condition as it develops. The dark patches on the retina create blind spots, which distort vision and make reality strange. Objects seem to vanish, quite suddenly, into visual holes. Friends slip in and out of sight like apparitions. Adding incongruity, these voids in sight are subtle, almost deceptive, because the brain fills in the gaps – guessing and reconstructing, patching up the scene.

It is quite possible that my preoccupation with blind spots and darkness drew me to the trials – although I didn't register it at the time. So much centres on vision, on what Miss X did or did not see. Undoubtedly, it's also what bound me to the bed trick and made the questions posed by the plot more potent, more necessary, more real.

In her study of the plot, Wendy Doniger identifies darkness as the most common way bed tricks are achieved. In another of Chaucer's tales, told by a drunken miller, the ruse takes place on a starless night. 'Dark was the night as pitch, aye dark as coal,' the Miller explains. In this bawdy story, a wife tricks her infatuated lover, who serenades her at a bedroom window. When the young man begs for a kiss, the wife responds with a prank. 'And through the window she put out her hole,' the Miller says, 'He kissed her naked arse/ Right greedily, before he knew of this.' Here, the bed trick becomes a 'bum trick', as the lover mistakes her bottom for a face, its hole for her mouth.

Meanwhile, in supernatural romances, spells of illusion allow bed tricks to take place. In Sir Thomas Malory's fifteenth-century reworking of Arthurian legends, *Le Morte D'Arthur*, the hero's mother is fooled when a lusty king employs Merlin's magic to disguise himself as her husband. The king comes to her bedchamber 'in the likeness of her lord'. In his deceptive embrace, Arthur is conceived.

Most of Shakespeare's bed tricks take place in the 'heavy middle of the night', in private locations, such as 'a garden circummured with brick' or dark bedchambers. But others are more fantastical. The bed trick in *A Midsummer Night's Dream*, for example, takes the form of eye trickery. Love-juice from a purple flower is dropped in the eyes of characters by a fairy. This play is a dream, a night of illusion, set in a forest outside Athens that is inhabited by fairies, whose king and queen are having a dispute. Oberon, the fairy king, concocts a plan that revolves around a magical juice from a flower hit by Cupid's arrow; the nectar, a kind of potion, 'on sleeping eyelids laid/Will make man or woman madly dote/Upon the next live creature that it sees', Oberon explains. In one of the various subplots, a group of amateur actors is rehearsing a play in the woods; in another, a set of Athenian lovers roams the forest. Dropped on actors' and Athenians' eyelids, the potion causes great confusion, in a plot that is both bewildering and funny.

This play enacts another form of bed trickery suggested by Doniger – tales of intoxication, sometimes literally drunkenness but also, as in *A Midsummer Night's Dream*, the 'drop of liquor' is a cipher for love, seductive beguilement and the clouding of reason. Distorted sight points to the delusion of romantic love, the enchantment of lust, and the way desire is not rational – we can be blinkered by desire, get transfixed, act almost against our will.

In Titania's famous scene with the amateur actor Bottom, the juice dropped on the queen's eye incites a kind of deluding lust; under the moon, in the magic of the night, with the liquor in her eye, she can't really see, and believes Bottom is an 'angel', her dream suitor (in another 'bum trick').

Wolfgang Mozart's opera *The Marriage of Figaro* (1786), based on the stage comedy *The Mad Day*, is also a kind of dream. A Countess conspires with her servants to trick her husband, the Count, who in turn plans to seduce his wife's maid, Susanna, right under her nose. Across this mad day, deceptions and misunderstandings stack up and collide. Identities change by darkness, by trick and by mistake. Nobody seems to know who anyone is. Fraudulent love letters are sent; rings are given to the wrong person.

The bed trick eventually takes place in a dark garden, 'under the pines', where the Count arranges to meet Susanna – but it's actually the Countess in Susanna's clothes. In the shadows, in the excitement, his senses are deluded and the Count does not recognize his wife. Susanna, peering on from the side, calls him 'the bizarre lover' – a man beguiled by lust, stupefied by the spell of passion.

*

Blindfolds are common sexual props; the loss of one sense (vision) tends to heighten others (touch, sound). As a prop, it's also caught up with excitement, sexual adventure and risk; usually only one person is blindfolded, surrendering power, which can be another kind of sensory overload. Blindfolds appear across erotic literature, from the classic French novel *Story of O* to the memoir *Nine and a Half Weeks* and the *Fifty Shades of Grey* series, all made into popular films. The stories feature rich, mysterious, powerful men (often bankers, or members of elite clubs) testing the sexual boundaries of the female protagonists. These women submit to their lovers' fantasies, taking part in erotic power games, including sexual role play with a blindfold on among other acts.

In stories, bed tricks happen by way of darkness or spells, on improbable dreamlike days – inspiring narrative delight. But in sexual fraud cases, the blindfold appears. Exhibit 5 is a black eye mask seized from Gayle's bedroom. Facts are produced in the courtroom, and this exhibit is one such fact, which the trials attempt to establish. Is it a blindfold as Miss X alleges, or a sleeping mask as sold? No forensic evidence will help; the answer must be found through the adversarial contest and in the stories produced at trial.

If the dildo is guilty, a kind of deodand, then the eye mask is different. It's ambiguously innocuous, an everyday object that doesn't have the same potency as the dildo. It could be read either way, as a blindfold or sleeping mask, and its interpretation is crucial.

Miss X says the blindfold was Kye's idea – one of his 'terms', the only way he'd agree to meet up. After all the injuries, illnesses, his long convalescence, Kye was shy. He explained that his body had changed. The first time they met, Miss X says she improvised a blindfold, using a silk scarf. When they began to meet at hotels, she says Kye bought an eye mask; he'd arrive first, wait in the bathroom, leaving the mask for her on the bed.

In romance settings, blindfolds are tied to risk, seduction and the sexual imagination. But Miss X's account wrests the blindfold away from kink and sexual play. She says the blindfold was about Kye's injury, his confidence, his feelings of bodily shame. He was a vanilla guy – a 'normal student', she insists; they had 'normal boy and girl' sex. It was nothing kinky or experimental; she thought she was in a tender rom-com, a fairytale.

'Obviously, in hindsight, looking back, you know, I wish I'd ripped that mask off sooner,' Miss X says at trial. But she trusted Kye, she goes on. These were his 'terms'. It felt okay.

The blindfold features in Gayle's story too; it's also a narrative lynchpin, but in negative form: there was no mask. She explains the exhibit was something else, 'just a sleeping mask'. She had trouble sleeping, she tells Power, when he asks about the mask found in her bedroom. 'I wear ear plugs when I go to sleep. I take sleeping tablets. It was a mere sleeping mask, nothing to do with Miss X,' she says.

Seemingly, sexual fraud trials take us back to reality – evidence is presented, as the courts attempt to establish facts. There are real-world consequences – conviction, prison time, the Sex Offender Register. Even so, courtroom stories tend to share the same sense of fantasy, confusion, unreality and extravagance as bed trick tales.

Take a case from the 1990s, which made headlines in the US. A businessman in his forties, Raymond Mitchell III, was accused of calling women late at night and pretending to be their boyfriends. He convinced them to open their front doors, put on a blindfold and wait for him. One woman described the phone ringing late at night, hearing a soft whisper on the line, and being persuaded it was her fiancé. On the phone, he referenced the erotic movie *9½ Weeks*, in which two obsessed, intoxicated lovers play out fantasies, including blindfolded sex with a white silk scarf; he explained he wanted to enact the scene.

Another woman described having sex with Raymond twice a week for two months; she believed it was her boyfriend, and said she only realized the truth when the blindfold slipped. This complainant also described a sexy whisper on the phone and a voice saying: *unlock your door, put a blindfold on, and wait for me.*

The case was a media sensation, with the defendant given the moniker 'Fantasy Man'. The women were ridiculed, but the man was finally convicted.

When it comes to recent gender fraud cases, the scarf or blindfold remains a common exhibit. A year after Gayle's second conviction, another gender fraud case reached a UK court; this time – in a new iteration – a man named Duarte Xavier was accused of pretending to be a cis-woman named Ana and tricking multiple straight men into sex. On Tinder, Ana was attractive and sexually adventurous, posting provocative pictures and proposing to meet her matches for blindfolded sex. They made contact in parks and gardens. One man explained he waited on a park bench with a scarf around his head for Ana. She led him to her flat, where he had sex without seeing her, the scarf covering his eyes. At trial, the man contended he chose a vagina and a woman, and that he had no idea he was having anal sex with a man.

At least four men claimed to be tricked in this way, drawn in by Ana's presentation as a fantasy woman, who was beautiful, horny, game. In the excitement of the moment, in the absence of sight, their genitals and senses were fooled. At trial, Duarte was described as setting 'bizarre conditions' and demonstrating 'extreme cunning'; he was eventually sentenced to fifteen years.

THE BLINDFOLD ON THE STAND: TOUCH

The women tricked by the Fantasy Man, Duarte's victims in parks, Miss X – in legal terms, these complainants lost their freedom and autonomy, their choices distorted by trickery, by deceit, a kind of spell.

Sexual fraud accounts are often bewildering, as complainants describe meeting in person, being tricked in real life and eventually in bed. The cases suggest that love (or its promise) can make a person susceptible to dupery. The medieval idiom 'love is blind', coined by Chaucer, describes the way romantic passion can blind a person, so that everything seems rosy sweet and it is impossible to see a lover's flaws. Oscar Wilde took this notion a step further in his novel *The Picture of Dorian Grey* (1890), by suggesting that love induces a kind of inner blinding. 'When one is in love, one always begins by deceiving one's self, and one always ends by deceiving others,' he wrote. Here, romance is figured as a delusion. The contemporary philosopher Jules de Gaultier concurred in an essay of 1892 outlining the condition 'Bovarysme'. Named after Gustave Flaubert's fictional heroine, Emma Bovary, the condition describes a romantic tendency towards escapist daydreaming. Emma imagined herself to be in a romance novel, and she preferred the fiction to reality. Those afflicted by Bovarysme have an overactive romantic imagination and live in a state of delusion.

Indeed, Doniger's list of how successful bed tricks are enacted includes self-deception, as fantasy prevails over life. For the plot to make sense, at some point the victim must turn from the truth or turn a blind eye, she suggests. 'People can be fooled because they want to be fooled,' Doniger writes; it is the 'will to believe' that allows a trickster to succeed.

This doesn't mean these complainants aren't victims of a trick. But it does make the situation more entangled, the dynamics more ambivalent.

*

The thing about Miss X and Gayle – they were friends. Best friends. And this is what makes the blindfold so key to Miss X's account. She knew Gayle as Gayle; the deception only worked if she never saw Kye, who would have been instantly recognizable as her best friend. The courtroom is preoccupied by the question: was Miss X wearing a blindfold *at all times*? Exhibit 5 is often presented as the fact on which this narrative turns. Was it a blindfold or sleeping mask? Worn always or never? It's binary, extreme.

And yet, during the trials, other details slip through:

A statement, written by Gayle, that describes Miss X wearing a 'light scarf' to cover her eyes.

A text, sent by Miss X to Kye, that describes seeing his penis, seeing his face.

The barristers jump on these details during the cross-examinations, impaling the friends on their own words. Both fight and flounder.

As the two sides in a trial do battle, opposing stories are produced. There is little room for nuance. These new details unsettle each of their stories, spoiling the claims on which they rely. By the time of the trials, both Gayle and Miss X are willing to say they've lied, to dismiss their earlier words – so they can expel nuance and preserve the purity, and thus integrity, of their stories.

But Miss X does admit to looking once. After the first encounter on Valentine's Day – the moment she'd been

THE BLINDFOLD ON THE STAND: TOUCH

waiting for, when Kye climbed the stairs to her bedroom, and they kissed on the bed; the first meeting that led to all that came after.

The admission comes up at the first trial as Miss X undergoes cross-examination. Power has been quizzing her about Kye's photos, which he suggests aren't credible – pointing to the American plug sockets in the background, or a photograph of Kye with a Hollywood celebrity (Miss X says she thought he was next to a dummy at Madame Tussauds).

Now, Power turns to Valentine's Day and goes over the story of Kye arriving from the hospital, climbing the stairs, his heart beating from the meds and the first kiss on her bed.

Miss X explains that she was feeling elated. They'd finally met in person after so many months. And when Kye was descending the stairs she says she took off her blindfold and looked for him on the street below.

MISS X. Erm, after, after, after Kye had gone, I looked, I looked from the window.

POWER. Right. And what did you see?

MISS X. I saw Gayle driving off.

This recollection doesn't appear in Miss X's statements – she's revealing it live, during cross-examination, for the first time.

Power appears stunned.

'So, let's just, let's just think about this,' he says, trying to slow things down. He mirrors her description back: Kye comes to see her, and leaves, and then she looks out the window, and sees Gayle? He calls the scenario 'ridiculous' at the first trial and 'daft' at the second, when they go over it again.

Miss X, stammering, says it made sense that Gayle was there. She'd dropped Kye off – she was being a good friend. Gayle helped him up the stairs, because he was sick and often needed assistance. Now she assumed Gayle was picking him up, driving him back to the hospital.

But, Power asks, what about Kye? This man had just left your flat. Wasn't it strange you didn't see him – that he had disappeared, and in his place stood Gayle?

But Miss X says that she thought he was in the vehicle already.

At the retrial, she admits she saw Gayle 'walking round to the side of the car', and getting in. 'How am I not to know that she's not put him in the passenger seat?' she says.

Kye leaving, Gayle driving off. In some sense, it's a *Figaro*-like confusion, as if Gayle and Kye had swapped costumes, switched places. Up the stairs, down the stairs, one appearing, the other disappearing – like a scene from a bed trick opera.

But also, it's not that at all. Gayle *is* Kye. There's only one. They share a body. They're the same.

*

After Valentine's Day, they met many more times. Miss X says she never looked out the window again – never tried to glimpse Kye in the car or on the street.

For so long Kye had been virtual. And for so long, he'd been ill. But finally in 2013, both agreed the treatment seemed to be working. At first, they met at hotels. It was easier to keep it private, avoiding housemates. But in April, Miss X moved to a new, one-room flat. It was small, and the bed was on a mezzanine. But it was all hers – she lived there alone.

Grilled by Power, Miss X says the times at her flat blur together, in part because of the eye mask. 'I can't tell you exactly what, what happened,' she says. 'Like . . . You've got a blindfold on, the only thing you've got is your other senses'. But Power keeps up the attack, quizzing her about her other perceptions, specifically in relation to the dildo.

Fingertips are some of the body's most sophisticated sensors – they can be trained to read tactile writing systems like Braille. But when Power asks about fingers, Miss X says she barely touched Kye during sex. She kept her hands behind her back – it was another of his 'terms'. At times, he bound them; at others, he'd let her rub his arms up and down. Occasionally, they'd 'clasp' hands.

In the absence of fingers and eyes, Miss X's vagina is cross-examined. 'Sometimes the devil is in the detail,' Power says, turning again to Miss X's sensory descriptions of Kye's penis and challenging her vaginal sensations.

'I think it's hard for you to understand as a woman, like we're just not a mould,' Miss X says at the retrial, as she argues her vagina isn't eyes, it isn't fingers, and it wouldn't necessarily know plastic from flesh – nor even, she goes on, one dildo from another. 'I'm not going to know that it's the same penis,' she tells him.

In her book *Vagina Obscura: An Anatomical Voyage* (2022), the science writer Rachel Gross explores the ways in which the vagina has been under-studied across history, beginning with the Ancient Greek doctor Hippocrates, who never studied a human vagina (he relied on the words of midwives). This neglect, argues Ross, has led to a 'vast knowledge gap' when it comes to the vagina, which until recent decades was viewed as 'a black box': more complex and obscure than the penis – more secret – because it was tucked up inside.

In Renaissance demonology, the vagina was seen as a place where devils hide; evil spirits could be discharged through 'genital exorcism'. In law, the vagina has been constructed as a secret place too – as a 'cavity' or hidey-hole, identified in legal documents when it is searched. In his 1997 book *Bodies of Law*, the legal scholar Alan Hyde points to a search warrant from 1991, which orders a search of a woman's 'apartment and vagina' – figured as a suspicious aperture and a place to smuggle drugs.

On the stand, Miss X quite boldly pushes back against the vagina as a thing, a mould, saying the organ must be taken on its own terms. When Power reads the transcripts back to her at the retrial, telling her what her vagina should have felt, she counters, '[If] you're wet, everything feels wet, doesn't it?' She suggests his understanding of the vagina is inadequate, as she defends the organ as having its own unique kind of wetness and touch.

Occasionally, Miss X's mouth is interrogated too. Power reads out text messages that Miss X sent to Kye, promising to give him a blow job when they next meet. Miss X admits that she went down on Kye with the blindfold on, though not very often (she can't remember how many times). Lips are known for their sensory richness; imbued with a high concentration of sense receptors, they are understood to be one of the most sensitive areas of the body, along with the tongue. Drawing on this rationale, Power suggests that she couldn't have taken the dildo in her mouth and given Kye head without knowing what it was.

'You knew all along', he accuses. But Miss X says she didn't know. She thought he'd put a condom on which explained the texture, the taste; he was thoughtful like that.

*

Both trials focus on sexual acts. But the story on trial is about so much more than bodies and sexual performance. Beyond the bed, the hours and hours at Miss X's flat, not just having sex but being together romantically. It is the story of a relationship.

Both agree that by late spring 2013, a routine had emerged. Miss X and Kye began to spend Sundays together and sometimes Wednesday evenings too.

By now, Miss X has moved to the new flat. When asked what they did on these Sundays together, she describes a normal lazy Sunday – watching TV, smooching, spooning, having sex – except that she wore a mask at all times.

These were happy months. Kye seemed to be getting better, 'he was able to go like one or two days without his treatment', Miss X remembers, although he was still living at the hospital. He would come over to her flat around lunchtime on Sunday, after his treatment finished, and stay until 7 or 8 p.m. Sometimes one of them would 'pop out' for food or Miss X might bake a cake in advance. They'd watch TV or a rom-com – films that Miss X concedes she 'heard' rather than saw because she had the mask on. Miss X says sometimes they didn't do much; she'd lie with an ear to Kye's chest, listening to him breathing, listening to his heartbeat; 'I was so happy being cuddled and lying there talking and kissing,' she remembers.

The blindfolded Sundays baffle Power – the logistics of popping out of the house, sharing cake, going to the loo. He suggests the choreography is ridiculous, implausible, incapable of belief.

Gayle remembers the Sundays too. She would come over as Gayle and become Kye, moving in and out of role. Miss X never wore a blindfold, she says. They'd lie on the couch and watch romantic movies or American sitcoms. On Sundays, they'd make a meal; sometimes Miss X would cook, but mostly they'd get takeaways. Those Sundays felt calm. They still hid the truth from family and friends, but in Miss X's flat, in the privacy of her room, they could be together as lovers. They'd fall into role play when she stepped into the strap-on, but she didn't go round just for 'sex', Gayle says. They were in love, and learning to be together, to feel 'comfortable'. Often they'd do nothing; she remembers lying body to body, the TV on, a Sunday passing by. She describes the afternoons as 'just normal, you know, chatting, erm, probably kissing, watching telly, eating'.

The whole days together spooning lead Power to ask about bodily contact – beyond the myopic focus of the Sexual Offences Act. 'It is not just about what you see,' he says at one point. He's trying to establish the importance of the other senses, and the many ways Miss X sensed Kye. Importantly, what she sensed on the couch, body to body, skin to skin. Power tries to interrogate touch, asking Miss X what she felt, and by extension knew. But the problem is, there is a certain mystery to this perception. In *De Anima*, Aristotle theorized the five senses as we know them today. He considered touch to be the most elusive sense; unlike the other senses, which have specialized organs (eye, ear, nose, mouth), the organ of touch is multifunctional. The skin, spread across the body, is a giant sense organ. Different areas of the body have different degrees of sensitivity. Scientists today distinguish between highly sensitive 'glabrous' skin, which is skin without hair follicles (such as the mouth, parts of the genitals, the fingertips), and the rest of the body, which has a different concentration of sense receptors.

This means that touch, under interrogation, can reveal itself to be a perplexing sensation – one without a stable lexicon and that is difficult to apprehend. Further, when it comes to desire and the power of the sexual imagination, touch can be even more elusive. The subjectivity of sexual sensation is illustrated by the variation of 'erogenous zones' – points on the body that experience arousal, that turn us on. Lists of erogenous zones include the earlobe, the nape of the neck, the inner wrist, the scalp.

Power – trying to find a line through – turns to the photos in the dossier. He asks about Kye's muscles. The body Miss X spooned on the couch could not have matched Kye's images, he suggests.

She admits that Kye's body didn't feel athletic. 'He'd pre-warned me,' Miss X explains, 'he said *"My body's not what it should be."*' He'd been in hospital for so long and his muscles had wasted away. That's why she wasn't surprised that they felt soft, 'like jelly under the skin'.

In Miss X's story, Kye is bedridden – a terminal romance figure, a wounded jock. Every time they met, he had come from the hospital to see her. 'They had to bandage him up,' she remembers. She says he had bandages around his head, to hide the scars from surgery; she says sometimes he put a hat on top, to keep them in place. He also had bandages around his chest and a heart monitor; the nurses would dress him in what she calls a medical 'circulation suit' before he left the hospital. The suit pressed the 'wires' of the monitor and a 'nozzle' to his chest and helped to regulate his heartbeats. It was the only way he could leave the hospital, she recalls.

In terminal romances, the principal characters look beautiful as they expire – they are young and pale, with sparkling eyes. Gus, at his 'pre-funeral' in *The Fault in Our Stars*, appears handsome as ever, beaming sadly as his eulogy is read, a single tear trickling down his cheek.

But in this story, Kye is bandaged, wasted, disfigured, covered in wires. The tragic romance seems to tip towards science fiction and perhaps even horror.

*

It's not only Kye's injuries and bandages that Miss X says deceived her senses; Kye's ethnicity was also part of the trick. She recalls that his arms and legs were smooth and hairless, almost feminine. But he told her it was because of his ethnicity, she contends; 'Filipino people aren't very hairy,' she remembers him saying.

At the first trial, the Crown takes up this argument. Corbett-Jones directs the jury to the photos of Kye in his closing speech.

'Look at the photographs, members of the jury,' he says, pointing to the images of Carlo, a half-Asian man. 'Can you see hair on the face, the arm, the torso? Those photos are designed intentionally to portray somebody who is completely smooth and without hair,' Corbett-Jones contends.

The prosecution suggests that Gayle, the cunning mastermind, cleverly identified Carlo's ethnicity to feminize Kye and aid her deception – so that when they eventually met, Gayle could explain away what Miss X felt. In making this argument, the Crown draws on an old racial trope that figures the male Asian body as feminine.

This trope is the legacy of racial science that emerged from colonial domination. To make sense of racial hierarchy, a logic needed to be established; 'lower' races were gendered (and sexualized), and Asian men were figured as hairless, feminine and more inclined towards homosexuality.

Gayle says very little about Kye's ethnicity. In the examinations, Power avoids race and the Crown follows suit – partly because race is not a legal focus and partly because racial electivity is a quagmire. The racial deception lawsuits of the 1930s identified by Jill Hasday revealed an anxiety about people passing as white. But nearly a century later, a new anxiety began to emerge: white people identifying and passing as Black or Asian – most famously, the case of Rachel Dolezal, a white American woman who presented as African-American for a number of years, working as a professor of African Studies and president of a branch of US civil rights organization the NAACP. In June 2015, in the months before Gayle's first trial, Dolezal was exposed by her white parents and widely condemned for racial 'masquerade'.

Other cases emerging in the years since include Ja Du, a white American trans woman who claimed to identify as Filipina in 2017, causing public outcry; and more contentiously Oli London, a white British pop singer who claimed to identify as South Korean. London underwent surgeries, beginning in 2019, to look like a K-pop star. By 2022, he had undergone thirty-two operations, and spoke of a (finally unrealized) plan for a penis reduction, which he said he needed as a finishing touch, to make him '100 percent Korean'.

*

Bed trick tales consider a victim's blindness but they are also about the trickster's performance. In Eliza Haywood's inventive novella *Fantomina, or, Love in a Maze* (1725), the protagonist tricks her lover in four disguises. Beauplaisir thinks she is a different woman each time. They have sex in dimly lit bedrooms; occasionally, Fantomina wears a 'mask'. Beauplaisir is a 'blinded' lover, the narrator explains, but Fantomina is also 'admirably skill'd'. She deludes him by changing her name, her hats and her hairstyles, in a set of brilliant performances worthy of a playhouse.

Miss X was blinded too. Her senses were tricked; she says the stories Kye told about his ethnicity and sickness explained a body that was soft and hairless, that was covered in bandages and that she could rarely touch.

At the trials, Gayle is accused of telling imaginative lies about Kye's body and of compounding these lies with a performance. She is figured as a creative writer devising an extravagant plot, but also in the final months 'play-acting', as Corbett-Jones puts it – choreographing the fiction and then acting it out. As part of this performance, the Crown describes Gayle wearing a 'bizarre costume' when she enacted Kye, cleverly designed to confound Miss X's touch: the bandages, the circulation suit, the strap-on dildo and a hat. She is accused of using these amateur objects to disguise her female body, a figure with breasts, with long hair. And also, to hide a best friend's body, a body that Miss X knew. It is argued that the disguise made Gayle's body feel like Kye's body. This theatrical 'costume' was allegedly glimpsed by Miss X when she finally ripped off the blindfold and ran from the room.

In the CCTV footage, Gayle is wearing a hat. She is questioned about it at the trials. Miss X told the police that Kye often wore a woolly hat to cover his surgical scars and shaved head; now she realized that all along it had been hiding Gayle's long hair.

The Crown tries to suggest that the hat, caught on CCTV, is evidence of the 'bizarre costume', the act. 'Why ... in the middle of the summer, were you wearing a woolly hat?' asks Medland at the retrial. He's trying to make the hat suspect – but it doesn't really work. Gayle says it was a 'beanie' anyway, and it was about fashion. 'I'd wear a beanie if it went with my outfit, to be honest,' she says.

But there's more evidence of the 'costume'. It appears in a statement made by the female police officer who arrived at the canal after Gayle jumped and followed her to the hospital. That statement included a description of Gayle's attire. Along with a cream jumper, a pair of trainers and the woolly hat, the officer described Gayle wearing a navy swimming costume 'on underneath her clothing' – she saw it when paramedics removed Gayle's wet clothes to wrap her in a blanket.

This item 'on underneath' figures in the transcripts and in court as a kind of reveal. Gayle does not deny wearing it. But she is unable to give a clear explanation for why she did so. Meanwhile, the Crown tries to use the swimsuit as a lightning rod of suspicion and guilt, arguing that it is this 'costume' that tricked Miss X's touch, evidence of the 'circulation suit' itself.

And yet, Kye's medical contrivance remains obscure. Medland, attempting to clarify it, describes it as 'a medically necessary body suit'. But nobody's heard of such a thing. It is an imaginary item, part of the fiction, the bamboozling plot.

*

Gayle is accused of wearing an extravagant disguise. But in Miss X's story, she's in costume too; 'every single time that I met Kye Fortune I had a mask and a scarf on', she insists.

In her account to police and on the stand, Miss X says the Sundays blur together – in part, because she couldn't see, and also because they were regular, average Sundays, each one the same. Once, though, they did something different – Miss X tells of a day trip with Kye. He came from hospital, as usual, wearing his hat and bandages and they went on an excursion, borrowing Gayle's car.

Miss X recounts it at the trials. Kye picked her up from her new flat. She doesn't describe how she got into the car with the blindfold on. Her flat was situated off a shopping street near the centre of town. But she does say she put sunglasses on top of the blindfold, 'so drivers-by wouldn't think, erm, you know, he was kidnapping me'.

Power asks for clarification. It's a surreal moment: the image of sunglasses over the eye mask; the joke about kidnapping.

Miss X hesitates, uncertain, aware she's being made to look silly. But she remains defiant. 'He wanted to take me somewhere. So, those were the rules,' she states. It was a 'surprise', she goes on. She was excited. She remembers they drove for about half an hour.

'Where did you go?' asks Power. But she doesn't know.

Gayle remembers the outing too – a scenic drive to her family home, twenty minutes out of town. They often went on outings as friends – for lunch at her parents' house, to see her dog Gypsy, who was Kye's dog too. But this time, Gayle says, her family was away. And this time, she went as Kye.

In Gayle's recollection, Kye picked up Miss X from her flat but there was no scarf, no blindfold. It was a sunny day. Kye was wearing normal clothes. When they arrived at the house, they went out to the patio and lay in the sun. 'We just spent most of the time sunbathing,' Gayle says. Kye cooked Miss X dinner and they played with the dog. They 'chilled', then drove home.

In Miss X's version, the location is anonymous. She had no idea where she was. Power, who is unsatisfied with this, asks her to describe arriving in more detail, and for any memories she has of moving through the space.

Miss X says that, when they arrived, Kye undid her seatbelt and helped her out of the car. 'He walked into, erm, somewhere, erm, sat me down.'

'A house?' Power asks. But she can't be sure. There was a door, she concedes, so it was 'a building'.

If Miss X's account is operatic (the mask, sunglasses, bandages), the setting is also mundane: a day trip, a Sunday afternoon, a patio, a family home. She remembers going somewhere to sunbathe. It might have been a garden. They lay there for a while. When he took her back inside, she sat down next to something that 'smelt like an oven' and he made some food. Then they drove home.

'It was Gayle's parents' house, wasn't it?' Power says at the retrial. She'd been there plenty of times, he accuses – for lunch, one Christmas. She should have recognized it, he says, blindfold or not. And there was Gypsy too, Gayle's dog – a dog that she'd met many times and that Power suggests 'jumped up and looked interested in Kye'.

But Miss X says no, she didn't know where she was. It didn't seem familiar. There was no dog, no recognition.

'I don't know what you're talking about, sorry,' she says.

*

Wendy Doniger suggests that all bed trick plots are failed bed tricks, 'for we, the readers, always learn the truth'. The stories turn on exposure. The arc of the bed trick moves towards the 'great moment' of the unmasking when a stranger is revealed.

Sexual fraud stories, too, turn on the revelation that leads to trial. Miss X says she was tricked on those Sundays, tricked on the outing, tricked time after time into sex. Looking at Kye on that final evening rendered it all so different. But there is so much she did seem to want, to choose: sex with a very sick person, a person with bandages on multiple parts of their body, a person with a circulation suit and nozzle going into their heart. Sex with a body that passed as male with some gender ambiguity. And a blindfold: sex with somebody she couldn't see.

These trials, along with other gender fraud cases – often blindfold cases – seem to suggest that when it comes to 'informed' consent (knowing what you're choosing, a legal yes) sight is key. Informed consent (true choice) is figured as consent that isn't 'blind'. In these cases, complainants knew their lovers carnally but they didn't see, so (the logic goes) didn't really know and didn't truly consent.

But while sex can involve looking, it can also be a sensual, physical knowing, caught up with touch, fantasy and want. At the heart of the bed trick plot – perhaps accounting for its eternal fascination – is this tension between intimacy and knowing, desire and choice. Fevered feelings collide with cooler choices as night becomes day, in a movement out of the bedroom and into the light. The plot seems to ask, what kind of knowing is sexual touch, sexual sensing? Can sex be an intimate form of knowing, and yet somehow general and impersonal, where *your* body is also *any* body?

On trial, Miss X's account is a bed trick plot – life seems to emulate fiction. She is blindfolded, under Kye's spell, in a boyfriend fantasy. She tells a story of gigantic dupery and blind love. For two years, she was caught in the story, under his spell. She says removing the blindfold changed everything. The dream, the spell, broke. Fantasy became horror and love became hate.

9

Kye Fortune on the Stand: Impostors

Early into researching this book, I borrowed a car and drove north. I'd spent weeks combing through the transcripts, trying to get my head around the two accounts. I'd spent hours online looking for Kye. By this point, I was feeling frustrated by the transcripts. They were perplexing to read. They didn't lay out the story from beginning to end. There were so many interruptions, narratives cut short and missing perspectives. There was so much I couldn't *see*.

I studied the list of locations, which I had scraped from the transcripts: the hotels the lovers stayed in after Valentine's Day. The bridge over the canal from which Gayle jumped. The police station where Miss X made her complaint. And then I went looking, trying to follow them all these years in the future. I wanted to feel closer to the people I was trying so hard to understand. So I drove north to the university where Gayle and Miss X studied, and where Kye was a student too (but he was never on campus – always bunking off, sick, away in Monte Carlo, writing song lyrics and posting on his blog).

I walked around the university and peered into the creative writing rooms. It was summer and I was hopelessly out of season. The campus was empty. Doors were locked and blinds were drawn.

I thought about my own years studying writing in my late twenties. During my first weeks in the classroom, I was troubled by a bout of impostor syndrome. I was no longer persuaded by my own fiction. The story I told myself – that I had enough talent, a real chance of becoming a writer – dried up. This wasn't just self-doubt. In that moment, I was struck by an intense feeling that I was going to be found out – revealed for what I was, busted as a pretentious nobody with delusions of creative grandeur. Perhaps everyone on the course felt that way as, crossing a threshold, we confronted that tenacious gap between the coherent self, presented to the world, and the messy one within.

Eventually, I went to the beach. The air was salty. Tiny birds were diving into blackberry bushes. This was the beach where the friends used to walk, and where the lovers dreamed of buying a house together. I passed by a cafe selling iced drinks and a row of commemorative benches engraved with the names of loved ones. Trinkets attached to the frames were rotting in the sun: a padlock, a glove, faded ribbons, key rings. I sat there and reflected. I thought about the story on trial – the bamboozling plot. I mulled over the madness, the mess, the sensory memories, the role play and the fiction. The investigators, as part of Operation Imperia, sought order – and often I did too.

By the time of the trials, Miss X is explicit. She says, clearly, Gayle and Kye were not the same person. Kye was her lover, her fiancé. And Gayle is a liar and an impostor.

By the trials, Gayle isn't so sure.

But there is one document in the evidence bundle that

speaks to the relationship between Gayle and Kye more than any other. It is an email from July 2013, sent in the days after the final argument. It is titled, 'Explanation as best I can at this moment'. 'Dear Miss X,' it begins. 'I really hope you're okay.'

> This all started when I was just 13 years old – a kid. I found more comfort and confidence in this person. I could be myself; and since then it just became the norm and I finally felt I had a way to channel the real me as I couldn't within my own skin. I've never been able to form any relationship or closeness with my friends or anyone else as me. It has been impossible. I know Kye is who I am. It is my personality and everything.

The email, which is about nine hundred words long, has a contentious status at the trials. For the Crown, it's evidence of the deception: in it, Gayle seems to admit to a secret life. But the email also speaks to identity, appearing to provide a missing testimony about Kye.

> You'll never understand what it is like to be physically unable to be yourself, and to live as someone that isn't who you were meant to be. With you I never intended it to go this far. It turned from a seed to a tree and I was stuck. Every day I felt guilty, but I couldn't leave you, as you needed me.

At trial, the email is discussed as Gayle's; she is considered to be the sender. But it's a little more complicated than that.

KYE FORTUNE ON THE STAND: IMPOSTORS

The email comes from Kye's address (kyefortune@). It's Kye writing.

> My intention all along was for you to find happiness and then eventually leave me, even though it would have left me heartbroken. All those times you thought I had let you down, I didn't. I was there on your birthday, Christmas, moving out when you were at your lowest.

The email becomes increasingly melancholy, circling back to identity and the body, and talking of suicide. This is the final section:

> It's impossible for me to fake my personality. You knew the real me. Everything I did was with good intentions. I'm so sorry, Miss X. If you need anything, anything at all, just ask. If you want me to kill myself so you can gain real closure, then I fucking will. Kye is who I am. Just in this world I've not been able to be that or given the correct skin to be that. Please just try to understand, even though I know it's pretty much impossible.

Several hours after reading the email, Miss X went to the police. It was important to the investigation and, along with Gayle's apologetic text messages, became central to the Crown's case. It seems to reinforce the allegation that Miss X didn't know.

But the email doubles as evidence of something else too. It is an example of the 'malleability of trial evidence' – Janet

Malcolm's term for evidence that is used to verify different accounts, and where the same records are used to prove contrary facts.

Gender fraud trials are, in one way or another, about a defendant's gender. The focus is on the defendant and the question of intentional deception. Today, the structure for validating legal gender is built around personal testimony. And as a document of self-revelation, this email can be read as a form of testimony. It's the clearest record we have on identity, gender and Kye.

The email admits to lies while also claiming integrity, saying: *It was me, as I am. I lied to be true. I'm Gayle and Kye. But I can't be Kye. I don't have the correct body, the right skin.*

The email attempts to provide an explanation 'as best I can at this moment' – the moment being July 2013. And this moment seems to pass quickly. The next day Gayle is arrested. She will not speak so clearly to herself, or to Kye, on record again.

At her first interview that evening she says nothing. Staying silent is a right but it can be dangerous too. There's another rule, Section 34, that says silence can be interpreted negatively at trial – what is called 'adverse inference'. And indeed, during Gayle's cross-examinations, the Crown makes the suggestion that her silence was suspicious.

'At no stage did you say to the police during the course of those questions, *"Hang on. She always knew that I was Kye"*,' Corbett-Jones accuses at the first trial. He's asking: why didn't she explain that she was Kye? Why hold back?

Gayle doesn't have an answer.

The next time she's interviewed, six months later, she still won't answer questions; she stays silent again. But this time she gives the police a prepared statement. It's short, a legal statement of just a few lines written in the third person. If the email was private and intimately directed, this statement is on record, for the police. The first lines address the friendship, stating, 'Gayle and Miss X were close friends . . . they met frequently and had many conversations . . . In addition, Gayle Newland communicated with Miss X using the name Kye.' Here, Kye is just a name. The real person is now singular, only Gayle. It's a different explanation to the email. The Kye phone, the profiles and the accounts are now described as a front. Then, with legal clarity, the next line about Kye states, 'At all times Miss X knew that the person she was with was not actually Kye, but was Gayle.'

In the statement, Kye begins to disappear.

*

Shakespearean or operatic bed tricks are often one-night stands. But many real-life cases are much longer affairs.

Take the case of Martin Guerre, a real-life story and trial from sixteenth-century France. When Martin went missing an impostor took his place, living as Martin for three years with his wife Bertrande, before being exposed in 1560. As time went on, suspicions grew and Martin was eventually tried in Rieux for imposture, with scores of witnesses testifying he was the real Martin and scores more that he was not. During a second trial, at which Martin pled his case claiming he was being falsely accused by a jealous uncle, the 'real' Martin dramatically appeared, hobbling into court on a wooden leg.

Martin's case exemplified the way courts in this period struggled to identify a real person from an impostor. And indeed, this question remained fraught right up until the late nineteenth century. Perhaps the most famous fraud trial in history reached English courts in the 1870s. Roger Tichborne had been missing for ten years after he boarded a ship bound for Jamaica, which sunk on its journey. His mother rejoiced when he finally reappeared, ready to inherit the family fortune – but other relatives declared the man was a fraud and determined to expose him. A set of sensational trials excited and befuddled the nation. Was this the real Roger? The witness was able to recount precise childhood memories and intimate details of Roger's life. And yet, he couldn't speak French, Roger's first language, and he even had a strong cockney accent. Finally, after a year-long criminal trial, he was exposed as an impostor – a butcher from Wapping named Arthur Orton.

In the late nineteenth century, new methods of identification emerged in the fields of criminology and forensics. A French police chief, Alphonse Bertillon, developed a method for identifying offenders by compiling photographs and bodily measurements. The 'spoken portrait', as Bertillon termed it, included a key for nose types, ear shapes and eye colours to accompany forensic mugshots. The method was effective but also laborious. Over the years, rare but compelling hiccups brought the system into question – famously, two people had the exact same facial measurements, leading to misidentification.

By the end of the century, a simpler and more reliable method of identification emerged: the fingerprint. The science was startling, as it became clear that no two individuals had the same markings. Fingerprints were unique – signs of individualization, a distinctive trace. (A century later, the method was succeeded by 'DNA fingerprinting', first used in 1987 at a rape trial.)

That was individuality: telling a real person from an impostor. But another, more complex question troubled society, and sometimes courts – namely, what is the line between self-invention and fraud?

The history of literature is full of stories in which women reinvent themselves as men. The collection of Arabic folktales known as *The Thousand and One Nights*, which circulated in Europe in the eighteenth century, is replete with tales of cross-dressing and gender switching, while in Shakespeare's plays characters such as Viola and Rosalind choose new names and disguise themselves as men.

In life too, women have cut their hair, bandaged their breasts and put on men's clothes. Historians occasionally discover such lives in letters or diaries, but mostly they are found in court records. By the eighteenth century, population growth and rural exodus led to the rapid expansion of English cities. Fears about trickery, artifices and seduction flourished. Pamphlets such as 'The New Cheats of London Expos'd' warned of 'tricks, impostures, frauds and deceptions' that were 'daily practiced in London'. Some of these impostors were women in disguise as men. Court records track female rogues sent to the pillory for pretending to be men. Most cases centre on the accusation of fraudulent marriage. Some of the defendants were literal fraudsters; in a case from 1777, a woman was convicted of tricking three wealthy ladies into marriage, and defrauding each one of their money and clothes. But other instances were more ambiguous. The 'female husband' cases followed by Caroline Derry and other historians were never short-term schemes of financial extraction, but rather something harder to name and prosecute, tied to identity and personal change.

By the following century, the division between men and women was being regulated with a new zeal. In 1836, a child's 'sex', based on the appearance of newborn genitals, was registered at birth for the first time as part of the Births and Deaths Registration Act. Before this, the responsibility of registering births fell to parishes, which had recorded the passage of the Christian soul in narrative form ('the son of...'). But now that shifted. Civil birth certificates included a new column recording sex, as birth registration was modernized and responsibility was transferred into the hands of the state – a development that aligned with the Victorian mania for statistics.

This newly enshrined civic system was supported by medical theories that became entrenched in this period. Increasingly, the distinction between the sexes was becoming essential to the maintenance of social and sexual hierarchies. A new logic was necessary to keep women in order. For centuries, the 'one-sex model', the perception of the female body as an inversion of the male body – the vagina an inverted penis – had prevailed in Europe. Indeed, as Thomas Laqueur argues in his study of the history of sexual difference, *Making Sex* (1990), up to the seventeenth century, it was a commonplace belief that women had the same genitals as men, except that theirs were tucked up inside. Across the eighteenth and nineteenth centuries, new medical technologies gave rise to a shift in thinking and the idea of a 'two-sex model', rooted in a biological understanding of sexual difference. This visual model – on which Victorian sex registration would rely – opposed the anatomy of the penis and the anatomy of the vagina, as well as the ovaries against the testes. But as Laqueur's study shows, a totalized thinking emerged, pitting male against female; by the early nineteenth century, doctors were arguing that not only were genitals and reproductive organs different, but the sexes were different in all aspects of body and soul (in outward expression – in 'the brow, the nose, the eyes, the mouth' – but also inside the body, in 'tissues' and 'fibres').

Cases of women usurping the sexual hierarchy, labelled impostors, cheats and frauds, received heightened attention in an era when male and female were emerging as opposed, and when women in particular were being sexed.

*

The 'female husband' trials are precursors to the gender fraud trials of the twenty-first century. But how did 'gender' come to the fore, replacing sex as the focus of identity, deception and fraud?

By the twentieth century, the riddle of the real versus the impostor had seemingly been solved by forensics and methods of fingerprinting, blood testing and eventually DNA testing. But questions now turned inwards with new force to the problem of self-invention. Self-determination was a modernist promise, particularly with regard to how a person could determine their own life, importantly in relation to class. In the first half of the century, novelists probed the slippery dreams of class transformation. The protagonist of F. Scott Fitzgerald's 1925 novel *The Great Gatsby* is a wannabe who takes it too far. As the novel closes, Jay Gatsby is revealed to be a striver and self-improver – actually Jimmy Gatz, a farm boy with delusions of grandeur, who climbed the social ladder and got 'newly rich' by breaking the law.

The question of self-determination also applied to sex, as new technologies challenged the established 'two-sex model'. In 1919, the German sexologist Marcus Hirschfeld established the Institute for Sexual Science in Berlin. The first medical transition took place at the institute a few years later, and Hirschfeld coined the term 'transsexual' soon after. The plot of Virginia Woolf's 1928 novel *Orlando* playfully reflects this new, shifting reality with the protagonist's spontaneous change of sex. Orlando is born a man but at age thirty he undergoes a mysterious transformation. One afternoon, the poet is found 'sunk in a profound slumber' and awakens days later as a woman. As Woolf explains, it was the same Orlando, with the same personality, mind and intellect, but a woman.

That was sex. It was not until 1955 that an American sexologist called John Money, researching intersex patients, began using the word 'gender'. Before this, gender was almost solely used in linguistics to describe grammatical structures, but it now took on another meaning. It changed fields, moving out of linguistics and into sexology, becoming a term in specialized medical literature.

Over the next decades, new terms proliferated including 'gender identity' (to describe a person's private sense of being male or female) and 'gender role' (how that identity was expressed in daily life). Some of these terms would be adopted by queer theorists and trans activists in the 1990s. Though these concepts were adapted, they came out of sexology and psychiatry. When devised, they were underpinned by ideas of disorder and dysfunction, and the normal versus the abnormal. For John Money, for example, there was a 'normal' gender – that is, a normal person (always outside the examination room, imagined to be living a happy, ordered life) who had a unified 'gender identity' and 'gender role', opposed to an 'abnormal' gender – patients he observed with, as Money described it, 'gender identity errors'. These terms would eventually inform the diagnosis 'gender identity disorder' – the title of a set of conditions that entered the DSM in 1980.

New identities, which resulted from these diagnoses, led to new questions for the law. People getting gender-confirmation surgery and becoming Orlandos were seeking rights (the right to change a birth certificate, say, for the purposes of inheritance or marriage). In these years, UK law ultimately limited self-determination when it came to gender and sex. Judgments stated that neither could be reassigned and were forever fixed at birth. But by the end of the century, this legal position was shown to be absurd. The European Court of Justice, responding to challenges brought against the UK, pointed to the reality of trans lives and the fact that gender reassignment had been happening for decades. The court described the matter as a fait accompli. The current situation was unfeasible, the court held, and UK law must adapt to this reality.

This led to the UK's Gender Recognition Act 2004, which set out a new path for self-determination, the freedom to choose – or affirm – gender and sex if steps are followed. The Act set out the 'evidence' required to authenticate gender and with it sex (in the Act, they come as a pair, with 'the male gender' attached to the 'sex ... of a man', and 'the female gender' attached to the 'sex ... of a woman'). Applicants first need medical approval, a diagnosis by two doctors confirming gender dysphoria. These notes must be presented to a Gender Recognition Panel made up of lawyers and psychologists. For a Gender Recognition Certificate to be awarded, notes must say the applicant declares loyalty to one gender (and matching sex) 'until death'. In the Act, there is no option for non-binary, other. There are just two choices, male or female. Identities outside of this binary are not legible.

The Act is now two decades old but rejected petitions and other judgments show that the state remains deeply invested in the two-sex model. For example, a December 2021 judgment by the Supreme Court considered a case by an appellant who had been trying, since 1995, to get a passport with 'X' instead of 'M' or 'F'. In a unanimous decision by five judges, the application was dismissed. The judgment defends the gender binary as a crucial sorting category. 'The record of a person's gender in their passport is used for a variety of purposes,' the judgment states, one being 'in order to prevent fraud'. (This decision contrasts with other jurisdictions, including Argentina, Australia, Canada, Colombia, Denmark, Germany, India, Pakistan and New Zealand, which offer an 'X' gender option to passport holders.)

Gender fraud trials are also invested in this Supreme Court logic. These trials are concerned with legal gender and sex, the matching pairs. Is the defendant male, a man, or female, a woman? Are they living openly this way? Are they certified? (That is, did they seek legal approval? Did they provide the right testimony, the right medical notes?)

Gayle's account on record is a mess. She tells varying stories about Kye. Her account is not standardized, not legally friendly. (Notably, her gender dysphoria diagnosis, which *is* legally friendly, enters the records once the trials are over.) There is so much evidence of Kye in the bundle and exhibits that evoke his life. But legally Kye is not a person. He has no gender certificate, no citizenship, no state records. He's an impostor. Legally, there's only Gayle.

Trials are visual. The audience – the jury – must read documents in the bundle and listen to testimonies, but there is so much looking too. Jurors, looking at a witness, at their facial expressions and body language, are asked to discern: is the person on the stand trustworthy, are they telling the truth?

Both juries are asked, 'Where does the truth lie?' and told to, 'Look for the truth.'

Gayle is so visible during the trials, and it must have felt scary. Photos are taken each day as she gets out of her parents' car. In some photos, her dad is captured trying to block photographers. She wears blazers, coloured shirts. She looks smart. Defendants are often told to dress up in suitable attire, to come to court well groomed. Sometimes I wonder, is being (just) Gayle a kind of suit? Reasonable attire in a cis-normative world? A world that is, as Shon Faye explains in *The Transgender Issue*, hostile to trans people. A world especially hostile to people that don't fit into the legal categories M or F. Who don't continuously present. Who don't present the right evidence, the right story (people of, say, gender unknown: X).

I think of Kye's email: 'Just in this world I've not been able to be that or given the correct skin to be that.'

I think of the impossibility of being both Gayle and Kye in these contexts. Did Gayle feel she had to choose? Is that why Kye is not spoken for?

Or – does this have something to do with Kye being half-Asian? Represented with pictures of a real person, with Carlo's photos, Carlo's face? Does this make it too hard to be Kye, too impossible? Outside of a private relationship, a private room – a closet?

*

As I reconstruct the evidence of the relationship, as I try to understand the two accounts, as I read and reread – I often turn to the email.

'Kye is who I am.'

Sometimes, I think of these as Kye's last words – the last time Gayle spoke as Kye.

At other times, I think it's Gayle/Kye writing. Not two distinct entities, this male, that female, but something blurry, messy.

I wonder, many times, what Carlo thinks – a real person, his surname unknown. Does he know Gayle used his face, repurposed his images? Was he ever alerted to his digital twin?

At the trials, nobody argues that it was Kye, or Gayle/Kye – or anyone other than Gayle at the keyboard, Gayle in the bed.

For the Crown, Kye is not real. And the email is just more evidence of Gayle's deceptive fiction. In it, she's still trying to manipulate Miss X with a cunning 'explanation'.

The gender fraud precedent means that, at the retrial, the Crown must prove all four elements of the offence, including 'd' – what the defendant was thinking at the time, the guilty mind.

The last element is famously hard to demonstrate. But during the retrial, Medland finds a solution. Midway

KYE FORTUNE ON THE STAND: IMPOSTORS

through Gayle's cross-examination, he suggests the email is ideal *mens rea* evidence. He calls it 'a confession... a simple confession'. This is an argument unique to the retrial – the statements about Kye are now advanced as evidence of Gayle's cunning behaviour, demonstrating her intention to deceive.

During the cross-examination, Medland directly questions Gayle about the assertion, 'Kye is who I am.' He suggests the statement reveals the deception, because it confirms that Miss X didn't know. Why say it otherwise? Why justify Kye? Why offer this 'explanation', this testimony? Why explain?

Gayle avoids answering, but he persists; he won't let it go.

'I want you to answer the question,' he commands. 'The same part I asked you about a minute ago. Quote, "*I know Kye is who I am. It's my personality and everything*." Why were you having to explain that to her?'

'I don't know why I wrote that,' Gayle says finally. 'There is no reason.'

It's like she's shutting down.

In court, you must have reasons. To have reasons is to be reasonable and reasonability is the final measure of innocence and guilt.

10

The Reasonable Person on the Stand: Legibility

Responsibility is a concern at the heart of modern criminal law. Notions of who can be held accountable for a wrongdoing, and why, have shifted over time, but a key condition of responsibility is personal autonomy, the sovereign mind.

Philosophers across the centuries, from Immanuel Kant to John Stuart Mill, have considered the ability to reason as essential to personhood. The capacity to make free, rational choices is what confers not only humanity, but also responsibility. Modern criminal law is premised on the idea that people are rational, choosing, thinking beings – free to choose how to act, and as such, deserving of punishment if they (knowingly) break the law.

Presumptions, for example sanity, and recognized defences such as diminished responsibility or automatism (actions that are involuntary, automatic) further demonstrate that a culpable defendant must be reasoning, rational, in control, sane.

*

THE REASONABLE PERSON ON THE STAND: LEGIBILITY

At both trials, Miss X and Gayle appeal to the social norms.

Miss X says her relationship with Kye was 'normal'. He was a 'normal' student, they had a 'normal' relationship. When they kissed, it felt like 'normal' kissing; the sex they had was 'normal' sex.

Gayle, who is slightly more hesitant, says over time their role play 'became the norm'. It was a way to be 'comfortable' – she uses that word a lot. She describes the Sundays on the couch as 'just normal . . . standard, almost'.

Meanwhile, the barristers focus on the plot hurdles, in an attempt to spoil the other side's story.

'It's just absurd,' says Corbett-Jones at the first trial, referring to the role play.

'It's just not normal,' Power says about the blindfold. Miss X has just described 'watching' movies with the mask on. 'That's not normal by anybody's standards, is it?' he contends.

Power is appealing to the ordinary person, 'anybody's standard'. But he's also invoking a literal standard embedded into law: the reasonable person standard. The standard can help a jury decide if a defendant is guilty or not, and whether a complainant should be believed. At criminal trials, a jury is asked to consider whether a person behaved 'reasonably' – whether they behaved like the reasonable person imagined by the standard. When invoked, jurors can ask: how would this person act? What would they think or do?

*

The reasonable person is a legal fiction – a character invented by the law. Legal fictions first appeared in Roman law. A jurist named Gaius, in a textbook for law students known as *The Institutes*, imagined a fictitious heir, a figure who could be employed by an unclaimed son to initiate legal proceedings. Imaginary defendants and complainants go by the names of Jane Doe or John Doe, and have been used in law since the Renaissance period, when a corpse can't be identified or a name is withheld.

Legal fictions are constructs, which are accepted by law as true even though they are known to be fictitious. These fictions tend to be thin – practical placeholders or legal devices. But in the nineteenth century, a new kind of fiction was required as standards of civility shifted. The law needed a standard of behaviour, a model subject with qualities, beliefs and interests – that is, a character. Enter, the reasonable person.

The figure first appeared in 1837 as 'the reasonable man', used to help solve legal problems in negligence law and later in contract law. The man mirrored his era, and was imagined to be fair-minded, informed, careful and nosey but unexceptional.

Over time, the character was almost irresistibly fleshed out. In the early 1900s, he became known as 'the man on the Clapham omnibus'. This figure was a Victorian social archetype, who appeared in the rhetoric of politicians and then slipped into law. It described an average Londoner, a distinctly middle-class man: that's why he lived in Clapham, a suburb of London; that's why he rode the bus. In another personification from the 1930s, the reasonable man 'took magazines home' and 'in the evening pushes the lawnmower in his shirtsleeves', in the words of one judge, evoking another middle-class figure who has a garden and cares about his lawn.

THE REASONABLE PERSON ON THE STAND: LEGIBILITY

When I first encountered these imaginary persons, I was startled; they were stark reminders that the law is a realm of text and interpretation, character, imagination and plot. I saw the way the law overlapped with fiction and how the law could be read as a kind of literature, populated by characters.

First used in civil law, by the 1950s the standard was being employed in criminal law.

Over time, the character has been reformed and blanked out: it is no longer a man, but a nondescript person (without class, race, sex or gender), constructed as an average adult – a kind of base avatar, humanoid but not yet customized.

Today, the person appears across UK legislation, from stalking and self-defence to alcohol sales and the use of sun beds. There are other hypothetical characters too, a 'group of personalities' used to set standards and help solve problems, who inhabit what's been called the 'legal village'. This is an imaginary dwelling, populated by friends and neighbours. In the village lives a character called the 'officious bystander' used in contract law – a nosey, self-important bystander, imagined to ask questions about a contract, to help work out how it should be interpreted. Another resident is the 'fair-minded and informed observer', a character used to help perceive whether there might be a bias during trial.

In some ways, these ordinary fictions reflect the collective psyche, but they are also distinctly legal, and though reformed and abstracted, they are still recognizable as Victorian men.

At criminal trials, the jury is asked to consider whether a person behaved 'reasonably' – like the person imagined by the standard. At the heart of the test, whoever behaves like the reasonable person is justified in their actions. Because, according to the standard, this normal, fair-minded, average person is justified. Their decisions, intentions, beliefs and goals are all justified. This hypothetical person is not flawless by any means, but if they act selfishly or fearfully or cowardly, it's in a reasonable way; they make the correct decision. In other words, their mistakes and errors and fears are reasonable too.

*

Who, in this story, behaved like the reasonable person? The problem for the barristers arguing the case is that neither Gayle nor Miss X acted sensibly. Each lawyer contends that the other side's account is 'absurd' and 'ludicrous'. And despite their appeals to the 'normal', Miss X and Gayle acknowledge that, at some point, things did get out of hand.

Kye, at the centre, is a dream man, a Romeo. Desire drives the action forward; the stories they tell on the stand are tales of irrationality, madness, love.

Miss X says she was mad about Kye. When Power asks if Kye was the love of her life, Miss X says yes. In her account, she was crazy for him; she describes feeling 'desperate'. She admits that she didn't behave rationally. After the years of chatting online, she says she would have done 'anything' to meet him. His absences, his refusal to meet, the special conditions when they did – she was willing to overlook all this. She was ready to agree to the blindfold, any terms.

Gayle's story is a mirror image. She was crazy for Miss X, whom she calls 'my first, my true love'. She says meeting Miss X was a kind of miracle; 'before her, I thought I'd never be able to experience love. I didn't think it was something that would ever happen to me,' she says. Over two years, her whole world came to revolve around Miss X; she would have done 'anything for her', she explains. 'Absolutely anything to make her happy.'

In Gayle's story, by 2013, things were getting out of control – the story was running away with both of them. But she couldn't pull back. 'At the time, she was the only person I truly cared about, she's the only person I thought about,' Gayle says. This mad, consuming love is part of her defence. Describing the apology messages and the email sent after the fight, Gayle says, 'love makes you do stupid, stupid, crazy, crazy shit'.

To read their stories is to find both entering a topsy-turvy world – their reason clouded by fantasy and hope, blinkered and madly doting. Both stepped over some line and their reason evaporated.

But also, can we expect people to fall in love with each other, to have sex with each other, in reasonable states of mind? Is the standard, the language of reason, the right fit? It conjures a fiction of careful, fair-minded, reasonable people, weighing up considerations, rather than driven by the strange phenomenon that is desire.

*

Courts require rational inner thought processes, capable of inspection. But in the context of love and desire, the language of reason can feel all wrong.

During Gayle's cross-examinations, the barristers home in on the final evening together, the breakdown of the relationship and the moments leading up to Miss X's complaint. Gayle must account for all the decisions she made that day in relation to sex, but also every act – from messages she sent, to what she was wearing and her gestures on the street. At both trials, she is asked about the suicide attempt, the apologetic texts, the email. At the first trial, she says, 'Do I know the reason of individual things? No.'

She is lacking the standard of self-knowledge required in court, the reasons to account for every act. Sometimes at the retrial, she seems to shut down. Medland turns to the swimming costume worn 'on underneath' her clothing, which features in the police officer's report, along with other items Gayle was wearing at the canal – a hat, blue trainers, a jumper. Gayle admits she wore the swimsuit, sometimes, because she didn't like her body. She talks about the gym. But Medland wants to know about sex. His style is polite, persistent, deadly.

'Miss Newland, forgive me, I will put the question again,' he says. He specifies the day of the argument: a Sunday with Miss X, the canal jump – in particular, a day they had sex.

'Why were you wearing a swimsuit whilst that was happening?' he asks.

'For no particular reason,' Gayle replies.

Her failure to take part in the reasonable person contest is dangerous. At trial, a defendant has got to provide reasons. And yet, accounting for every action can be hard. Sometimes the reasonable person, with reasons for everything, who is always responsible, in control, can feel like an impossible standard. The problem is, the person is an ideal, that people on the stand rarely live up to.

'Because I got changed,' Gayle eventually declares when Medland turns to the other items she was wearing, including the (unseasonable) woolly hat. 'Why would I put a hat on?' she asks, desperately, as she searches, and fails, to give reasons for her actions, to know. 'Why was I wearing shoes? Why was I wearing a top?'

*

Jurors watch the trial unfold, listening to the testimonies, reading evidence, studying character. Ultimately, they have to come to conclusions. 'Common sense is what you are required to use,' Judge Dutton explains at the end of the first trial. But the problem with common sense – as the philosopher Antonio Gramsci has observed – is that it is hard to pin down, and can reveal itself to be local, chaotic and even fickle. Gramsci, writing from prison in 1930s fascist Italy, considered the complicated roots of collective knowledge, and the bundle of assumptions that are encountered as self-evident truths.

Juries are asked to 'pool' together in the deliberation room and make a decision. To be judged by twelve ordinary citizens rather than experts is a democratic ideal. But in the context of sexual offences trials, it can also be treacherous. Countless studies have shown juries' susceptibility to rape myths, which are perceptions about 'real' rape stories. It is impossible to know what actually happens in the deliberation room, because in the UK a jury can never be asked to explain how a decision was reached. The jury room is a closed universe. Its internal workings are opaque. The task is onerous and the responsibility is high. After watching the trial, jurors are finally given directions by the judge, a route to verdict – summarized first in a speech, and then on a piece of paper, which outlines the steps to find a defendant guilty, or not.

Here, both juries are told to deliberate with an objective lens, a 'cool head'. At the retrial, the McNally Principle is at work. The route to verdict is different; there is no Section 76, no short cut. The last elements of the offence are back, with the spotlight on the consent parts.

'What is consent in law?' Judge Stockdale asks rhetorically, before giving the jury the definition (freedom, capacity and choice). Consent, he goes on, is 'at the heart of the case'. He evokes the sexual contract, identifying 'the agreement'. But unlike a contract, no articulation is required, he notes. 'Consent, members of the jury, is a state of mind,' he explains.

Assault by penetration has four elements or ingredients. The retrial turns on the last two and on consent – its definition and its conditions, via the principle that gender deception can vitiate consent. Stockdale outlines the third element, which is, 'Miss X did not consent.' This is what Miss X says in her testimony. When it comes to making a decision, no corroboration evidence is required. Her word alone is enough, if she is believed. Jurors must ask themselves, is she trustworthy, credible? (Do we believe her? Are we sure?)

After this comes the last element. 'If you are sure that Miss X did not consent then you will move on to the final element of the offence,' Stockdale explains.

Liability is a central tenet of criminal law. The judge will explain there are two steps. First, jurors must ask, was the defendant's state of mind honest? Specifically, when it comes to Gayle, did she honestly think Miss X was consenting at the time?

But that's only the first step. Before 2003, honest belief was enough. A second step was added to the new Sexual

THE REASONABLE PERSON ON THE STAND: LEGIBILITY

Offences Act asking, was a defendant's belief in consent 'reasonable'? This standard is written into the last element of the offence, which Stockdale now outlines: 'Gayle Dawn Newland did not reasonably believe that [Miss X] consented.'

The second step supposedly made it easier to demonstrate a defendant's state of mind and thus to convict, because the standard is objective, employing the test of reasonableness. Even so, the consent wall remained high, because *mens rea* is hard to demonstrate. Belief in consent – whether just honest or also reasonable – is an intangible thing. The prosecution must prove an 'absence of belief' or an 'unreasonable belief'. But how is an absence, a belief, to be demonstrated?

And when it comes to this last element, a judge's directions, however careful, can also feel tricky, technical and elusive. Speaking to the jury, Stockdale puts it like this: 'If . . . you were to conclude that whilst Miss X was not in fact consenting, Gayle Newland honestly believed or may have believed that she was consenting then you must consider whether that belief or possible belief was reasonable in the circumstances.'

What a sentence! All the conditionals. There's so much going on; it's thorny, edging on the inscrutable.

This final part of the test is meant to offer jurors a specific tool, the yardstick of reasonableness. The jurors are told they can 'draw inferences', using the reasonable standard. 'It is for you to decide what the truth of the relationship was,' Stockdale tells the jury.

In the private room, jurors must 'find' what was going on in the minds of Gayle and Miss X at the time: 'that depends on your finding as to what happened', Stockdale says, 'your finding of what was going on in Gayle Newland's mind at the time.'

To infer is to deduce, to calculate, to conclude. Stockdale simplifies: 'What was reasonable in the circumstances?'

This question seems to open a can of worms in the context of sexuality, queerness, confusion and embodiment. Was it reasonable for Gayle to become Kye as well as Gayle? For Miss X to know that? (Want that?)

The dildo, the blindfold, the closet, role play: we're so far from the familiar here.

*

In the courtroom, the reasonable person is a fiction used to construct truth – helping a jury to decide what happened in the private room and on the facts of a case. In the context of a sexual offences trial, the standard also seems to invite the question, what is a reasonable person's desire?

The line between sexual behaviour figured as reasonable or intolerable is not stable. But no society allows complete sexual permissiveness. Every culture has rules, the most ancient and unvarying of prohibitions being incest. Sexual science emerging in the Victorian period imagined a normal, healthy sexual life (heterosexual, reproductive and within a marriage). This was the correct way to be. Anything outside of this paradigm was labelled perverse. But the notion of a uniform sexual life, where one size fits all, is a fiction, and under these rules 'unnatural' desires were hidden and repressed. 'People do not show their sexuality freely,' Sigmund Freud wrote in 1909. 'To conceal it they wear a heavy overcoat woven of a tissue of lies, as though the weather were bad in the world of sexuality.' The weather *was* bad. It's no wonder people concealed desires, and lied, in a time when anything outside the norm was judged to be perverse, and when women were rarely expected to have any desires at all.

In the 1920s, Freud theorized 'the id' as a primitive, instinctual part of the mind surging below conscious thought. Urges and impulses, he suggested, were trained by society – domesticated and shaped by any culture's notion of a reasonable desire. But the reality was far more unnerving. For Freud, the objective of psychoanalysis was to understand 'the id', to discover ourselves and our desires rather than to judge, repress and deny.

When it comes to regulating sexuality, rules change and boundaries shift. Over the twentieth century, the rise of the 'consent model' led to a reassessment of sexual behaviour along the new axis of autonomy. Desires and preferences once figured as wrong and kept secret, from homosexuality to kink practices like BDSM (bondage and related activities), were slowly legitimized by the logic of consenting adults and 'compatible' kink. For BDSM, the shift in attitude was very recent (and indeed is ongoing), following changes to its definition in the *Diagnostic Statistical Manual of Mental Disorders* in 2013.

New definitions have resulted in a lessening of stigma. But even so, the logic of the word 'kink' – meaning a sharp twist or back pain – assumes there is an objective straightness to desire, a standard of reasonableness. And yet sexologists today suggest the idea of 'normal' desire is ludicrous. It is impossible to generalize because desire defies the science of averages. '[T]here is no norm in sexual medicine for what our levels of sexual desire should be,' writes Karen Gurney in her book on sex and desire, *Mind the Gap* (2020). 'Amazing, right?' she continues. 'Where else in science is there no norm? We have norms for height, norms for intelligence, norms for how long it takes men to come etc., etc. ... Not desire.'

The method of discovering what's average, normal, emerged in the nineteenth century. A Belgian astronomer called Adolphe Quetelet developed a method of combining many measurements together into a single average measurement. Quetelet used a graph to determine the average, which took the shape of a bell. At the very top of the bell, known as the 'normal curve', was the average calculation.

Initially utilized by astronomers, Quetelet had the idea of applying the method to society. By the 1830s, he'd come up with the term 'the average man' – a man made up of the measurements of many men. The curve of the bell accounted for the 'normal' 90 per cent of the population, with the average man found in the very middle. Quetelet hoped this figure could help novelists and poets to create characters appropriate for their age.

In the same era, the reasonable man was emerging too, a fair-minded, average man, later 'the man on the Clapham omnibus' – an expression of this ordinary person in the happy middle of the curve. This figure would later take form in other statistical fictions such as Average Joe and Plain Jane.

The thing about the normal, average, ordinary: it has always found its way against its opposite, and asks the shadow question, who is abnormal, who is unreasonable? (Who is kinky or bent?)

Indeed, in the nineteenth century a fixation grew with the two ends of the curve. The bell curve became popular among race scientists – eugenicists believed it described the social hierarchy, with the mighty few at one narrow end of the curve and the degenerates at the other. In this same period, the abnormal individual was being theorized by sexologists and criminologists alike – an individual who needed to be institutionalized and corrected. Bodies once figured as 'vile', 'unnatural', 'monstrous' – from the hermaphrodite to conjoined twins – shifted to the abnormal individual found at the end of the curve (as 'vile' became 'disordered'). And in the twentieth century, gender variance was also understood along this axis, with the diagnosis 'gender identity disorder' pitting people with a 'normal' gender identity against others with gender identity 'errors'.

*

If once Kye passed as the reasonable person (the hetero prom king, handsome fiancé), a way to get on script, into the normal village (a Guy, a Joe), by the time of the trials, he is sick, missing – the dossier, his email, used as evidence of how unreasonable Gayle is.

In his closing speech, Medland describes Kye as 'a complete illusion'. Pointing to the profiles and phone records, the years of intricate messages, he asks: 'What was she presenting it as? The life of Kye Fortune.' (As if giving a title to a hoax memoir.)

Gayle's account of Kye is not standardized. The figure that ultimately emerges in the bundle and the testimonies is a messy Gayle/Kye. A half-Asian man, built from the torso of random guys, with Carlo's face; and also Gayle, with the same birthday, same voice, a student and creative writer; and a role – a man who was sick, dying, absent. Together it's a patchwork that is hard to make sense of.

This mishmash – one as two – is not favourable or legible in a legal context.

The reasonable person, once the reasonable man, can be hard to visualize. Feminist legal scholars have sought to reveal his suppressed qualities. Despite reform, these scholars argue that the default person – once openly a man – remains front-loaded and invisibly marked. He is in all likelihood white, heterosexual and cis-gender too. And, in ways that are rarely noted, presumed to have a clearly bounded single subjectivity.

The bounded individual is an axiom of law. In her 1997 essay 'The Body Bag', the legal scholar Ngaire Naffine uses the metaphor of a sealed bag to evoke the persons imagined by law. These persons 'come in a closed body bag', she writes. Each bag is bounded and separate. Inside is a single subject.

In law, cohabiting or sharing a body bag, is disruptive to Western notions of bodily integrity and autonomy, which are seen as a natural right. When it comes to Gayle and Kye, 'the same person', there's a suggestion of cohabitation, a shared body. But before the law, Gayle/Kye amounts to a category crisis. They are unreasonable, absurd.

By the time of the first trial, Gayle has distanced herself from Kye. He's gone. She distances herself from the email and from his life. Even so, her story, her sexuality and her subjectivity are far from reasonable, and she knows it. 'It sounds stupid . . . It sounds ridiculous,' she tells the Crown as she tries to explain the phones, the role play, Kye's life.

THE REASONABLE PERSON ON THE STAND: LEGIBILITY

'Yes, it looks stupid. Yes, I look fucking stupid. I look like a fucking weirdo,' she sobs.

But she's not alone. Miss X's story, and even her preferences, are not particularly reasonable either – choosing a bandaged lover, consenting to a blindfold, getting engaged to a person she'd never seen.

In the absence of reasonable narratives, reason gives way to belief. The question becomes, whose story do you believe?

11

Storytelling on the Stand: Fiction

Trials are storytelling competitions. Lawyers are making a case and constructing stories, as each side's account is shaped into a legal narrative. But what makes a good story, one that works on the imagination, that convinces – that convicts? Is a good story realistic – trying its best to render real life as we recognize it? Or must it be coherent, well plotted, as illustrated by the Russian playwright Anton Chekhov's famous rule that a gun introduced in the first act must, by the third act, be fatally discharged? Is a good story also satisfyingly familiar? Must it thrill, like a finger on the hair trigger (we know it will blow, but when?)?

At both trials, the jurors hear two incredible stories. They are finally asked, who do you believe? Narratives are in competition. The lawyers attempt to put evidence in order, presenting it persuasively. It is an adversarial battle. 'Thus, members of the jury, the battle lines are drawn,' Stockdale pronounces at the end of the retrial. And those battle lines, put forward in the final arguments, offer two implausible stories.

The Crown contends the story on trial is a real-life bed

trick. It's an unlikely ruse – but Gayle, highly skilled, pulled it off. She is cast as the devious author in control of the plot. In this version, Miss X is the naive reader – a credulous, innocent hopeful, looking for love. And Gayle, the false friend, cunningly fitted her deception into a romantic framework (namely, the marriage plot) to enact a bed trick. This was rape under the guise of romance, the whole relationship deceptively structured by courtship, love and the promise of marriage. Gayle's apologetic texts and email, her messy testimony, along with the other evidence she can't explain, together reveal her guilt.

Meanwhile, the defence says the bed trick is not credible (it is 'quite literally impossible to believe', says Power). Speaking to the jury, Power appeals to common sense. The trick is 'in-credible' (and he's using this word in its pure sense, as *not*-credible) because of the constant blindfold, the whole Sundays together, the mask never slipping. Because Gayle and Miss X were best friends, and because Kye is Gayle – they share the same body, the same voice.

And yet, despite the rhetoric of good sense, the defence relies on a plot that's bound up with fiction too. The messages to Kye are explained as 'role play', a story between them, with Gayle 'in role' as Kye. Behind it all was a queer plot – a secret lesbian romance, the two friends in the closet, and no one knew.

In surprising ways, both sides' stories are infused with fiction – to the point that Stockdale is compelled to tell his jurors, 'You may have been surprised by some of the evidence that you've heard, you may even on occasions have been frankly astonished but, members of the jury, this case is not fiction, this case is not make believe, it is real life.'

THE BED TRICK

*

Sexual offences law is public, but it's also intimate law, which tells us what we are allowed to do with another person's body and sometimes with our own.

One of the complications of regulating intimate acts is that they can have private meanings, which can't always be grasped from the outside. Compounding this difficulty, sex and desire defy norms – there is no average, no bell curve, as Gurney notes, which can make it hard to put sex in the public realm and to judge it. In the absence of clear facts, plots and popular narratives end up setting standards and shaping behaviour. Alongside medicine and law, minds are steered by fiction. Literature can inform what is reasonable to want – what's normal, credible and acceptable.

Seduction is an old theme in literature. In the eighteenth century, a new, heightened literary realism took shape. Lengthy seduction novels employed the epistolary format, following characters day by day, almost in real time, creating a 'reality effect' – as in Samuel Richardson's colossal novel *Clarissa*. The author's technique of presenting the novel as letters written between his characters was dazzling to contemporary readers, giving them a sense of being privy to the ebb and flow of thought and the secret recesses of the heart. Some seduction novels, such as Richardson's, were intended as conduct books, which set out to warn young women, set standards and inform behaviour. But while actual conduct books were full of platitudes, novels were far more exciting to read – and far more affecting.

The gentleman-seducer is a staple of the seduction novel, a literary archetype epitomized by characters such as Lovelace, the mythic rake who ensnares Clarissa, and Alec in Thomas Hardy's *Tess of the D'Urbervilles*. These ruthless libertines are romantic antagonists who endanger heroines while enthralling readers; as the critic Elizabeth Hardwick wryly notes in her 1973 essay on seduction literature, 'the most interesting seducers are actually rapists' – a pointed reminder that literary allure is often reserved for predators. In these novels, love is often depicted as a risky tournament. Gentlemen-seducers procure romance through falsehood – by trickery, seduction and deceit. Take the story of Hardy's protagonist, Tess. She never really likes her seducer (and employer), Alec. His mode of seduction, Hardwick writes, is 'by flattery, pretence and finally a rude, overwhelming insistence'. The scene of Tess's 'seduction' was controversial from the outset (Hardy was forced to censor it). Tess is tricked by Alec late at night, when he takes her into the fog and into the woods. She falls asleep. Then she is a 'maiden no more'. The event defines and ruins her life; she can never quite escape it. Hardy himself claimed it was 'a seduction, pure and simple'; Alec thinks so too. But it's far more ambiguous; Tess's consent was dubious at the very least. She was tricked, vulnerable and possibly asleep.

Hardwick's essay drew out the ambiguity of seduction practices – looking at the characters who got away with it, interpreted as seducers, pure and simple, and those viewed as tricksters, burglars and rapists.

*

The term 'date rape' emerged in the 1970s. From the outset, it sparked cultural controversy, like the Victorian-era questions about a true rape act. Critics asked, was rape on a date 'real' rape?

In the 1980s, the feminist researcher Diana Russell conducted a new study of rape, examining in particular 'acquaintance rape', a new term describing rape by someone you know – a husband, friend or suitor. In the same era, the journalist Robin Warshaw, using another study on sexual assault, wrote a book on date rape, which she called a 'hidden epidemic'. Both studies argued – against contemporary logic, which focused on 'stranger-rape' (by a strange man in a dark alleyway) – that, actually, the most prevalent type of rape was by someone you know, occurring at home or on a date.

During these decades, debates intensified within feminism. These studies received backlash in the 1990s from figures such as Camille Paglia, who – appearing on CNN, writing in daily newspapers and giving lectures – described 'date rape' as 'propaganda'. 'I think real rape is an outrage,' Paglia would often opine (she defined it as rape by a stranger). But at the same time, she would go on, 'I consider the propaganda and hysteria about date rape equally outrageous.' Paglia turned the focus on female responsibility. Of a woman, going on a date, entering a sexual setting, wearing a short skirt, she asked brutally: what do you expect? In Paglia's view, as in the nineteenth-century novel, courtship is a 'dangerous game'. It's risky – she compared it to gambling; you might lose. Society can't make rules to legislate this kind of behaviour, she argued: 'we cannot legislate what happens on a date.' (Other feminists such as Lynne Henderson responded by saying that date rape is unacceptable, and we should stop finding arguments to excuse men and shift the blame.)

In her study of rape across the centuries, Joanna Bourke pointed to alarming evidence of rapists, in this era in particular, fitting actions to romantic frameworks. 'A rapist, in the twentieth century, would take the trouble to drive the victim to her home, dropping her off politely at her doorstep,' she explained. Just like the gentlemen-seducers in classic literature, the romance plot overlays (and obscures) the rape plot, as the victim is given flowers, gifts, teddies, sweets, a romantic dinner – then raped. This idea was reflected in psychiatric theories, emerging in this period, in which rape was conceived as a 'courtship disorder' – that is, a 'flawed performance' of normal courtship.

Across the 1990s, 'real rape' was pitted against date rape as feminists debated the law and responsibility, and searched for bright lines. An autobiographical essay by the writer Mary Gaitskill, published in 1994, changed the terms and managed to stay with the ambiguity, escaping reactionary debates. 'The Trouble with Following the Rules' describes the experience of being raped, twice – one, a violent rape by a stranger, and another in a softer, intimate context. Both were harmful in different ways. The first was violent and terrifying. Gaitskill's attacker threatened to kill her, and she thought he might. But the extremity of the situation actually made it easier to process, she suggested. 'For me the rape was a clearly defined act, perpetrated on me by a crazy asshole whom I didn't know or trust . . . so, when it was over, it was relatively easy to dismiss,' Gaitskill wrote. Meanwhile, rape by someone intimate – who might even say they love you when they do it – has a haunting and troubling ambiguity. 'Its motives are often impossible to understand,' she wrote. 'Nearly always it's hard to know whether you played a role in what happened and, if so, what the role was. The experience sticks.'

Here, intimate rape becomes the hardest to judge from the outside and sometimes the inside too. But this ambiguity, rather than making the rape less 'real', actually works in the opposite direction, making it the most haunting and damaging, the one that sticks.

*

The line between seduction and deception in law, and the difficulty of creating a set of rules, is an old and persistent trouble. Across the 1990s, journalists and judges alike worried about the over-criminalization of seduction (what would become the 'pure view'), where any active lie – whether false promises of undying love, exaggerations or pretences – could turn sex into rape. Many worried this would limit male sexual freedom, arguing that seduction shouldn't count. Law would be overreaching and overregulating the private sphere. This position revealed a romantic idea of seduction, where love and trickery were tied together – at least when it came to gentlemen-seducers. (As one Canadian Supreme Court judge put it in 1998, 'Deceptions, small and sometimes large, have from time immemorial been the by-product of romance and sexual encounters.') Conservative journalists worried about the 'end of romance', and a new feminist 'morality' taking the fun and spontaneity out of sex, for some eviscerating the erotic, where sex and danger are entwined. This concern was also raised in light of the MeToo movement that consumed public discourse in 2017.

Since 2003, under the Sexual Offences Act, there has been a patchwork of judgments and rulings on hidden HIV status, condom removal, gender history deceptions, undercover cops and fertility lies. Some deceptions count (condoms, gender). Most others don't. These uneven judgments are part of an ongoing, unresolved question: what are the deceptions that count, that we want the state to censure? To put it another way, when is it an illegal, state-censured 'trick'? When is it an 'ordinary seduction' (as one judge memorably put it), a minor wrong?

For me, there's a scale. Some deceptions feel wrong – the Spy Cops, for example, who lived with women for years under 'legends', their deceptions intentional, active, state-sanctioned. Other deceptions appear too private and involve conduct that's difficult to measure or judge – for example, saying 'I love you' when you don't mean it. But it's hard to find a middle ground. When I audit this question among friends, writers and scholars, I get so many different answers. It always leads to more questions about why *these* lies count, and which lies shouldn't – as if, at this moment in time, there is no agreed reading, no 'common' sense.

In the public forum, the conversation can lead to binaries, with one side saying, 'all's fair in love and war', dismissing the whole conversation, and the other wanting a (penal) code, protection in private life and a strong, carceral state.

The deeper questions when it comes to intimate deception, emotional harm and lies inside a relationship might be: is the law (always) the right tool? Is more law, refined law, the right answer? Sometimes it can feel like a category error.

To me, the recent patchwork of judgments is a stark reminder that 'deception' is culturally inflected, a loose concept, informed by time and place. I think of the McNally judgment, which stated it was 'common sense' that gender counted, and it was 'obvious' that other deceptions, like wealth, should not. (As always, common sense is never defined, but the buck stops there.) I think of the Australian man convicted of tricking a woman into believing he was white, the Palestinian man convicted of rape in Israel on the basis of ethno-religious fraud, and the continuing streak of gender fraud cases.

Who gets to seduce and lie and mislead in the course of 'seduction'? And who is criminalized? Rape by deception has been described as a 'riddle', which 'drives a stake through the very heart of modern rape law' and its central principle, consent. Where does one person's sexual autonomy end, and another's begin? Is it fair that some deceptions are singled out, when others are seen as ordinary, permissible? When it comes to deceptions that count and those that don't, we must ask, whose sexual freedom, autonomy and interests are being protected? And whose are being restricted, criminalized and feared?

*

The love plot is part of the cultural script, once centre stage in fairytales and plays, now in romance novels and rom-coms. Shakespeare's problem play *All's Well That Ends Well* drew on folktale and romance sources. In the play, a healer named Helena is given a set of labours in a fairytale trope known as 'the fulfilment of the tasks'. To win her man, Bertram, she must complete the tasks – including getting his ring upon her finger, which she does via a bed trick.

In movie scripts, an invitation to the prom, a first kiss, becoming prom queen and prom king – all these lead towards the ring. Prom, with its special dress and grand entrance, is a kind of rehearsal for the wedding (in the 2004 rom-com *A Cinderella Story*, Samantha wears an actual wedding dress to prom, to meet her cyber prince).

Kye's love letters and the ring he sent are evidence of a love story. But to follow Miss X's and Gayle's accounts is to find they are in different plots. Miss X is in a marriage plot, symbolized by the ring. She says that in December 2012, Kye posted her an eternity ring and they were engaged. The proposal was just another sign that Kye really was 'that boyfriend fantasy', the 'best of both'. She felt she'd been chosen by the popular guy, the guy whom loads of girls fancied. He wasn't afraid of commitment – she was going to be 'Mrs Fortune'.

Meanwhile, Gayle is in a different plot. It's not the marriage plot. 'We were never engaged,' she says; that was Miss X getting carried away. Gayle's story is a secret queer romance, surfacing at trial – a coming-out plot layered by fantasy, secrecy and shame. This plot is symbolized by the dildo, which is held up at the trials and figured as guilty and queer.

The ring and dildo are both fetish objects – but in so many ways they are at odds. While the engagement ring is precious, the ultimate prize, a symbol of the marriage plot, worn as a token of respectability and protection (designed to be eye-catching), the dildo is erotic and private, hidden away, connected to touch and play. In some ways, it figures as a kind of smoking gun; in the dominant (heterosexual) reading, the dildo can't be in a legitimate romance or seduction but is unwanted, predatory and fraudulent.

When it comes to romance, will the ring plot always be more public, more familiar and ultimately more credible than the dildo plot? Is queer rape more legible than straight rape?

Miss X is an impressive witness. She's consistent and firm, and she holds onto her story despite Power's many attempts to pull it apart. The same cannot be said of Gayle, who tells a messy story; narratively, it is as if she's guilty of (courtship) disorder. The Crown contends her convoluted account is a sign of unreliability, as if she's struggling to get her story 'straight'. 'Your story is changing,' Corbett-Jones accuses, 'because it's a story and not the truth.' Her story is multiple, contradictory, lacking an elegant narrative line (and against what the Crown argues about her 'skills', she's often a poor storyteller). She doesn't follow the rules of a good story, one that works on the imagination, that convinces. In other words, her story is not coherent enough, not familiar enough, not straight enough.

*

In the context of the trials, there is one truth teller and one liar. Ultimately, the jury must vote; Gayle is found guilty both times.

After the verdict comes the sentencing. A judge, following guidelines, decides on a punishment. At each sentencing, the judge chooses 'Category 2A'. 'A' is for culpability. It is the highest category, for cases where there has been a significant degree of planning or abuse of trust. '2' is for harm and describes 'particularly vulnerable' victims and 'severe' psychological harm. The sentencing range for this category is from five to thirteen years.

At the first sentencing, Dutton says, 'you are an intelligent, obsessional, highly manipulative, deceitful, scheming and thoroughly determined young woman'. He's speaking to Gayle, who is back in the glass box. 'As for culpability these offences required a lengthy and complex degree of planning over many many months,' he continues.

'This was a deceit of such subtlety and cunning in its planning,' says Stockdale at the second sentencing. Miss X was 'completely in the thrall of a fictitious persona, created by you', he continues. 'It is difficult to conceive of a deceit so degrading or a deceit so damaging for the victim upon its discovery.'

Both judges noted that Kye had other victims, women he also spoke to online and who believed he was 'real' – increasing culpability – though 'none of that led to the commission of offences', Dutton observed. The 'Category 2A' paradigm evokes the dominant and the vulnerable – Gayle, the cunning specialist, and Miss X, a gullible girl who continues to suffer the consequences of abuse; her medical records, presented at sentencing, list various conditions including post-traumatic stress disorder.

And yet, at each sentencing, there's a suggestion that the dynamics are a little more complicated. Gayle's guilt is evaluated by way of mitigating factors through the assessment of psychiatric reports. At the first trial, Dutton notes that Gayle has been diagnosed with various disorders, 'including social anxiety disorder, personality disorder, depression and OCD'; he adds, 'Your history of low self-esteem and blurred gender lines is important.' As 'an aspect of mercy', she is sentenced to eight years.

At the second trial, Stockdale reads a new report that adds gender dysphoria to the list, along with Asperger's Syndrome. On the latter, Stockdale acknowledges that Gayle will be 'particularly vulnerable in a prison environment to manipulation'. Her sentence is reduced to six years as the judge makes it clear that Gayle, as well as being 'cunning', is vulnerable too.

*

Today, the shock of substitution continues to entertain in body swap movies. This popular genre is part of the bed trick lineage, a kind of contemporary cousin. Scores of films have been released over the decades, from *18 Again!* (1988) to *Freaky Friday* (2003) to *The Swap* (2016). In these Hollywood fairytales, protagonists wake up in a different body. Typically, the magic swap is triggered by an exotic spell, activated by a fortune cookie in a Chinese restaurant, a pair of African earrings or an Aztec statue in a museum. As part of the comedy, romantic intimacies are carried out in somebody else's skin. But unlike adult tales of deceptive sex, these are softer stories of wishful thinking, magic and personal growth. The protagonists must live a life, for a period of time, in a new body – a frenemy's body, a younger body, or a body of the 'opposite' gender. Often, the protagonists get to be teenagers again – to go back to high school, like Josie in *Never Been Kissed*, except these highschoolers aren't undercover. This second chance is by magic.

The films speak playfully to the riddle of identity, asking, if you have a different body, are you still you? Where does identity lie?

This is an old preoccupation; in the seventeenth century the philosopher John Locke pondered the same questions. In one essay, he asked his reader to imagine a body swap, where the mind of a prince, with all its 'princely thoughts', is transferred into the body of a cobbler. He asked, who is the resulting person, the cobbler or the prince? Locke went on to argue that a person goes where their consciousness goes; as in body swap movies, identity is located in the mind and in the continuity of psychological life.

*

In Miss X's telling of the final night, when she rips off the blindfold, the ring and dildo collide. It's her ring, of all things, that alerts her. Eternity rings, with their continuous line of gems, can often get caught on fabric. Miss X describes her ring catching on the wool of Kye's beanie, the one he wears over the bandages around his head, which is shaved and covered in scars. The hat slips, releasing hair that Miss X says feels 'like a Barbie doll's hair'. As Kye is feminized, his hair switching with Gayle's hair, he begins to disappear – first by touch, then by sight.

Miss X describes it as a 'bad movie'. She's not in a rom-com with Kye any more, a terminal romance with a sick Valentine, who is beautiful, in danger, doomed. She's in another script entirely. She seems to acknowledge the movie's gone wrong – her boyfriend has vanished; in his place, there's a 'stranger'. Recounting this moment of looking for the first time, she remembers the strap-on, and then seeing a person pulling down the woolly hat, hiding their face, and realizing, in shock, that she doesn't know who this person is. She says the stranger starts talking about a body swap movie – using it to explain.

This part of Miss X's account has always fascinated me. The body swap plot coming in. Life emulating fiction, imitating art.

In her account, Miss X says the moment doesn't feel real. She can't believe what she sees. It's not Kye. To the police, she repeats, 'I just couldn't believe it. I just couldn't believe it. I couldn't believe it.'

Time seems to slow down. They're on the bed. She's naked. She grabs the sheet, looking for her clothes. The stranger is following her around the room. 'You have to let me explain,' they're pleading. 'It's not what you think.'

That's when the stranger starts talking about the body swap movie *17 Again*. Miss X watched the film with Kye months ago. They'd watched it on the phone when Kye was in hospital, hooked up to a machine. In her complaint, Miss X recounts the plot.

In *17 Again*, the main character is a dissatisfied dad called Mike. One day, he is magically transported into his younger body. It's still Mike but he is no longer recognizable. To his friends, his wife, his kids, he looks like someone else, a random teenager.

Miss X recalls that when she watched the film with Kye, he'd asked her jokingly: *If I changed bodies, do you think you would recognize me?* And Miss X remembers playing along, saying: *Well, I'd have to ask you some personal questions, which only the two of us would know.*

This is how it happens in the movie. In a plot point of the genre, the main character must prove it's them – usually to a friend; some kind of 'evidence' is required. In *17 Again*, Mike's bestie is called Ned. The scene takes place in Ned's flat. 'It's me, Mike O'Donnell, your best friend,' Mike declares, but Ned doesn't believe him. He assumes it's a burglar. To prove it's really him, just in a new body, Mike starts to reference things that only a bestie would know – eventually winning Ned over.

Miss X says that the stranger reminds her of this

conversation she had with Kye. 'It's me. It's me,' Miss X remembers the stranger saying. 'I told you this would happen.' 'You said you'd believe me. You said you'd believe me.'

I find this moment compelling, because the boundary between life and art, reality and fiction, seems to slip. And it's more than this – art, the film script, seems to overlay real life. The scene also cuts to the heart of the bed trick plot – a juncture that turns on belief, knowledge, intimacy and recognition. What pieces of knowledge can change someone, erase someone, make them into someone else? What makes someone knowable or unknowable? (Can we draw a line?)

In bed trick plots, to demonstrate intimacy and knowledge, and to prove it's really you, the protagonist must tell a secret, reveal a scar, or offer up a token (often a ring).

Miss X, using her eyes for the first time, has to decide: who is it in front of her? In the moment of the unmasking, which senses or ways of knowing does she trust the most? Her eyes, her touch? Knowledge, a secret? The mask has come off, but it feels like a fiction, madness. Miss X had the conversation with her boyfriend, Kye. Now this person, this stranger, is referencing the secret question, the film. 'It's me,' the body says.

And for a second, Miss X says she believes it's Kye.

It's Kye's voice. It's Kye speaking.

He tells her he's 'better'. 'They put me in this body,' he says. It's like he's not dying any more. He's cured. For a moment, it's a miracle.

But then, reality returns.

She stops believing it's Kye. The intimate question – it's not enough. Her eyes are winning. It's not Kye with his scars and bandages, his circulation suit, his wires, his nozzle, his shaved head. And not a half-Asian man.

She starts to realize, *every time, it's been Gayle.*

She starts to realize, *there's no Kye.*

Now she's shouting, telling Gayle she's evil, a psycho, a freak. Gayle is sobbing, begging, using the same words, 'It's me, it's me. You said you'd believe me.'

But she pushes Gayle out of the way, down the stairs, as she runs into the street.

*

In Gayle's account, this is one of the many Sundays they spend together in role. Over these months, the line between their lives and Kye's is becoming increasingly blurred. But they are in so deep. It's a way to be together, their own rom-com. Every Wednesday and Sunday, they follow the script. Gayle brings the strap-on and they have sex, but it's about so much more – the drive, the days on the couch, moving in and out of role. She is becoming Kye, or Gayle/Kye, for longer periods. But the script is a fragile thing, conjured between them. It relies on both of them being in it, a circle of two.

That week, they have the terrible argument. Gayle, who wants to come out to her family, is accused of breaking the pact. Something begins to split. Miss X is so angry that Gayle backs down, but the sense of fracture lingers.

In this account, Gayle/Kye comes over on Sunday. They follow the routine and the argument is dormant. They're in role as Gayle/Kye, as Kye. They watch TV, talk, kiss and have sex, on the chair and on the bed. But Miss X is quieter than usual and Kye notices.

STORYTELLING ON THE STAND: FICTION

That's when it happens, as Kye takes off the strap-on.

As in the bed trick or the movies, there's a moment of change, of substitution. But in this version, it's Miss X that disappears.

Miss X 'switched, like *switched*', Gayle says. It's not Miss X in front of her. At first, it seems like a bluff. She thinks it's a performance, a pretence. Miss X is 'like, acting or, or acting like she was almost shocked', Gayle remembers. It's a subtler disappearance. Miss X is gone. Gayle can see her, but there's been a departure, a change. In this version, Miss X's body is the same, but it's a psychological switch, as in tales of mind control, lobotomy, alien takeover – another mind, a substituted brain.

In this moment, everything seemed to change. Gayle says that sometimes she still can't believe it. Even when she's arrested and under investigation, Gayle says it still feels mad, like a fiction. She's in denial – until the first day of the first trial, she says she never thought 'for one second' that Miss X would come to court. Never thought Miss X would take the stand 'and look me in the eyes and say the things that she did', Gayle says. That's when reality finally hit. 'The second that she did that is the second that everything changed,' she says.

At trial, Gayle is still baffled. 'I wish I knew,' she repeats, over and over, when asked why Miss X went to the police, why she's here. 'I don't know the reason. Even to this day I don't know the reason,' she says.

She still doesn't know what happened to Miss X that night. After the 'switch', the unreal moment, Gayle says that Miss X starts shouting, pointing to the strap-on, saying, 'What the hell! What's this? What're you doing?'

In this version, Miss X is the mad lover, losing it. Gayle is confused, starting to get scared. Her anxiety is spiking. She asks Miss X what she means. It feels like reality is slipping.

Miss X keeps accusing, pointing, asking for Kye. It's like she's gone. She's been taken. In her place, a stranger.

Now they throw accusations back and forth. Gayle calls Miss X 'tapped', in the sense of being mad – which is one of the worst things she could have called her. In return, Miss X calls Gayle sick, a rapist; she calls 999, hangs up. It's the beginning of the terrible things they say – an arsenal of terrible things that only people who know each other so intimately could fire.

It's war. Miss X pushes her and she falls.

This is a scene of devastation and disorientation. Missing bodies and missing minds. The confusion, the hurt, never quite goes away. But in the aftermath, there is one thing they both agree on – a shared fact. Kye is gone.

Miss X suggests he 'died' on that Sunday.

Gayle stays silent. When she finally speaks about Kye, he's in the past tense, just a name. (Thinking about the canal jump later that night, I sometimes wonder, was it Kye's suicide?)

By the time of the trials, Kye is missing, an absentee and an enigma – described as 'a cipher, a code word', a missing key.

*

Half a century earlier, Pauline Parker and Juliet Hulme were on trial for murder. Their diaries and letters, examined by prosecutors, were full of codes and fictions, making them difficult to interpret. In the run up to the trial, the best friends confessed, and the only possible defence was madness of two, *folie à deux*. This is a form of the 'diminished responsibility' defence. The disorder described a delusion shared by two people, defined in psychiatric terms as 'paranoiacs'. As one doctor explained at the trial, 'The lone paranoiac makes slow progress', but as two, the shared fantasy escalates. This diagnosis would make the friends not responsible for murder – as defendants who didn't act freely or know what they were doing, because they were 'mentally ill', not rational and therefore not guilty.

At trial in 1954, Pauline and Juliet were still in the fantasy. They sat together in the dock, whispering and giggling, sometimes putting their fingers in their ears. The delusion continued.

Meanwhile, for Gayle and Miss X in 2015 and 2017, it's different. If they once shared a fantasy, bound together by the promise of Kye, by the time of the trials it's broken. The story has shattered; they've split. Whether they were friends or lovers, the dossier and the events point to a profound misreading of each other. They're not just in different plots, but in different books. The misinterpretation is so severe, the breach so profound, that they have ended up in court, with twelve strangers judging them – deciding from the outside on the truth of the relationship, on the facts.

*

So often, as I read and write, as I construct this book, I'm reminded of how much can't be known. The transcripts are a partial record. 'There is little silence, but much that is silenced,' writes Caroline Derry in her study of the criminal law, pointing to the rules of evidence, which limit and shape what can be presented at trial. There are precedents and statutes too; the barristers tell their stories under constraints, according to the elements of the Sexual Offences Act, and in the light of principles such as McNally.

But also, there are things that I'm withholding too. In writing this, I've had to decide what not to say, in relation to both parties, but especially when it comes to Miss X. Anonymity rules are outlined in the Sexual Offences (Amendment) Act 1992, which lists material that it is necessary for journalists to avoid, including the complainant's name, address, place of work and place of study. These rules locate responsibility in the reporting. That is to say, it is my responsibility. The stakes are high; it is criminal to reveal this information. After all, I'm a writer who is free to choose how to act and, as such, deserving of punishment if I break the law.

Legislation outlines the bare minimum; beyond this are industry standards. The UK's Independent Press Standards Organisation publishes guidance on reporting sexual offences and warns of 'jigsaw identification'. This is the process by which different pieces of information, revealed at trial and appearing in various news outlets, can allow people reading multiple reports to work out who the victim is.

I spent time in the aftermath of the reporting – in 2019 and 2020 – looking back at what was reported, from when the trial first hit the headlines in 2015, to when Gayle was sentenced for a second time in 2017. I assembled all the pieces of the jigsaw. And as I evaluated other journalists' decisions, I found some details revealed in reports to be misguided – like the university they both attended, which was widely reported. This detail narrowed them down to a specific group, at a specific point in time, in a way that seemed unnecessary – and even violated the law (which restricts the naming of 'any . . . education establishment').

STORYTELLING ON THE STAND: FICTION

In writing this book, I have chosen to retract that information, anonymizing it to 'the university' and refraining from recounting the specific context of the city and their life there in any detail. At other times, I understood what pieces had been left out already. And I also understood that I must not add significant new pieces to the jigsaw. Some things would have to remain anonymous; some histories, some facts, cannot be told.

When it comes to reporting, defendants are considered fair game. From day one of the first trial, before any facts had been found, Gayle was totally exposed.

During a trial itself, defendants are protected in various ways, by the presumption of innocence and by the standard of proof ('beyond reasonable doubt' is a high bar). The rules of evidence too can exclude certain facts or histories in service of a fair trial. For example, a defendant's antecedents – information about previous crimes – are often not revealed until conviction. And indeed, at the second sentencing, Stockdale reveals what had been held back. Gayle has six months tagged onto her sentence for another, unrelated crime committed over eighteen months, which only came to light after the first trial. She had pled guilty already but the jurors didn't know. Now, the judge says that between March 2014 and September 2015 Gayle was working for a marketing agency. The company paid bloggers to endorse products, and Gayle created a number of fictional blog accounts, writing fake endorsements and extracting £9,000 – defrauding the company.

The journalist Trevor Grove served as a juror at the Old Bailey in 1996 and wrote of his experience at trial in *The Juryman's Tale*. The book offers a rare insight as Grove found a way to chronicle the process without breaking the rules (jurors are told they can't ever discuss the specifics of the deliberation). At the end of the book, Grove described the stage, once the verdicts had been delivered, when information hidden from the jurors was finally revealed. At this trial, a defendant, whom the jury had very nearly found not guilty, had multiple previous convictions revealing a shady criminal past. Grove describes the antecedents as 'missing bits of the jigsaw . . . It was a moment of the most intense relief, a vindication,' he writes.

Gayle has been convicted of sexual fraud; now there is proof she's committed financial fraud. Is this the missing puzzle piece? Perhaps it felt that way to the jury. The parallel offence appears in the transcripts and in the reporting as a revelation. Clearly Gayle was a kind of addict. She'd been living online and speaking as Kye since she was a teenager. Now, at this crucial juncture, we learn she has also been caught creating fictional blogs.

Here's the moment in the text when I could reveal something about Miss X's life, her history, her record. Something with equal weight that would counterbalance this revelation, which could shed equal doubt and tip the scale back. Because that's what I've been doing – weighing back and forth, striving for balance. But I've reached my limit of jigsaw pieces; I can't reveal any more; I'm held back by anonymity constraints.

The truth is, like the barristers, I'm telling a story. In my attempt to know, I construct a plot. In a way, this book is a shadow trial. I'm using literary tools, like suspense and points of view. Don't forget that I'm using these tools.

The thing about storytelling is it can be enlisted in the

service of any cause. It is never innocent. I have spent five years studying and researching this case. I'm not neutral. How could I be? I want to understand, I want to imagine. 'Writing cannot be done in a state of desirelessness,' observed Janet Malcolm, 'if the writer *actually* didn't care one way or another how the things came out, he would not bestir himself to represent them.' I have my own biases and interests, desires, wants and motives, as I try to inform you.

Why?

Because I'm drawn to difficult stories, to arguing hard things, to ambiguity.

Because of my interest in the bed trick, in blind spots, in sex and lies.

Because of my own assault case, sleeping in my unconscious, surfacing at the very end.

Because I'm queer.

And because, after reading Gayle's words spoken at the first verdict – 'How can you send me down for something I haven't done?' – I wanted to try to answer that question. 'How? How? How? How? How? How?' How was Gayle convicted? How was she sent down?

While jurors have to make a decision, you, the readers, don't.

When it comes to Gayle and Miss X, I have tried to refuse choosing sides. Yes, I'm withholding information, but actually the missing pieces won't solve it. By this point in time, there is no piece that will complete the puzzle.

Gayle and Miss X believe their own stories, despite the (often devastating) flaws in each account. Both are willing to deny evidence and admit to lying, in order to uphold their stories.

I think back to those words written by a forensics expert describing Miss X's laptop. 'Continued use', the statement explained, had 'degraded [the] ability to recover evidential artefacts ... The effect is akin to the tide washing away footprints in the sand.' In some ways, the legal processes work as a kind of 'continued use' of their memories and stories, their accounts. That's how it seems to me. In the end, the legal retellings prevail – overriding the actual events, the actual memories, as the complicated, messy, contradictory story is lost, washed away, like footprints in the sand.

Epilogue

I started this book thinking about rape law, my research subliminally triggered by my own assault. But I ended somewhere else, thinking about the relationship between law and literature, between the trial and fiction. I wondered if rape was ever reducible to law, and I saw how, so often, the truth doesn't emerge through law – it disappears; the trial produces a fiction.

Looking back to my assault in 2006, I remember how quickly the story was taken out of my hands. It was reported in the papers. I didn't get to choose who knew. It stopped being my story, or his story, and it became a public story. In the years after, the dreaded summons arrived year on year. Since I never gave evidence at trial, I did not undergo cross-examination. Today, there are few records to pick apart.

Alongside the summons, there was another set of letters that I received in these years from weekly magazines, bearing my name. Editors, having seen the report in *The Sunday Times*, invited me to tell my story in the first person. I particularly remember a letter from *Bella* magazine (the name I go by), a weekly aimed at women, which includes 'true life stories' alongside health tips and gossip. I didn't respond to these letters. I wasn't insulted or enticed. But the requests did unnerve me. Why was my story so appealing? Why did it have such a ready audience? What made it so alluring, so publishable, so 'good'?

Was it because I was *nearly* raped, making the account more palatable, while retaining a shock factor, a thrill? Was it because I was, on the face of it, a wholesome white girl, while my assailant was foreign, a man with brown skin? Was it compelling as a (rare) example of the 'right' scenario, the credible scene, the one we already believe, and indeed almost want to believe – that rape is random, violent, far away, over there, the assailant a crazy asshole you don't know? Was it because the story was unresolved, missing a testimony, a legal narrative – as yet untold?

The law is a set of rules, inherited and created, implemented and interpreted. It can remedy injustice and create oppressions – sometimes both at once. Gender fraud case law is, I think, an example of just this. The cases present a complex double bind: on the one hand, the imperative to believe victims of sexual assault, usually women; but on the other, the imperative to face the reality of homophobia and transphobia, and the queer defendants – lesbians, women with male aliases, trans men, occasionally gay men – threatened by conviction. Whose narratives are heard? Whose stories do we believe? Given the 2021 government statistic already quoted – that only 1.6 per cent of rape reports result in a charge – why are gender fraud complaints being taken forward? Is there something stronger than misogyny? Is it homophobia and transphobia?

EPILOGUE

In 2015, Gayle's trial was the first of its kind to reach court under the 2003 Act. But since her second conviction in 2017, there have been more trials. The advocate Alex Sharpe records at least ten prosecutions since 2012. Two such trials took place in English courts in 2023: the trial of Blade Silvano in May, and the trial of Georgia Bilham in June. Both resulted in convictions.

In recent years, there have been two major developments. First, in 2022 the Crown Prosecution Service began a public consultation on its rape and sexual offences guidance. CPS guidance assists prosecutors in making 'appropriate' and 'consistent' decisions when charging suspects. In other words, the guidance relates to that crucial stage, the step that so many complaints don't get past. The 2022 consultation focused on one area in particular: deception as to gender. Open for three months, it invited 'interested groups' to provide feedback on proposed revisions to the gender fraud guidance. The consultation received over four hundred responses, a high volume, as the CPS entered the fray, stepping right into the highly charged 'sex and gender debate', shaped by two opposing camps: trans rights advocates on one side and gender-critical feminists on the other. Responses came in from academics, police organizations, healthcare professionals, as well as charities at the centre of the battlefield, including Mermaids (which supports gender-diversity and trans rights) and Sex Matters (which campaigns for birth sex rights).

The responses were reviewed over a prolonged two-year period. Alex Sharpe, writing in October 2024 before the guidance was published, expressed cautious optimism about the proposed revisions. But when the guidance was finally published two months later in December 2024, she described it as a 'considerable row back' from the original consultation.

The new guidance is dense and guarded, and runs over 4,500 words, making it far lengthier than other sections on consent. But one major change stands out. In a significant reinterpretation of McNally, 'deception as to gender' is refigured as 'deception as to sex'. This was a revision proposed by Sex Matters in response to the consultation. In the guidance, the CPS explains the new focus on 'birth sex' by way of the established 'closely connected' test, because sex is considered 'so connected to the nature of the sexual activity' that it offers a more robust focus for prosecutors. Here, McNally is cited as the authority on the somewhat shaky grounds that 'although the court in McNally used the word "gender" with regard to the deception in question, *it was probably referring to a deception as to sex*' (my italics). It is sex fraud that will be the subject of future prosecutions, the guidance states, not gender. The final, amended principle is this: 'deception as to sex can vitiate consent'. In other words, the terms have changed once again.

At the very same time, other legal challenges are taking place. In November 2024, judges at the UK Supreme Court considered a case brought by Scottish campaigners about how women are defined in law. This dispute concerned the Equality Act, and challenged whether a person with a full Gender Recognition Certificate (reassigning their sex as 'woman') is a 'woman' for the purposes of the Equality Act. At its most basic level, the case asked what 'sex' means in law. One side, representing For Women Scotland (supported by Sex Matters), described the reassignment of sex as a 'legal

EPILOGUE

fiction', arguing for a 'common sense' meaning of the words 'man' and 'woman' and the immutability of birth sex. The other side countered these claims, describing sex and gender recognition as a 'fundamental right', similar to adoption (also a legal fiction).

The case was decided in April 2025. The Supreme Court judges unanimously sided with For Women Scotland, ruling that 'woman' means 'biological woman' for the purposes of the Equality Act. This judgment disproportionately affects trans people by eroding protections they have under their reassigned sex and gender. It also has implications for sexual fraud law under the CPS's shift from 'gender fraud' to 'sex fraud' in ways that are yet to be tested.

Broader uncertainties concerning the law of sexual deception also remain unresolved. A recent report on deceptive sex by influential UK reform group the Criminal Law Reform Now Network revealed inconsistencies in case law, splits among experts and the difficulties of constructing a consistent legal framework for deceptive sex. Across ten papers by experts, a rare point of consensus was the need for reform. In an attempt at synthesis, the network recommended in its final chapter the creation of a new and bespoke offence for deceptive sex to be added to the Sexual Offences Act. If implemented, the offence would expand the scope of deceptions that count beyond the 'closely connected' test to include any intentional deception that matters to a complainant. Future Spy Cops could be prosecuted under this offence, along with many other sexual deceivers.

The proposed reforms do not close the door on deceptive sex so much as open it. Explicit conditions and preferences that count are not limited, meaning that many new factors could emerge through the courts and turn sex into a sexual offence. Sexual deception, I believe, requires redress. It is a particularly corrosive wrongdoing because it manipulates a person into acting against their will and ultimately against themselves. At the same time, I think about the way desire doesn't come out of a vacuum. When is a sexual preference also a sexual prejudice? Why *do* we desire what we desire? How much freedom do we really have?

I agree with reforms that may stop future Spy Cops getting away with it. But I also worry about a future where a lover's health or other new factor is legible as a sexual choice and lie that could turn sex into a sexual offence. Could a cancer-free body be recognized as a sexual preference? What about bodies of a certain race, or minds of a certain belief – are these desires and choices that the state could one day be willing to get behind and to prosecute?

These questions matter because desire and deception are old bedfellows. This is what makes the bed trick speak across time and what makes it such a captivating plot. These are familiar stories; we pretend to be something so others will desire us; we can be made to desire things that aren't true.

The impossible question is where we draw the line. Studying this case and writing this book has been one attempt to explore that question. In the end, what I find so compelling about this case, and about Gayle and Miss X's story, is that – despite pages of evidence, two trials, my own years of enquiry – there is no final answer to what is deception and what is true.

I think back to the evidence bundle, and the many pages of messages sent from the three different phones. There are thousands of texts, an overwhelming volume that has been

EPILOGUE

ordered and colour-coded. Miss X's are in blue, Gayle's in orange and Kye's in green.

In the story that wins, Gayle is the puppet master, Kye is the sock account and Miss X the dupe.

But Kye's performance is often confusing and messy. The green messages are described as 'the phone that Gayle was using mostly as Kye'. And mainly it is him – arguing with Miss X, making up, declaring his love, getting sick. And sometimes it's Gayle.

I love you, I miss you, I need you.

He wouldn't ever do anything purposely to upset you.

You are my world, my light in the darkness.

He kept saying your name.

I love my best friend and wanna chat.

I want my partner in crime back.

When the authors spill together, green bleeding into orange to create a muddy brown, it becomes impossible to separate reality from fiction, truth from deception, the partners from the crime.

Miss X often takes the messages in her stride. She's stoic, committed. Nothing feels strange. She's dreaming of a future when everything is better. Of her wedding day. Kye will be waiting at the altar, and Gayle will be at her side.

Just rest babe.

We'll chat tomorrow.

I love you too.

Notes

Author's Note

My primary sources were the trial transcripts *R v Gayle Newland* [2015] Chester Crown Court (Judge Dutton); *R v Gayle Newland* [2017] Manchester Crown Court (Judge Stockdale).

Prologue

p. 1

Miss X alleges that the person in the dock, Gayle Newland The spelling of Gayle's name is contested. Sophie Wilkinson, in 'Consent, Dildos and Deception: Reexamining the Trial of Gayle Newland', VICE (21 December 2017), claims that 'there was a typo in a court report and it caught on, which is why she has always been referred to as Gayle'. I decided to repeat the misspelling 'Gayle' so as to afford Gayle a small degree of anonymity. See https://www.vice.com/en/contributor/sophie-wilkinson

p. 5

Gayle had been accused of an old and rare offence called 'sexual fraud' Writer and advocate Alex Sharpe has described this offence as 'sexual fraud'. See Alex Sharpe, 'Gayle Newland and the problem of equating ignorance with non-consent',

NOTES

The Conversation (3 July 2017), https://theconversation.com/gayle-newland-and-the-problem-of-equating-ignorance-with-non-consent-80407

p. 6

'On this good wife did he vigorously lie/No such merry time she'd known in years gone by' Geoffrey Chaucer, 'The Reeve's Tale', 375–6, Librarius, http://www.librarius.com/canttran/reevtale/reevtale345-379.htm

p. 6

Night-games are a theme of medieval folktales Antti Aarne and Stith Thompson, *The Types of the Folktale: a Classification and Bibliography* (Suomalainen Tiedeakatemia, 1973).

p. 7

Gayle was described as a 'lesbian sex abuser', seeking 'bizarre satisfaction' See https://www.thetimes.com/uk/crime/article/jail-for-lesbian-sex-abuser-gayle-newland-who-posed-as-a-man-to-seduce-student-qk993lrrw and https://www.dailyrecord.co.uk/news/uk-world-news/woman-who-tricked-female-friend-10837851

p. 7

Was Gayle 'an imaginative and persuasive liar' See Helen Pidd, 'Woman who posed as man to dupe friend into sex is jailed after retrial', *The Guardian* (20 July 2017), https://www.theguardian.com/uk-news/2017/jul/20/gayle-newland-jailed-for-tricking-female-friend-into-sex

p. 8

'The transcripts of a trial at law – even routine criminal prosecutions and tiresome civil disputes – are exciting to read,' Janet Malcolm, *The Crime of Sheila McGough* (Knopf, 1999), p. 12.

1   Miss X on the Stand: Consent

p. 17

The promise of lifetime anonymity, automatically given to Miss X, entered legislation in 1976. Sexual Offences (Amendment) Act 1976, https://www.legislation.gov.uk/ukpga/1976/82

p. 19

In a shift away from a reliance on live testimony Home Office, 'The Stern Review: A report by Baroness Vivien' (2010), pp. 14–5.

p. 20

a measure available to vulnerable witnesses by request. See Youth Justice and Criminal Evidence Act 1999, Section 23, https://www.legislation.gov.uk/ukpga/1999/23/part/II/chapter/I/crossheading/special-measures

p. 20

Reporters describe a heatwave in Manchester Simon Hattenstone, '"I was pretending to be a boy for a variety of reasons": the strange case of Gayle Newland', *The Guardian* (15 July 2017), https://www.theguardian.com/uk-news/2017/jul/15/gayle-newland-retrial

p. 22

Power has had the prosthetic penis on his desk at the ready, asking his legal team to place it there 'discreetly' that morning. Hattenstone (15 July 2017).

p. 24

Under this rubric, only violent attacks (comparable to breaking and entering) were legible as rape to the law. Susan Brownmiller, *Against Our Will: Men, Women and Rape* (Bantam, 1975); and Lane Kirkland Gillespie and Laura King, 'Legislative Origins, Reforms and Future Directions' (2014), in Tara N. Richards and Catherine D. Marcum (eds), *Sexual Victimization: Then and Now* (Sage, 2015).

p. 24

But a shift in interpretation across the twentieth century culminated in a revision to the Sexual Offences Act, altering the definition of rape. Judith Bourne and Caroline Derry, *Gender and the Law* (Routledge, 2018).

p. 24

In a 1976 amendment, rape was redefined by whether 'a woman' did or did not 'consent to it . . . at the time'. Sexual Offences (Amendment) Act 1976, https://www.legislation.gov.uk/ukpga/1976/82

NOTES

p. 25

This process was furthered by revisions to the Sexual Offences Act in 2003 Home Office, 'Setting the Boundaries: Reforming the Law on Sex Offences', Volume 1 (2000). This paper informed the Sexual Offences Act 2003, which defined consent in Section 74: 'A person consents if he agrees by choice, and has the freedom and capacity to make that choice'. https://www.legislation.gov.uk/ukpga/2003/42/section/74

p. 25

And in a courtroom, this results in a heightened focus on the complainant. Victor Tadros, 'Rape Without Consent', *Oxford Journal of Legal Studies*, vol. 26, no. 3 (2006), 515–43, pp. 515–16.

p. 26

Contract law solidified during the industrial revolution Simon Deakin, 'Legal Origin, Judicial Form and Industrialisation in Historical Perspective: The Case of the Employment Contract and the Joint Stock Company', CLPE Research Paper 36/2008.

p. 26

For a contract to be valid, it must be formed in precise steps. Law Commission, 'Smart Legal Contracts. Advice to government' (November 2021), p. 39.

p. 26

Crucial to the valid contract is a stage known as 'the meeting of minds' Randy E. Barnett, 'Contract Is Not Promise; Contract Is Consent', in Gregory Klass, George Letsas and Prince Saprai (eds), *Philosophical Foundations of Contract Law* (Oxford University Press, 2014), pp. 42–57.

p. 26

(Nor would it help to actually have a contract Emma Batha, 'After #MeToo, phone app allows you to legally consent to sex', Reuters (18 January 2018), https://www.reuters.com/article/world/after-metoo-phone-app-allows-you-to-legally-consent-to-sex-idUSKBN1F72EZ/

p. 28

The law, fixed in books and evolved in case law, did not recognize,

or refused to name, rape by another actor Caroline Derry, *Lesbianism and the Criminal Law: Three Centuries of Regulation in England and Wales* (Palgrave, 2020), p. 86.

p. 28

But in 2003, the Sexual Offences Act was amended Andrew Ashworth and Jennifer Temkin, 'The Sexual Offences Act 2003: (1) – Rape, Sexual Assaults and the Problems of Consent', *Criminal Law Review* (2004), 328–46.

p. 29

The new offence was viewed as gender-neutral, because, unlike any previous definition, a woman could rape, since a woman can have a penis. The definition of rape in Section 1 includes surgically reconstructed male and female genitalia. See 'Part 1: general interpretation', Section 76(3) of the Sexual Offences Act 2003. In addition, under the Gender Recognition Act 2004, the process of legally reassigning gender and sex does not require confirmation surgery. See Stephen Whittle and Lewis Turner, '"Sex Changes"? Paradigm Shifts in "Sex" and "Gender" following the Gender Recognition Act?', *Sociological Research Online*, vol. 12, no. 1 (2007), 75–89, p. 85.

p. 29

To describe the phenomenon of rape without a penis lawmakers would have to find new words Sexual Offences Act 2003, Section 2, https://www.legislation.gov.uk/ukpga/2003/42/notes/division/5/1/2

p. 29

The new offence had almost the same wording as rape Ashworth and Temkin (2004), p. 329.

p. 30

There's an absurdist quality to the body parts Nikolai Gogol, *The Nose* (1836; Penguin Classics, 2015).

p. 35

Since the Gender Recognition Act 2004, a person can legally reassign their gender. Gender Recognition Act 2004, https://www.legislation.gov.uk/ukpga/2004/7/contents

p. 35

'a strong desire for the primary and/or secondary sex characteristics of the other gender' American Psychiatric Association, *Diagnostic and Statistical Manual of Mental Disorders, Fifth Edition* (American Psychiatric Publishing, 2013), 'Gender Dysphoria in Adolescents and Adults', pp. 452–3.

2   Rape on the Stand: Myths

p. 39

only 1.6 per cent of rape reports result in a charge. Home Office, *End-to-End Rape Review Report on Findings and Actions* (June 2021), p. vii.

p. 40

(less than one in five, research suggests). Home Office, *Crime Outcomes in England and Wales, year to December 2020* (May 2021).

p. 40

The review suggested the entire apparatus was beset with problems at every stage Home Office (2021).

p. 40

In recent years, persistent prejudicial assumptions, such as the notion that 'real' victims fight back or report immediately, have been demonstrated by mock jury studies. Fiona Leverick, 'What do we know about rape myths and juror decision making?', *The International Journal of Evidence and Proof*, vol. 24, issue 3 (2020), pp. 225–79.

p. 40

Although the rape trial's (infamous) 'cautionary instruction' was abolished in the 1990s Michelle J. Anderson, 'The Legacy of the Prompt Complaint Requirement, Corroboration Requirement, and Cautionary Instructions on Campus Sexual Assault', Villanova University, Charles Widger School of Law (2004).

p. 40

'No injured party [is] more distrusted than the rape victim' Joanna Bourke, *Rape: A History from 1860 to the Present* (Virago, 2007), p. 23.

p. 40

Rape (along with murder) has been a fixation of criminal law Joel Feinberg, *The Moral Limits of the Criminal Law Volume 1: Harm to Others* (Oxford University Press US, 1984), p. 10.

p. 41

As such, rape is viewed as a *mala in se* R.A. Duff, *Answering for Crime: Responsibility and Liability in the Criminal Law* (Hart Publishing, 2007), p. 90.

p. 41

'carnal knowledge of a woman, by force and against her will' A common law definition in William Blackstone, *Commentaries on the Laws of England* (1765); notably, Blackstone declined to elucidate the offence, describing it as 'highly improper to be publicly discussed'. This interpretation of rape persisted in English common law judgments; in the 5th edition of *Russell on Crime* (1877), the definition of rape includes 'by force and against her will'. In a 2001 judgment Judge Williams JA notes, regarding the 1877 interpretation, that in this period 'the use of force rather than the absence of consent was the critical element' (*R v Pryor* [2001] QCA 314); this remained the case up to the 1950s.

p. 41

In fact – jurists and doctors argued – the act of rape was extremely difficult, if not impossible, to achieve. Bourke (2007).

p. 41

A popular notion known as 'the vibrating sword' theory posited that it was 'almost impossible' to rape a woman who resisted Michael Ryan, *A Manual of Medical Jurisprudence* (Renshaw and Rush, 1831), cited in Bourke (2007), p. 24.

p. 41

This notion was repeated time and time again in nineteenth-century textbooks of medical jurisprudence Horatio Robinson Storer, in 'The Law of Rape', *The Quarterly Journal of Psychological Medicine and Medical Jurisprudence II* 55 (1868), cited in Bourke (2007), p. 24.

p. 42

If a woman *was* to be raped, it was generally agreed that one man

NOTES

could not do it alone Charles Graham Grant, in *Practical Forensic Medicine: A Police Surgeon's Emergency Guide* (Lewis, 1924), p. 46, claimed that rape was 'rare . . . it took four men to do it', cited in Bourke (2007), pp. 26–7.

p. 42

The parable of Potiphar's wife Genesis 39:7–20.

p. 42

In one episode, Dumas's hero D'Artagnan tricks his enemy Alexandre Dumas, *The Three Musketeers*, tr. Lord Sudley (1844; Penguin Classics, 1982), p. 532.

p. 43

It wasn't Thomas but a stranger. *R v William Williams* [1839], full judgment: https://vlex.co.uk/vid/r-v-william-williams-801986653

p. 43

Other wives described the moment of apprehension after lovemaking was complete *R v Dee* [1888], full judgment: https://ie.vlex.com/vid/r-v-dee-803988373; *R v William Williams* [1839], full judgment: https://vlex.co.uk/vid/r-v-william-williams-801986653; and accounts in Jocelynne A. Scutt, 'Fraudulent impersonation and consent in rape', *University of Queensland Law Journal*, vol. 9, December (1975), 59–65.

p. 43

A spate of cases led to some rare convictions. See Scutt (1975), p. 60: *R v Jackson* [1822], *R v Saunders* [1838], *R v Williams* [1839], *R v Dee* [1884].

p. 44

It explained how the stranger had got around her defences and thwarted her (pelvic) 'resistance'. Judge Alderson B., in *R v William Williams* [1838], in *R v Pryor* [2001], p. 5.

p. 44

'resistance is prevented by the fraud of the man who pretends to be her husband' Judge Gurney B., in *R v Saunders* [1838], in Scutt (1975), p. 60.

p. 44

At first, tricked wives were compared to blind women, or seen as victims of a kind of property offence comparable to 'theft in the dark'. Judge O'Brien, in *R v Dee* [1884] in Scutt (1975), p. 61.

p. 44

'It cannot be said that he agreed to the terms of the latter document . . . although his signature appears thereon,' Judge Murphy, in *R v Dee* [1884] in Scutt (1975), pp. 61–2.

p. 44

the proliferation of fraud. James Taylor, 'White-collar crime and law in nineteenth-century Britain', *Business History*, vol. 60, no. 3 (2018). Following a series of 1850s bank scandals, new legislation was passed in Parliament, resulting in the Punishment of Frauds Act 1857.

p. 44

A series of financial scandals unfolding in the 1850s stirred up fears about 'white-collar crime' Hartmut Berghoff and Uwe Spiekermann, 'Shady business: On the history of white-collar crime', *Business History*, vol. 60, no. 3 (2018), note that it took a long time to categorize this malfeasance (the term was coined by the criminologist Edwin Hardin Sutherland in 1939).

p. 44

Sexual fraud was legislated against in 1861; its scope was then crystallized in a judgment of 1888 Sexual fraud enters the Offences Against the Person Act 1861 in Section 49 as 'a misdemeanor' [*sic*]; it was later amended in the Criminal Law Amendment Act 1885, Section 3 ('fraud' – a misdemeanour) and Section 4 ('husband impersonation' – rape). Then in 1888, the leading judgment, *R v Clarence* [1888], written by Judge James Fitzjames Stephen, clarified what frauds counted. See Ngaire Naffine, *Criminal Law and the Man Problem* (Hart, 2019), p. 70; Karl Laird, 'Rapist or rogue? Deception, consent and the Sexual Offences Act 2003', *Criminal Law Review*, issue 7 (2014), p. 494.

NOTES

p. 45

New provisions, titled Section 76 – still in place today – set out circumstances where consent is gained by deception and is thus not consent. Alex Sharpe, *Sexual Intimacy and Gender Identity 'Fraud': Reframing the Legal and Ethical Debate* (Routledge, 2018), pp. 32–3. The provisions provide that where particular types of deception are used to obtain consent, the person is deemed not to have consented to the sexual conduct. Even more powerful is that it is irrelevant if the defendant can show that the complainant did in fact consent – once the relevant deception or imitation has been proven, the consent discussion is concluded.

p. 45

This stage takes place after police have investigated, often months after an initial complaint. Rights of Women, 'Reporting an offence to the police: A guide to criminal/police investigations' (2017), p. 6, https://www.rightsofwomen.org.uk/wp-content/uploads/2023/12/reporting-an-offence-to-the-police-a-guide-to-criminal-investigations.pdf

p. 45

The step requires CPS lawyers to ask whether there is a 'realistic prospect of conviction', and whether a jury is 'more likely than not' to find a defendant guilty. CPS Code (2018), https://www.cps.gov.uk/publication/code-crown-prosecutors

p. 45

Given these conditions, rape is sometimes referred to as 'a black box'. Shiori Ito, *Black Box: The Memoir That Sparked Japan's #MeToo Movement* (Tilted Axis Press, 2021), p. 8.

p. 50

some prosecutors refer to this barrier, laid in the 1970s, as 'the consent wall' Ito (2021), p. 8.

p. 50

Section 76, which is found towards the end of the Act, is rarely triggered. Laird (2014), 'What is evident is a narrowing of the applicability of the conclusive presumptions in s.76 to near vanishing point [since 2003]', p. 927.

p. 52

Instead of proving negatives, Section 76 offers the Crown a short cut. Ashworth and Temkin (2004), p. 233.

p. 53

(the phrase in the relevant part of Section 76 is 'intentionally deceived' as to 'the nature' of the act) Section 76(2)(a): [if] 'the defendant intentionally deceived the complainant as to the nature or purpose of the relevant act'. There is an additional provision, Section 76(2)(b), which states, '[if] the defendant intentionally induced the complainant to consent to the relevant act by impersonating a person known personally to the complainant'.

3 Gayle Newland on the Stand: Deception

p. 54

By Tuesday, before she's taken the stand, news items appear online, and the case goes viral. See https://www.theguardian.com/uk-news/2015/sep/09/woman-allegedly-tricked-into-sex-with-friend-pretending-to-be-man-lesbian-court-told

p. 58

But consent-rule jurisdictions continue to recognize that deception can turn sex into rape. Amit Pundik, 'The Law of Deception', *Notre Dame Law Review Reflection*, vol. 93, issue 1 (2018), 174–86, p. 175.

p. 58

This makes consent – saying yes, saying no – an exercise in sexual autonomy. Shivam Kaushik, 'The Impossible Trinity of Deception, Sex and Consent', *Journal of Criminal Law*, vol. 85, no. 6 (2021), 415–24, p. 420.

p. 58

And deception meddles with this – it erodes a person's autonomy, warping it. Vera Bergelson, 'Sex, Lies and Law: Rethinking Rape-by-Fraud', in Chris Ashford, Alan Reed and Nicola Wake (eds), *Legal Perspectives on State Power: Consent and Control* (Cambridge Scholars Publishing, 2016), p. 157.

NOTES

p. 58

Because deception takes away the freedom to choose, and it distorts the choices available. Nora Scheidegger, 'Balancing Sexual Autonomy, Responsibility, and the Right to Privacy: Principles for Criminalizing Sex by Deception', *German Law Journal*, 769–83 (2021), p. 772.

p. 59

Philosophers of deception have made a distinction between 'active' and 'passive' deception Sharpe (2018), p. 89.

p. 59

the first, to actually invent information, to intentionally lie; the second, to conceal, to withhold a piece of information, to not correct an assumption. Thomas Carson, *Lying and Deception: Theory and Practice* (Oxford University Press, 2010), pp. 3–5.

p. 59

But the question of exactly which 'active' deceptions spoil consent is one that has troubled modern sexual fraud law across this century. Bergelson (2016), p. 153.

p. 59

People lie all the time, especially when it comes to intimacy, seduction, sex. Jed Rubenfeld, 'The Riddle of Rape by Deception and the Myth of Sexual Autonomy', *Yale Law Journal*, 122 (2013), 1372–443, p. 1416; and Ben A. McJunkin, 'Deconstructing Rape by Fraud', *Columbia Journal of Gender and Law*, vol. 28, no. 1 (2014), 1–47, pp. 22–3.

p. 59

'I love you', told as a lie to seduce someone into bed, violates sexual autonomy; it distorts someone's choice; therefore, the act that follows isn't sex: it's rape. Jonathan Herring, 'Mistaken Sex', *Criminal Law Review* (2005), 511–24, pp. 516–18.

p. 59

some frauds recognized as criminal (like husband impersonation), and others (promises of marriage) seen as 'minor wrongs' Kaushik (2021), p. 416.

p. 60

Deception fascinated Victorians in a society alarmed by fraudulent practices and the dangers facing women. Mary Ann Irwin, '"White Slavery" as Metaphor: Anatomy of a Moral Panic', *Ex Post Facto: The History Journal*, vol. 5 (1996).

p. 60

In a case from 1850, a young woman believed that she was undergoing medical treatment, rather than sex Sharpe (2018), p. 32, *R v William Case* [1850].

p. 60

She let him 'operate' on her, without knowing what the act really was. Sharpe (2018), p. 32, *R v Flattery* [1877].

p. 61

The accusations centred on one group with unparalleled access to the drug: doctors. Bourke (2007), p. 57.

p. 61

'If fraud vitiates consent . . . many seductions would be rapes'. Naffine (2019), p. 71 on *R v Clarence* [1888] by Judge James Fitzjames Stephen.

p. 61

fraud relating to 'the nature of the act itself' (the doctors), 'or as to the identity of the person who does the act' (the husband impersonators). Naffine (2019), p. 69.

p. 61

This dichotomy, fixed in law, would become known as 'fraud in the factum' and 'fraud in the inducement'. See Sharpe (2018); Kaushik (2021).

p. 61

Irregular as they were, the allegations proved persistent. See *R v Williams* [1923], in Sharpe (2018), p. 32.

p. 61

Take *People v Minkowski* (1962), a case from California McJunkin (2014), p. 10, *People v Minkowski* [1962] California Court of Appeal. The complainants were known as Miss X, Miss Y and

Miss Z. See *People v Minkowski* [1962], https://casetext.com/case/people-v-minkowski

p. 61

As the girls lay on the examination table Stuart P. Green, 'Lies, Rape, and Statutory Rape', in Stuart P. Green, *Criminalizing Sex: A Unified Liberal Theory* (Oxford University Press, 2020), pp. 198–9, *State v Atkins* [1926]; *Boro v Superior Court* [1985]; Wendy Doniger, *The Bedtrick: Tales of Sex and Masquerade* (University of Chicago Press, 2000), p. 520, *State v Ely* [1921], *People v Borak* [1972] and *Story v State* [1986].

p. 62

'an act of an altogether different nature . . . penetration by a medical instrument'. McJunkin (2014), p. 10, quoting a judge in *Boro v Superior Court* [1985] who in turn cited *People v Minkowski* [1962].

p. 62

Police would later describe him as the 'perfect rapist' Kathy Marks, 'Seven more say they were rapist's victims', *Independent* (1 December 1992), https://www.independent.co.uk/news/uk/seven-more-say-they-were-rapist-s-victims-kathy-marks-reports-on-the-harley-street-doctor-who-was-jailed-for-sex-offences-yesterday-1560755.html

p. 62

The Act was touted as 'a new code of sex offences [for] the new century', which would 'set the boundaries' for society by way of consent. Home Office, *Setting the Boundaries: Reforming the Law on Sex Offences* (2000), pp. i, 1.

p. 62

the key words being 'freedom', 'capacity' and 'choice'. See Sexual Offences Act 2003, Section 74.

p. 63

This section was at once old and new Kaushik (2021), p. 422.

p. 63

The second, and much rarer, is 'conclusive' (or irrebuttable). House of Commons, 'Fifth Report of Session 2002–3' (2003), p. 10, discussing rebuttable and irrebuttable presumptions.

p. 63

If a deception described in the provisions is demonstrated, the defence is prevented from making its case Ashworth and Temkin (2004), p. 334.

p. 69

Sexual trickery is a story that has fascinated humans for centuries. Julia Briggs, 'Shakespeare's Bed-Tricks', *Essays in Criticism*, vol. XLIV, issue 4, October 1994, p. 293.

p. 69

'You go to bed with someone you think you know . . . Doniger (2000), p. ii.

p. 70

Playwrights of this period were fixated on outdoing each other in increasingly tangled and ingenious plots. Marliss C. Desens, *The Bed-trick in English Renaissance Drama: Explorations in Gender, Sexuality, and Power* (University of Delaware Press, 1994).

p. 70

Later dramatists actually tried to 'improve' the play David Bevington, 'Measure for Measure on Stage', in William Shakespeare, *Measure for Measure, All's Well That Ends Well, Troilus and Cressida* (Bantam Classic, 1988), p. 14.

p. 70

Doniger argues that, over the next century, bed tricks lost popularity following the invention of night lights Doniger (2000).

p. 70

A critic in 1858 bemoaned the 'blind submission' necessary for the device to work William Watkiss Lloyd, 1858, in George L. Geckle (ed.), *Measure for Measure* (The Athlone Press, 2001), p. 137.

p. 70

the following decades saw an increasing intolerance of the trick's lack of realism and general foolery. William Bowden, *The Bed*

NOTES

Trick, 1603–1642: Its Mechanics, Ethics, and Effects (Shakespeare Studies, 1969) in Doniger (2000); and John Wain, *The Living World of Shakespeare: A Playgoer's Guide* (St. Martin's Press, 1964) in Desens (1994), p. xv.

p. 72

Never before at a trial had this strain of sexual fraud law, rooted in the 1880s, been applied to queer acts or to a dildo Sharpe (2018), pp. 44–7, notes the various convictions before 2015, but none of the cases made it to trial. Defendants pled guilty in the run up to trial, including in the landmark case *R v McNally* [2013].

p. 76

'Woman, 25, who pretended to be a man to dupe female friend into sex is found GUILTY'. Stephanie Linning, 'Woman, 25, who pretended she was a man to dupe female friend into sex is found GUILTY of three counts of sexual assault', *Daily Mail* (15 September 2015), https://www.dailymail.co.uk/news/article-3235421/Woman-pretended-man-dupe-female-friend-sex-GUILTY-sexual-assault.html

p. 76

'Convicted After Duping Friend Into Sex. Gayle Newland, 25, cries and shouts in court'. Sky News, 'Woman Convicted After Duping Friend Into Sex', Sky News (15 September 2015), https://news.sky.com/story/woman-convicted-after-duping-friend-into-sex-10346222

p. 76

'Fake penis trial verdict – Gayle Newland found GUILTY. Jonathan Humphries, 'Fake penis trial verdict – Newland found GUILTY of three counts of sexual assault', *Liverpool Echo* (15 September 2015), https://www.liverpoolecho.co.uk/news/liverpool-news/re-read-fake-penis-trial-10060599

p. 76

She will be sent to a maximum-security prison and, Dutton explains, be placed on the Sex Offender Register 'indefinitely'. Tom Rawstorne, 'Why this fraudster needs help, not prison', *Daily Mail* (29 July 2017), https://www.dailymail.co.uk/news/

article-4741312/Is-fraudster-Gayle-Newland-really-sex-offender.html

4 The Closet on the Stand: Sexuality

p. 77
'Rapists who end up being convicted in a court of law must regard themselves as exceptionally unlucky,' Bourke (2007), p. 389.

p. 78
As the entry shows, 'closet' has long signified a private room, 'for privacy or retirement', 'an inner chamber', often a place of 'secluded speculation'. Eve Kosofsky Sedgwick, *Epistemology of the Closet* (University of California Press, 1990), p. 66.

p. 78
'the defining structure of gay oppression in this century' Sedgwick (1990), p. 71.

p. 79
government ban on openly talking about homosexuality in schools. Section 28 of the Local Government Act 1988 banned local authorities and schools from 'promoting homosexuality'. See Local Government Act 1988, https://www.legislation.gov.uk/ukpga/1988/9/section/28/enacted

p. 79
It was the subject of Plato's *Lysis* David Roochnik, 'Plato's Lysis and the Erotics of Philia', *Archai: Revista de Estudos Sobre as Origens Do Pensamento Ocidental*, 32:e-03242, pp. 1–23.

p. 79
In this era, new fragments of erotic poetry by Sappho of Lesbos were circulating in Victorian England. Yopie Prins, *Victorian Sappho* (Princeton University Press, 1999), p. 3.

p. 83
making a joke was a form of release. Sigmund Freud, *Jokes and Their Relation to the Unconscious* (1905; White Press, 2014).

NOTES

p. 83

(an example being the public mockery in 2012 following the 'Twitter Joke Trial'). *R v Paul Chambers* [2010], popularly known as the Twitter Joke Trial.

p. 84

The term 'sexuality' came into being in the 1870s meaning 'sexual feeling'. Véronique Mottier, *Sexuality: A Very Short Introduction* (Oxford University Press, 2008), p. 31.

p. 84

in his 1886 manual of disorders, *Psychopathia Sexualis*. Richard von Krafft-Ebing, *Psychopathia Sexualis* (1886; William Heinemann, 1939).

p. 84

'sexual inversion', 'Uranian love', 'the homosexualist' and 'frauds against nature'. Benjamin Kahan, *The Book of Minor Perverts: Sexology, Etiology, and the Emergences of Sexuality* (University of Chicago Press, 2019), pp. 3–4.

p. 84

The term 'lesbian' also emerged in the 1870s Mottier (2008), p. 31.

p. 84

What had, before, been illicit acts Michel Foucault, *The History of Sexuality, Volume I*, tr. Robert Hurley (Pantheon Books, 1978).

p. 85

The theory of sexual inversion Ivan Crozier (ed.), *Sexual Inversion: A Critical Edition. Havelock Ellis and John Addington Symonds (1897)* (Palgrave Macmillan, 2008).

p. 85

The defendants were Ella Klein and Margarete Nebbe Todd Herzog, 'Crime and Literature in the Weimar Republic and Beyond: Telling the Tale of the Poisoners Ella Klein and Margarete Nebbe', in Richard F. Wetzell, *Crime and Criminal Justice in Modern Germany* (Berghahn Books, 2014), p. 228.

p. 86

'morbid' was a favoured term See Kraft-Ebbing (1939), p. 191, and Crozier (2008), p. 165.

p. 86

This view persisted well into the twentieth century Jack Drescher, 'Out of DSM: Depathologizing Homosexuality', *Behavioural Sciences*, vol. 5, no. 4 (December 2015), 565–75.

p. 86

a 'cure' available until the early 1970s. Helen Spandler, 'The shocking "treatment" to make lesbians straight', Wellcome Collection (22 January 2020), https://wellcomecollection.org/articles/XhWjZhAAACUAOpV2

p. 87

When the lesbian 'vice' was debated in Parliament in the 1920s In 1921, the Criminal Law Amendment Act was discussed in Parliament, including Clause 3, 'acts of indecency by females'. See transcript of discussion: https://api.parliament.uk/historic-hansard/lords/1921/aug/15/commons-amendment-2

p. 90

In the 1950s, a spectacular murder trial caught the eye of the world Peter Graham, *So Brilliantly Clever: Parker, Hulme and the Murder That Shocked the World* (Skyhorse Publishing, 2013).

p. 94

'every encounter with a new classful of students, to say nothing of a new boss, social worker, loan officer, landlord, doctor, erects new closets' Sedgwick (1990), p. 68.

p. 94

'A gay bar . . . affords refuge . . . We go out to be gay.' Jeremy Atherton Lin, *Gay Bar: Why We Went Out* (Hachette, 2021), pp. 37–9.

p. 95

This obfuscation lingers in the vocabulary they both use at the first trial. The night was officially LGBT and aimed at students. See Grietje Baars, 'Queer Cases Unmake Gendered Law, or, Fucking

Law's Gendering Function', *The Australian Feminist Law Journal*, vol. 45, no. 1 (2019), p. 23.

p. 95

The word 'gay' has always been an umbrella term, explicitly used since the 1920s to broadly describe homosexuality. Lin (2021), p. 63.

p. 97

The 'gay panic defence' Sedgwick (1990), p. 19.

p. 97

The 'Portsmouth defence' Julian Meldrum, 'On the Streets', in Bruce Galloway (ed.), *Prejudice and Pride: Discrimination Against Gay People in Modern Britain* (Routledge, 1983).

p. 97

in what the judge called a 'clear . . . case of provocation'. *R v Thomas Somer* [1963], Judge Paull, quoted in *The Birmingham Post and Birmingham Gazette*, 22 January 1963, quoted by Michael J. Buchanan-Dunne, Murder Mile UK True-Crime podcast – #194: The Gay Panic (2022).

p. 97

The 'good homosexual' . . . was expected to be 'a law abiding, disease free, self-closeting homosexual figure' Carl F. Stychin, *Governing Sexuality: The Changing Politics of Citizenship and Law Reform* (Hart Publishing, 2003), p. 28.

p. 98

and the film *Heavenly Creatures*. *Heavenly Creatures*, dir. Peter Jackson (Miramax, 1994).

p. 98

Written by lesbian academics, *Parker and Hulme* grappled with the way this trial exacerbated fears in New Zealand Julie Glamuzina and Alison J. Laurie, *Parker and Hulme: A Lesbian View* (Firebrand, 1995), p. 12.

p. 99

In the same era, in the UK, lesbian historians such as Rose Collis published books unveiling lesbian lives, referencing these trials

Rose Collis, *Portraits to the Wall: Historic Lesbian Lives Unveiled* (Cassell, 1994).

p. 99

In 2002, the Portsmouth defence was discredited, following new guidance published by the CPS CPS, 'Policy for Prosecuting Cases with a Homophobic Element' (2002). As Michael Halls, LGBT Community Safety Officer, Letter, 'No Portsmouth defence', *Independent* (6 November 2003), explains, 'There was a major reform at the end of 2002 . . . In the new policy and guidance, crown prosecutors are told, in detail, how they should actively challenge any attempt by the accused to use the Portsmouth defence.'

5   Identity on the Stand: Fraud

p. 107

In 2014, for example, Facebook launched fifty-eight gender options Mark Liberman, '58 Facebook genders', Language Log (18 February 2014), https://languagelog.ldc.upenn.edu/nll/?p=10604; Peter Weber, 'Confused by All the New Facebook Genders? Here's What They Mean', Slate (21 February 2014), https://slate.com/human-interest/2014/02/gender-facebook-now-has-56-categories-to-choose-from-including-cisgender-genderqueer-and-intersex.html

p. 107

Soon after, *TIME* magazine triumphantly pronounced the 'transgender tipping point', whereby heightened visibility was enkindling 'trans consciousness'. Kate Steinmetz, 'The Transgender Tipping Point', *TIME* magazine (29 May 2014), https://time.com/135480/transgender-tipping-point/

p. 109

celebrities such as Caitlyn Jenner had come out as transgender in highly public ways Buzz Bissinger, 'Caitlyn Jenner: The Full Story', *Vanity Fair* (25 June 2013), https://www.vanityfair.com/hollywood/2015/06/caitlyn-jenner-bruce-cover-annie-leibovitz

NOTES

p. 110

As publicity around Gayle's case mounted, the conviction was revealed to be the latest in a series of cases, accelerating since 2012 – the fifth in a sequence. Sharpe (2018), pp. 44–8.

p. 110

All suspects were accused of falsely presenting as men; some identified as trans *R v Chris Wilson* [2013]; *R v Kyran Lee (Mason)* [2015].

p. 110

others as lesbians. *R v Barker* [2012]; *R v McNally* [2013]; *R v Newland* [2015].

p. 110

she called it 'gender identity fraud' Sharpe (2018), p. 1.

p. 110

She watched the appeal hearing from her cell via a live link. Sara C. Nelson, 'Prosthetic Penis Case: Gayle Newland Conviction Overturned', Huffington Post (12 October 2016), https://www.huffingtonpost.co.uk/entry/prosthetic-penis-case-gayle-newland-conviction-overturned_uk_57fe32dce4b08e08b93d6149

p. 110

A judge, speaking at the Royal Courts of Justice in London, ruled the original verdicts were 'unsafe' See *R v Newland* [2016] EWCA Crim 1577 (12 October 2016), para 25.

p. 111

The Court of Appeal ruled that his summary of evidence was biased in favour of the prosecution. *Newland* [2016], para 24.

p. 111

'in no doubt what . . . their verdicts should be'. *Newland* [2016], para 23.

p. 111

All the other defendants had pled guilty at pre-trial hearings. Guilty pleas: *R v Barker* [2012]; *R v McNally* [2012]; *R v Wilson* [2013] – see Sharpe (2018), pp. 44–8.

p. 112

it was the complainant's mother who had lodged the first complaint at her daughter's school *McNally* [2013], paras 6–10.

p. 112

after finding a dildo in Scott's rucksack. See *R v Justine McNally* [2013] EWCA Crim 1051 (27 June 2013).

p. 112

But the appeal backfired – leading to a precedent, the McNally Principle. There were three grounds of appeal: bad legal advice; the elements of the offence not being made out; and an 'equivocal' plea. But the judgment goes beyond this. *McNally* [2013], para 15, 'Against that background we first consider the offence'. Paras 15–27 then consider sexual fraud case law and uses of Section 76 versus Section 74, crystallizing the Section 74 route to prosecution.

p. 113

'[Miss A] chose to have sexual encounters with a boy,' he states, before citing the definition of consent: 'Her freedom to choose whether or not to have a sexual encounter with a girl' was 'removed by the appellant's deception' *McNally* [2013], para 26.

p. 113

'We conclude that, depending on the circumstances, deception as to gender can vitiate consent.' *McNally* [2013], para 27.

p. 113

The reporting caught the attention of transgender activists. See 'Support Gayle Newland', Facebook (2016), https://www.facebook.com/supportgaylenewland/?locale=en_GB

p. 114

'the sexual nature of the acts is, on any common sense view, different' *McNally* [2013], para 26.

p. 114

He even used the word 'obviously' about other deceptions not counting *McNally* [2013], para 25.

NOTES

p. 114

Both defendants identified as transgender men Sharpe (2018), pp. 49–51, *R v Kyran Lee (Mason)* [2015]; *R v Jason Staines* [2016].

p. 116

Sita Balani considers 'the trickery of race'. Sita Balani, *Deadly and Slick: Sexual Modernity and the Making of Race* (Verso, 2023), pp. xxiii, xi.

p. 117

In many states, 'one drop' of non-white ancestry Christine B. Hickman, 'The Devil and the One Drop Rule: Racial Categories, African Americans, and the U.S. Census', *Michigan Law Review*, vol. 95, no. 5 (1997).

p. 117

Jill Hasday unearthed a score of American lawsuits from this era Jill Hasday, *Intimate Lies and the Law* (Oxford University Press, 2019), pp. 118–20, *Rhinelander v Rhinelander* [1925].

p. 118

The pure view, put forward by Jonathan Herring, is that no deception is too trivial or too uncomfortable Herring (2005).

p. 118

Herring doesn't use the example of race specifically, but other scholars have, arguing that racial deception should count, alongside other identity lies Matthew Gibson, 'Deception, Consent and the Right to Sexual Autonomy' (2023), p. 49, and Amit Pundik, 'Deception about What? Subjectifying the Criminalisation of Deceptive Sex' (2023), p. 80, in Criminal Law Reform Now Network, *Reforming the Relationship between Sexual Consent, Deception and Mistake*, Report (2023), http://www.clrnn.co.uk/media/1031/clrnn3-deception-report.pdf. The arguments are for an expansion of the scope of sexual fraud law.

p. 118

'we must respect other people's wills as they actually are, not as they ought to be' Tom Dougherty, 'Sex, Lies, and Consent', *Ethics*, vol. 123, no. 4 (2013), 717–44, p. 730.

p. 118

Conditions that can vitiate consent were restricted See Kyle L. Murray and Tara Beattie, 'Conditional Consent and Sexual Offences: Revisiting the Sexual Offences Act 2003 after Lawrence', *Criminal Law Review*, issue 7 (2021), 556–74, pp. 556–7, on *R v Lawrence* [2020] EWCA Crim 971.

p. 119

Several months before Gayle's first trial, a man was convicted of 'procuring sexual penetration by fraud' Deepak Dhankar was found guilty at Victoria County Court in Melbourne in February 2015. See Adam Cooper, 'Blond-haired Caucasian', The Age (10 February 2015), https://www.theage.com.au/national/victoria/blondhaired-caucasian-deepak-dhankars-online-dating-lies-lead-to-sexfraud-charges-20150210-13au1u.html

p. 119

She claimed she kept her eyes closed during the encounter at his request News.com.au, 'Indian-born man who duped woman into sex by pretending he was Caucasian avoids jail', News.com.au (25 February 2015), https://www.news.com.au/national/victoria/indianborn-man-who-duped-woman-into-sex-by-pretending-he-was-caucasian-avoids-jail/news-story/3defd87c9b97f40bf53dd789a8114570

p. 119

At his sentencing, the judge reportedly said that if Dhankar hadn't shown contrition and pled guilty, she would have incarcerated him. News.com.au, 'Indian-born man who duped woman into sex by pretending he was Caucasian avoids jail', News.com.au (25 February 2015), https://www.news.com.au/national/victoria/indianborn-man-who-duped-woman-into-sex-by-pretending-he-was-caucasian-avoids-jail/news-story/3defd87c9b97f40bf53dd789a8114570

p. 119

In another variation, this time from Israel, a man was convicted of rape by deception, on the basis of ethno-religious fraud. Pundik

(2018), p. 174. Sabbar Kashur was convicted of rape on 19 July 2010 at the District Court of Jerusalem.

p. 120

the CPS's 'Full Code Test'. CPS, 'The Code for Crown Prosecutors' (2018).

p. 120

The CPS is effectively a 'gatekeeper'. House of Commons Justice Committee, 'The Crown Prosecution Service: Gatekeeper of the Criminal Justice System', Ninth Report of Session 2008–09 (2009), p. 3.

p. 120

The step is generally understood to be there to weed out complaints that are trifling, unbalanced or uneven Notably, the public interest step has more significance in lesser charges (e.g., shoplifting) than in serious crimes (e.g., sexual offences).

p. 120

Shon Faye tracks the way transgender rights became a culture war 'issue' in the 2010s, reduced to a 'talking point' and chewed over as a 'toxic debate'. Shon Faye, *The Transgender Issue: An Argument for Justice* (Penguin, 2021), p. 8.

p. 120

The optimistic 'tipping point' of 2014 soon morphed into a gloomy 'transgender dipping point' of 2017 Samantha Allen, 'Whatever Happened to the Transgender Tipping Point?', Daily Beast (31 March 2017), https://www.thedailybeast.com/whatever-happened-to-the-transgender-tipping-point/

p. 121

'Perhaps no topic – other than Brexit and, latterly, the coronavirus pandemic – has received such a consistently high and recurring level of popular media coverage' Faye (2021), p. 17.

p. 122

It does not conform to a standardized narrative – specifically, the legal narrative about gender recognition. Kit Heyam, *Before We Were Trans: A New History of Gender* (Seal Press, (2022), p. 20.

p. 122
The Act outlines the way gender identity can be legally affirmed by the state See Gender Recognition Act 2004, Section 3, 'Evidence'.

6   Kye Fortune on the Stand: Avatars

p. 125
'Online I could be whoever I wanted, and so my twelve-year-old self became sixteen, became twenty, became seventy,' Legacy Russell, *Glitch Feminism: A Manifesto* (Verso, 2020), p. 4.

p. 127
A spate of books published by lawyers and cyber scholars outlined the field and its concerns. Benjamin Duranske, *Virtual Law: Navigating the Legal Landscape of Virtual Worlds* (TradeSelect, 2008); Angela Adrian, *Law and Order in Virtual Worlds: Exploring Avatars, Their Ownership and Rights* (IGI Global, 2010); Greg Lastowka, *Virtual Justice: The New Law of Online Worlds* (Yale University Press, 2011).

p. 127
Based on the US Bill of Rights, he argued that avatars should be treated as 'actual people in an online medium' not 'soulless puppets'. Raph Koster, 'Declaring the Rights of Player' (27 August 2000).

p. 128
leading to an identity overlap termed 'character attachment' or 'bleed' Davide C. Orazi and Tom van Laer, 'There and Back Again: Bleed from Extraordinary Experiences', *Journal of Consumer Research*, vol. 49, issue 5 (February 2023), 904–25, p. 908.

p. 128
'Perhaps the most apt candidate for an avatar-like object is the prosthetic limb,' Lastowka (2011), p. 46.

p. 128
in many jurisdictions corporations are, by statute, legal persons, entitled to certain rights Tiffany Day, 'Avatar Rights in a

NOTES

Constitutionless World', *UC Law SF Communications and Entertainment Law Journal*, vol. 32, 137–56 (2009).

p. 128

Virtual law emerged in response to the growth and popularity of virtual worlds, and crucially in response to avatar complaints. Farnaz Alemi, 'An Avatar's Day in Court: A Proposal for Obtaining Relief and Resolving Disputes in Virtual World Games', *UCLA Journal of Law and Technology*, vol. 11, no. 2 (2007).

p. 129

Capturing legal (and media) attention, the case seemed to be based on a new allegation – avatar infidelity. Lastowka (2011), p. 30.

p. 129

In 1993, a journalist in an early virtual world witnessed a rape; he subsequently wrote an article entitled 'A Rape in Cyberspace'. Julien Dibbell, 'A Rape in Cyberspace: How an Evil Clown, a Haitian Trickster Spirit, and a Cast of Dozens Turned a Database into a Society', *The Village Voice* (23 December 1993).

p. 129

Was the harm, then, a rape of the mind, emotional distress? Notably, two decades later, digital sexual offences such as cyberflashing are recognized as criminal offences in the UK in the Online Safety Bill 2023. See UK Gov, 'Cyberflashing to become a criminal offence' (13 March 2022), https://www.gov.uk/government/news/cyberflashing-to-become-a-criminal-offence

p. 129

Think pieces circulated online, with titles like 'Virtual Rape . . . Is It a Crime?' Wired, 'Virtual Rape Is Traumatic, but Is It a Crime?', Wired, 4 May 2007.

p. 129

Or was it the avatar – as a prosthesis, an extension of the self – that was, in some way, harmed? Litska Strikwerda, 'Present and Future Instances of Virtual Rape in Light of Three Categories of Legal Philosophical Theories on Rape', *Philosophy and Technology*, vol. 28, no. 4 (2015), 491–510.

p. 131
In his 2013 book *The Psychodynamics of Social Networking* Aaron Balick, *The Psychodynamics of Social Networking: Connected-up Instantaneous Culture and the Self* (Routledge, 2013), p. 131.

p. 132
Traditions of 'avatar drag' are customary Avi Marciano, 'Living the VirtuReal: Negotiating Transgender Identity in Cyberspace', *Journal of Computer-Mediated Communication*, vol. 19, no. 4 (2014), 824–38.

p. 132
This is not a crime in itself in the UK (although it is in other jurisdictions such as France). Catfishing debated in Parliament, 2017, https://hansard.parliament.uk/Commons/2017-07-18/debates/F5CF658F-CB53-4A57-93D3-70457CA69F28/CatfishingAndSocialMedia. Online impersonation was criminalized in France in 2011, https://fra.europa.eu/sites/default/files/access_to_data_protection_remedies_country_fr.pdf

p. 132
To be prosecuted, online impersonation must intersect with other crimes, such as fraud or theft. Specific crimes online impersonation could intersect with include obscene messaging (Communications Act 2003) and plans for financial gain (Fraud Act 2006).

p. 133
Facebook admitted that 83 million profiles were fakes or dupes in these years Nev Schulman, *In Real Life: Love, Lies & Identity in the Digital Age* (Hodder, 2014), p. 25.

p. 134
***Catfish* (2010) followed Nev Schulman** *Catfish*, dir. Ariel Schulman and Henry Joost (Universal Pictures, 2010).

p. 134
'digital human beings' Schulman (2014), p. 40.

NOTES

p. 137

'High school hasn't changed,' Josie writes in her article ... *Never Been Kissed*, dir. Raja Gosnell (20th Century Studios, 1999).

p. 140

That is the storyline of the 2004 rom-com *A Cinderella Story* *A Cinderella Story*, dir. Mark Rosman (Warner Bros., 2004).

p. 145

But, across the 2000s, increasing reports began to surface Róisín Lanigan, 'The Internet Has a Cancer-Faking Problem: Munchausen by internet', *The Atlantic* (6 May 2019), https://www.theatlantic.com/health/archive/2019/05/faking-cancer-online/588334/

p. 146

take the pale, sick seamstress Mimi Giacomo Puccini, *La Bohème* (1895; Cambridge University Press, 1986).

p. 146

In *Sweet November* *Sweet November*, dir. Pat O'Connor (Warner Bros., 2001).

p. 146

in *P.S. I Love You* *P.S. I Love You*, dir. Richard LaGravenese (Warner Bros., 2007).

p. 146

in *A Little Bit of Heaven* *A Little Bit of Heaven*, dir. Nicole Kassell (The Weinstein Company, 2011).

p. 146

This genre was epitomized by *The Fault in Our Stars* John Green, *The Fault in Our Stars* (Penguin, 2012); *The Fault in Our Stars*, dir. Josh Boone (20th Century Studios, 2014).

p. 147

The film was so popular that it spawned an abundance of other terminal romances Films include: *Everything, Everything*, dir. Stella Meghie (Warner Bros., 2017); *Midnight Sun*, dir. Scott Speer (Open Road Films, 2018); *Five Feet Apart*, dir. Justin Balgoni (Lionsgate, 2019).

7 The Dildo on the Stand: Bodies

p. 154
Nev Schulman writes that catfish are 'doomed'. Schulman (2014), p. 38.

p. 155
'CyberSkin' is made of an elastomer called SEBS Nils H. Nilsson et al., 'Survey and health assessment of chemicals [*sic*] substances in sex toys', Danish Technological Institute (2006), p. 10.

p. 155
Elsewhere, it is described as a 'dream penis', a 'lifelike lover'. 'Cyberskin Dream Penis', sold on Amazon, https://www.amazon.com/Cyber-Color-Cyberskin-Dream-Penis/product-reviews/B0001FUWPC; and 'Lifelike Lover Ultra Realistic Dildo', sold on Sex Toy Sutra, https://sextoysutra.co.uk/shop/dildos/lifelike-lover-ultra-realistic-dildo-with-balls-9-5-inch/

p. 156
In Ancient Greece, objects could be accused of committing crimes; indeed they had a court, the Prytaneion, dedicated to trials of murderous objects. Geoffrey C.R. Schmalz, 'The Athenian Prytaneion Discovered?', *Hesperia: The Journal of the American School of Classical Studies at Athens*, vol. 75, no. 1 (2006), 33–81, p. 34.

p. 156
('[He] flogged the bronze image as though he were ill-treating Theagenes himself,' Pausanias, *Description of Greece* (AD 2), 6.1–18, in 6.11.6, various translations. W.H.S. Jones. https://www.theoi.com/Text/Pausanias6A.html

p. 156
According to Plato, the Prytaneion was a court where 'a thing' could be 'defeated'. Raphael Seale, 'Trial of Animals and Inanimate Objects for Homicide', *The Classical Quarterly, New Series*, vol. 56, no. 2 (2006), 475–85, p. 477.

p. 157
The accused items, named 'deodands', were murderous, seemingly

with agency, described in law as 'a thing that moved to cause death'. Anna Pervukhin, 'Deodands: A Study in the Creation of Common Law Rules', *American Journal of Legal History*, vol. 47, no. 3 (2005), 237–56, p. 252.

p. 157

Legal rolls record hundreds of prosecutions across the centuries See Sara M. Butler, 'Carts, Ships, and Trains: Abusing the Deodand', *Legal History Miscellany*, May 2020, https://legalhistorymiscellany.com/2020/05/29/carts-ships-and-trains-abusing-the-deodand/

p. 159

This is a difference rooted deep in law, which dates back to the Roman era. Christoph Bublitz, 'The body of law: boundaries, extensions, and the human right to physical integrity in the biotechnical age', *Journal of Law and the Biosciences*, vol. 9, issue 2 (2022), p. 8.

p. 159

Objects, meanwhile, are in a different legal category, seen as property and not protected to such a degree. Rachel Clement Tolley, 'Criminal Law, Battery and Bodily Harm: Reforming the Criminal Law for Users of Mobility Aids', Milestone Lecture 2019, Trinity Hall Cambridge, https://www.youtube.com/watch?v=kioV5fyydrM

p. 159

And, in the other direction, things that can become part of the body, from cochlear implants to pacemakers and artificial joints. Muireann Quigley and Semande Ayihongbe, 'Everyday Cyborgs: On Integrated Persons and Integrated Goods', *Medical Law Review*, vol. 26, no. 2 (2018), 276–308.

p. 159

In *Visceral Prosthesis* (2022), the theorist Margrit Shildrick tracks the shift in meaning of prostheses Margrit Shildrick, *Visceral Prostheses: Somatechnics and Posthuman Embodiment* (Bloomsbury, 2022), p. 3.

p. 160

The tip of the cane 'is transformed into a sensitive zone', he wrote,

becoming an 'instrument of perception'. 'The world of feelable things recedes and now begins, not at the outer skin of the hand, but at the end of the stick.' Maurice Merleau-Ponty, *Phenomenology of Perception* (1945; Routledge Classic, 2002), p. 176.

p. 160

Strike a wheelchair, kick a prosthetic limb, and it is property damage, not assault. Craig Murray, *Amputation, Prosthesis Use, and Phantom Limb Pain: An Interdisciplinary Perspective* (Springer, 2010); Lisa Folkmarson Käll et al., 'Disability and Prostheses', *Women, Gender & Research*, vol. 5, no. 2 (2021).

p. 161

'I can feel the Joystick penetrating my partner, can experience an orgasm inside my partner' Chris Straayer, 'Trans men's stealth aesthetics: navigating penile prosthetics and "gender fraud"', *Journal of Visual Culture*, vol. 19, no. 2 (2020), 255–71, p. 262.

p. 161

'The trans man inhabits the prosthetic, incorporates it into his body, brings it to life' Straayer (2020), p. 256.

p. 163

The artificial penis has probably been around as long as the natural one, and used as a masturbation aid by women and men alike. Hallie Lieberman, *Buzz: The Stimulating History of the Sex Toy* (Pegasus Books, 2017).

p. 163

Onanism was diabolical, a crime against nature – worse, some argued, than the so-called natural sins of fornication, incest and rape. Michael S. Patton, 'Masturbation from Judaism to Victorianism', *Journal of Religion and Health*, vol. 24, no. 2 (1985), 133–46.

p. 163

in Aristophanes' play *Lysistrata*, for example, women used 'olisbos' (leather penises) to satisfy their needs Max Nelson, 'A Note on the ὄλισβος', *Glotta*, vol. 76, nos. 1–2 (2000), 75–82.

NOTES

p. 163

Dildos take the form of stolen penises that witches would fatten up ('with oats') and keep in a secret place (either 'in a bird's nest' or 'in a box'). Heinrich Kramer, *Malleus Maleficarum* (1486), Part 2, Chapter VII, 'How, as it were, they Deprive Man of his Virile Member', describes various cases of men losing their 'members', and witches' practices of breeding penises: https://sacred-texts.com/pag/mm/mm02a07a.htm

p. 164

In a rare trial from fifteenth-century Germany, a woman named Katherina Hetzeldorfer was tried for sexual relations with women. Helmut Puff, *Sodomy in Reformation Germany and Switzerland, 1400–1600* (University of Chicago Press, 2003), p. 33.

p. 164

At trial, Katherina scandalized the court by describing a home-made penis, which she fashioned with 'a wooden stick' and 'a piece of red leather'. Julie Peakman, *Pleasure's All Mine: A History of Perverse Sex* (Reaktion, 2013), p, 144.

p. 164

The baffled, angry judges issued a death sentence and Katherina was drowned in the Rhine. Puff (2003), p. 34. A century later, in 1547, another woman, Agatha Disetschi, was arrested for heresy, after she was found to have manufactured a dildo, and used it on her lover 'behind a willow tree'.

p. 164

But Casanova revealed that, actually, Bellino was Theresa, a girl who had been fooling inquisitors with a lifelike penis, which tricked the naked eye and attached to her crotch with 'glue'. Giacomo Casanova, *The Complete Memoirs*, tr. Arthur Machen (1774; Start Publishing, 2012).

p. 164

One famous case, featuring a quack doctor named Charles Hamilton, appeared in broadsheets (early newspapers), exciting public interest. Jen Manion, *Female Husbands: A Trans History* (Cambridge University Press, 2020).

p. 165

something 'scandalous' was found in the doctor's medical bag, something 'vile' and 'wicked' Henry Fielding, *The Female Husband: or, the Surprising History of Mrs. Mary, alias Mr. George Hamilton, who was Convicted of having Married a young Woman of Wells and Lived with her as her Husband* (1746).

p. 165

Legal historian Caroline Derry traces the many other 'female husband' cases in England and Wales in the nineteenth and twentieth centuries, which she reads as precursors to gender fraud. Derry, *Lesbianism and the Criminal Law* (2020), pp. 41–82.

p. 165

One described the baggy clothes Jimmy wore and the 'sharp' feel of his penis. *R v Saunders* [1991]. Excerpts of the official court documents during the Crown Court trial at Doncaster County in 1991, p. 5, http://mauvaiscontact.info/texts/reginaVSaunders_court_excerpts.pdf

p. 166

'I suspect both those girls would rather have been actually raped by some young man than have happened to them what you did,' Diane Hamer, 'The Invention of the Dildo', *Australian Gay and Lesbian Law Journal*, 2 (1992), 41–54.

p. 167

Women, coming forward since 2012, said they did not consent to sex with these 'random' actors. Carole McCartney and Natalie Wortley, 'Under the Covers: Covert Policing and Intimate Relationships', *Criminal Law Review*, issue 2 (2018), 137–56.

p. 167

As of 2025, more than fifty women have come forward. Rob Evans, 'Revealed: at least 25 UK "spy cops" had sex with deceived members of public', *The Guardian* (2 March 2025), https://www.theguardian.com/uk-news/2025/mar/02/revealed-at-least-25-uk-spy-cops-sexual-relations-deceived-women

NOTES

p. 167

One case was taken forward under the pseudonym 'Monica'
Caroline Derry, 'Sustained Identity Deceptions', in Criminal Law Reform Now Network, *Reforming the Relationship between Sexual Consent, Deception and Mistake* (2023), 19–27, http://www.clrnn.co.uk/media/1031/clrnn3-deception-report.pdf

p. 167

The refusal to charge Spy Cops in 2018 and in the years since contrasts sharply with the dildo trials, suggesting a willingness to prosecute the dildo over the penis. E.g., in September 2023, a case was taken forward by 'Mary', who was deceived for 19 years by a Spy Cop. The CPS declined to charge, saying 'there was insufficient evidence to provide a realistic prospect of conviction', https://www.theguardian.com/uk-news/2023/sep/27/cps-declined-to-charge-undercover-police-officer-who-deceived-woman-into-19-year-relationship

p. 167

The only deceptions that would be taken seriously, the court stated, must be connected to the 'performance of the sexual act'. Murray and Beattie (2021), pp. 556–7.

p. 168

A 'good dramatist', noted a Shakespeare critic, does not 'flaunt' the implausibility of the bed trick Bowden (1969), p. 121.

p. 169

such as the prosecution of Carlos Delacruz in Scotland in 2018
R v Carlos Delacruz [2018] Edinburgh Sheriff Court.

p. 169

Blade Silvano in England in 2023 *R v Blade Silvano* [2023] Cambridge Crown Court.

p. 169

A wooden spoon? A bottle? A loo brush? A knife? David Davis, 'XVII: Part 2: On genital preference'; https://itsdavid.substack.com/p/david-davis-xvii-part-2 'Cucumber? Bottle? Knife? Hand?'

8 The Blindfold on the Stand: Touch

p. 172
She weighs evidence without the distraction of visual judgements.
Adriano Prosperi, *Justice Blindfolded: The Historical Course of an Image* (Brill, 2018).

p. 172
In a popular woodcut from the allegorical poem *The Ship of Fools* (1494), a jester ties a scarf over the eyes of Lady Justice. 'The Litigants' (woodcut) in Sebastian Brant, *The Ship of Fools* (1494), in Prosperi (2018), p. 9.

p. 172
In another woodcut from the same period, a group of judges are pictured wearing blindfolds and jester hats 'The madness of blind judges' (woodcut) in *Constitutio penalis Bambergensis* (1507), in Prosperi (2018), p. 39.

p. 172
Writers who have lived with retinitis pigmentosa Ryan Knighton, *Cockeyed* (Atlantic, 2007); Andrew Leland, *The Country of the Blind: A Memoir at the End of Sight* (Penguin, 2023).

p. 173
In her study of the plot, Wendy Doniger identifies darkness as the most common way bed tricks are achieved. Doniger (2000), p. 441.

p. 173
Here, the bed trick becomes a 'bum trick' Geoffrey Chaucer, 'The Miller's Tale', 623–7, Librarius, http://www.librarius.com/canttran/milltale/milltale615-635.htm

p. 174
In his deceptive embrace, Arthur is conceived. Sir Thomas Malory, *Le Morte D'Arthur Volume 1*, Book 1 (Penguin, 2004), p. 8.

p. 174
Most of Shakespeare's bed tricks take place in the 'heavy middle of the night', in private locations, such as 'a garden circummured

NOTES

with brick' or dark bedchambers. William Shakespeare, *Measure for Measure*, edited by Barbara A. Mowat and Paul Westerine (1604; Folger, 2020), Act 4, Scene 1, and *All's Well That Ends Well* (1604; 2020), Act 4, Scene 2.

p. 174

'on sleeping eyelids laid/Will make man or woman madly dote/ Upon the next live creature that it sees' William Shakespeare, *A Midsummer Night's Dream* (1600; 2020), Act 2, Scene 1.

p. 174

'drop of liquor' Shakespeare, *A Midsummer Night's Dream* (1600; 2020), Act 2, Scene 1.

p. 175

she can't really see, and believes Bottom is an 'angel' Shakespeare, *A Midsummer Night's Dream* (1600; 2020), Act 3, Scene 1.

p. 175

The bed trick eventually takes place in a dark garden Burton D. Fisher, *Mozart's Da Ponte Operas: The Marriage of Figaro, Don Giovanni, Così fan tutte* (Opera Journeys Publishing, 2007), p. 126.

p. 175

Susanna, peering on from the side, calls him 'the bizarre lover' Fisher (2007), p. 129.

p. 175

Blindfolds appear across erotic literature *Story of O* (erotic novel 1954; film 1975); *Nine and a Half Weeks* (erotic memoir 1978; filmed as *9½ Weeks* 1986); *Fifty Shades of Grey* trilogy (books 2011–12; films 2015–18).

p. 177

One woman described the phone ringing late at night *State v. Mitchell*, 01C01-96129702-CR-005702 (Tenn. Crim. App. 7-30-1999), https://www.casemine.com/judgement/us/59147f44add7b0493445ecea

p. 178

The case was a media sensation 'Fantasy Man Found Guilty', *The*

297

Spokesman-Review, 19 January 1996, https://www.spokesman.com/stories/1996/jan/19/fantasy-man-found-guilty-man-who-duped-women-into/

p. 178

a man named Duarte Xavier was accused of pretending to be a cis-woman *R v Duarte Xavier* [2018] Kingston Crown Court.

p. 178

On Tinder, Ana was attractive and sexually adventurous 'Man who posed as "attractive and adventurous" woman online', *The Standard* (9 November 2018), https://www.standard.co.uk/news/crime/man-who-posed-as-woman-online-then-tricked-men-into-blindfold-sex-jailed-for-15-years-a3986091.html

p. 178

At trial, Duarte was described as setting 'bizarre conditions' and demonstrating 'extreme cunning' Derry, *Lesbianism and the Criminal Law* (2020), p. 246.

p. 179

'love is blind' Geoffrey Chaucer, 'The Merchant's Tale', 366, Librarius, http://www.librarius.com/canttran/merchtrfs.htm

p. 179

'When one is in love, one always begins by deceiving one's self, and one always ends by deceiving others,' Oscar Wilde, *The Picture of Dorian Grey* (1890; Penguin, 2007), p. 42.

p. 179

The contemporary philosopher Jules de Gaultier concurred in an essay of 1892 outlining the condition 'Bovarysme'. Jules de Gaultier, *Le Bovarysme* (Nouvelles Editions, 1892).

p. 179

'People can be fooled because they want to be fooled,' Doniger writes; it is the 'will to believe' that allows a trickster to succeed. Doniger (2000), p. 445.

p. 184

This neglect, argues Ross, has led to a 'vast knowledge gap' when it comes to the vagina, which until recent decades was viewed as 'a

black box' Rachel Gross, *Vagina Obscura: An Anatomical Voyage* (W.W. Norton, 2022), pp. 5–8.

p. 184

evil spirits could be discharged through 'genital exorcism' Samuel Harsnett, *A Declaration of Egregious Popish Impostures* (1603) on the Denham Exorcisms of 1585.

p. 184

In his 1997 book *Bodies of Law*, the legal scholar Alan Hyde points to a search warrant from 1991, which orders a search of a woman's 'apartment and vagina' Alan Hyde, *Bodies of Law* (Princeton University Press, 1997), p. 4.

p. 184

Lips are known for their sensory richness Ashley Ward, *Sensational: A New Story of Our Senses* (Profile, 2023), p. 316.

p. 186

In *De Anima* (c. 350 BC), Aristotle theorized the five senses as we know them today. Ward (2023), p. 3.

p. 187

He considered touch to be the most elusive sense Daniel Heller-Roazen, *The Inner Touch: Archaeology of a Sensation* (Zone Books, 2007), p. 26.

p. 187

Scientists today distinguish between highly sensitive 'glabrous' skin Ward (2023), pp. 194–5.

p. 187

Lists of erogenous zones include the earlobe, the nape of the neck, the inner wrist, the scalp. Lara Maister et al., 'The Erogenous Mirror: Intersubjective and Multisensory Maps of Sexual Arousal in Men and Women', *Archives of Sexual Behavior*, vol. 49, no. 8 (2020), 2919–33.

p. 189

To make sense of racial hierarchy, a logic needed to be established Balani (2023), pp. 31–2.

p. 189

In June 2015, in the months before Gayle's first trial, Dolezal was exposed by her white parents and widely condemned for racial 'masquerade'. Tamara Winfrey Harris, 'Black Like Who? Rachel Dolezal's Harmful Masquerade', *New York Times* (16 June 2015), https://www.nytimes.com/2015/06/16/opinion/rachel-dolezals-harmful-masquerade.html

p. 190

London underwent surgeries, beginning in 2019, to look like a K-pop star. Oli London (@OliLondonTV), 20 June 2021.

p. 190

By 2022, he had undergone thirty-two operations, and spoke of a (finally unrealized) plan for a penis reduction, which he said he needed as a finishing touch, to make him '100 percent Korean'. Ryan Smith, '"Transracial" Influencer Oli London Reveals Plans for Penis Reduction Surgery', *Newsweek* (19 January 2022), https://www.newsweek.com/transracial-influencer-oli-london-reveals-plans-penis-reduction-surgery-1674040

p. 190

They have sex in dimly lit bedrooms; occasionally, Fantomina wears a 'mask'. Beauplaisir is a 'blinded' lover, the narrator explains, but Fantomina is also 'admirably skill'd'. Eliza Haywood, *Fantomina; or, Love in a Maze* (1725; Renard Press, 2021), p. 70.

p. 194

Wendy Doniger suggests that all bed trick plots are failed bed tricks, 'for we, the readers, always learn the truth'. Doniger (2000), p. 437.

9 Kye Fortune on the Stand: Impostors

p. 199

It is an example of the 'malleability of trial evidence' Janet Malcolm, *Iphigenia in Forest Hills: Anatomy of a Murder Trial* (Yale University Press, 2011), p. 12.

NOTES

p. 200

'adverse inference' CPS, 'Adverse inference', legal guidance, Criminal Justice and Public Order Act 1994, Section 34, https://www.legislation.gov.uk/ukpga/1994/33/section/34

p. 201

During a second trial, at which Martin pled his case claiming he was being falsely accused by a jealous uncle Natalie Zemon Davis, *The Return of Martin Guerre* (Harvard University Press, 1984).

p. 202

Finally, after a year-long criminal trial, he was exposed as an impostor Rohan McWilliam, *The Tichborne Claimant: A Victorian Sensation* (Bloomsbury Continuum, 2007).

p. 202

Over the years, rare but compelling hiccups brought the system into question Suzanne Bell, *A Dictionary of Forensic Science* (Oxford University Press, 2012), case from 1903.

p. 202

The science was startling, as it became clear that no two individuals had the same markings. Francis Galton, *Finger Prints* (Macmillan, 1892).

p. 202

(A century later, the method was succeeded by 'DNA fingerprinting', first used in 1987 at a rape trial.) *R v Colin Pitchfork* [1987] Leicester Crown Court.

p. 203

The collection of Arabic folktales known as *The Thousand and One Nights* Translated by the French orientalist Antoine Galland c. 1704, https://www.kent.ac.uk/ewto/projects/anthology/index.html

p. 203

in Shakespeare's plays characters such as Viola and Rosalind choose new names and disguise themselves as men. Viola in *Twelfth Night* (1601), Rosalind in *As You Like It* (1599).

p. 203

population growth and rural exodus led to the rapid expansion

of English cities. Enclosures, 1750, common land to private ownership. Rural exodus, https://www.bbc.co.uk/history/british/victorians/exodus_01.shtml and https://www.britishlibrary.cn/en/articles/the-rise-of-cities-in-the-18th-century/

p. 203

Pamphlets such as 'The New Cheats of London Expos'd' warned of 'tricks, impostures, frauds and deceptions' that were 'daily practiced in London'. Julie Peakman, *Libertine London: Sex in the Eighteenth-Century Metropolis* (Reaktion, 2024), citing Richard King, *The New Cheats of London Expos'd; or, The Frauds and Tricks of the Town Laid Open to Both Sexes* (c. 1780), p. 67.

p. 203

Court records track female rogues sent to the pillory for pretending to be men. Julie Peakman, 'Sexual Perversions in History: An Introduction', in Julie Peakman (ed.), *Sexual Perversions: 1670–1890* (Palgrave Macmillan, 2009), p. 16. In *Lesbianism and the Criminal Law* (2020) Derry also unfolds fraudulent marriages from the 18th century, p. 46.

p. 203

Some of the defendants were literal fraudsters Peakman (2009), p. 16.

p. 203

The 'female husband' cases followed by Caroline Derry and other historians were never short-term schemes of financial extraction See Manion (2020).

p. 204

In 1836, a child's 'sex', based on the appearance of newborn genitals, was registered at birth for the first time as part of the Births and Deaths Registration Act. Births and Deaths Registration Act 1836, see https://www.legislation.gov.uk/ukpga/Vict/37-38/88/enacted

p. 204

Civil birth certificates included a new column recording sex
Jess Smith, 'The Future of Legal Gender and the Challenge of Prefigurative Law Reform, pt. 1', Future of Legal Gender podcast,

NOTES

16.00 mins, https://futureoflegalgender.kcl.ac.uk/cookie-lists/resources/podcasts-2/

p. 204

For centuries, the 'one-sex model', the perception of the female body as an inversion of the male body – the vagina an inverted penis – had prevailed in Europe. Paul B. Preciado, *Can the Monster Speak? Report to an Academy of Psychoanalysts*, tr. Frank Wynne (Fitzcarraldo, 2021), p. 51.

p. 204

Indeed, as Thomas Laqueur argues in his study of the history of sexual difference, *Making Sex* (1990) Thomas Laqueur, *Making Sex: Body and Gender from the Greeks to Freud* (Harvard University Press, 1990), pp. 4–5.

p. 204

Across the eighteenth and nineteenth centuries, new medical technologies gave rise to a shift in thinking and the idea of a 'two-sex model' Preciado (2021), p. 53.

p. 205

in 'the brow, the nose, the eyes, the mouth' – but also inside the body, in 'tissues' and 'fibres'). Laqueur (1990), p. 5.

p. 205

Cases of women usurping the sexual hierarchy, labelled impostors, cheats and frauds, received heightened attention Terry Castle, '"Matters not Fit to be Mentioned": Fielding's *The Female Husband*', in Terry Castle, *The Female Thermometer: Eighteenth-Century Culture and the Invention of the Uncanny* (Oxford University Press, 1995), citing 'The Whole Life and Adventures of Miss Davis, Commonly Called the Beauty in Disguise' (1785), p. 71.

p. 205

The 'female husband' trials are precursors to the gender fraud trials of the twenty-first century. Derry, *Lesbianism and the Law* (2020), p. 2.

p. 205

a farm boy with delusions of grandeur, who climbed the social

ladder and got 'newly rich' by breaking the law. F. Scott Fitzgerald, *The Great Gatsby* (Charles Scribner's Sons, 1925; https://www.planetebook.com/free-ebooks/the-great-gatsby.pdf), p. 115.

p. 206
The first medical transition took place at the institute a few years later, and Hirschfeld coined the term 'transsexual' soon after. Heyam (2022), p. 151.

p. 206
As Woolf explains, it was the same Orlando, with the same personality, mind and intellect, but a woman. Virginia Woolf, *Orlando: A Biography* (Hogarth Press, 1928), p. 45.

p. 206
It changed fields, moving out of linguistics and into sexology John Money, 'Hermaphroditism, Gender and Precocity in Hyperadrenocorticism: Psychologic Findings', Bull Johns Hopkins Hosp., vol. 96, no. 6 (June 1955), 253–64, cited in Lisa Downing, Iain Morland and Nikki Sullivan, *Fuckology: Critical Essays on John Money's Diagnostic Concepts* (University of Chicago Press, 2015).

p. 206
Over the next decades, new terms proliferated including 'gender identity' (to describe a person's private sense of being male or female) and 'gender role' (how that identity was expressed in daily life). Downing, Morland and Sullivan (2015), p. 21.

p. 207
patients he observed with, as Money described it, 'gender identity errors'. Downing, Morland and Sullivan (2015), p. 26.

p. 207
These terms would eventually inform the diagnosis 'gender identity disorder' DSM-III (American Psychiatric Association, 1980).

p. 207
People getting gender-confirmation surgery See Zoë Playdon, *The Hidden Case of Ewan Forbes: And the Unwritten History of the Trans Experience* (Bloomsbury, 2021).

NOTES

p. 207

Judgments stated that neither could be reassigned and were forever fixed at birth. *Corbett v Corbett (otherwise Ashley)* [1970].

p. 207

The current situation was unfeasible, the court held, and UK law must adapt to this reality. Stephen Whittle and Lewis Turner, '"Sex Changes"? Paradigm Shifts in "Sex" and "Gender" following the Gender Recognition Act?', *Sociological Research Online*, vol. 12, no. 1 (2007), 75–89.

p. 207

(in the Act, they come as a pair, with 'the male gender' attached to the 'sex . . . of a man', and 'the female gender' attached to the 'sex . . . of a woman'). Gender Recognition Act 2004, Section 9.

p. 208

For a Gender Recognition Certificate to be awarded, notes must say the applicant declares loyalty to one gender (and matching sex) 'until death'. Gender Recognition Act 2004, Section 2(1)c.

p. 208

For example, a December 2021 judgment by the Supreme Court considered a case by an appellant who had been trying, since 1995, to get a passport with 'X' instead of 'M' or 'F'. *R (on the application of Elan-Cane) v Secretary of State for the Home Department* [2021] UKSC 56 before Lord Reed, Lord Lloyd-Jones, Lady Arden, Lord Sales, Lady Rose, 15 December 2021, para 5, https://supremecourt.uk/uploads/uksc_2020_0081_judgment_557c0b206c.pdf

p. 208

In a unanimous decision by five judges, the application was dismissed. Rachel Savage, 'UK Supreme Court rejects gender-neutral "X" passport', Thomson Reuters Foundation (15 December 2021), https://www.reuters.com/article/britain-lgbt-rights/uk-supreme-court-rejects-gender-neutral-x-passport-idUSL8N2T02TI/?edition-redirect=in

p. 208

'The record of a person's gender in their passport is used for a

variety of purposes,' the judgment states, one being 'in order to prevent fraud'. *R (on the application of Elan-Cane) v Secretary of State for the Home Department* [2021], para 9.

p. 208

(This decision contrasts with other jurisdictions Erik Niewiarowski, 'These 18 countries legally recognise non-binary people – but the UK isn't among them', *Pink News* (18 September 2024), https://www.thepinknews.com/2024/09/18/countries-that-legally-recognise-non-binary-people/#page/3. Notably, on 20 January 2025 under the second presidency of Donald Trump, the White House issued an Executive Order under which passports will no longer be issued with an X gender marker. See https://travel.state.gov/content/travel/en/passports/passport-help/sex-marker.html

p. 209

A world that is, as Shon Faye explains in *The Transgender Issue*, hostile to trans people. See Faye (2021), pp. 40–49.

10   The Reasonable Person on the Stand: Legibility

p. 212

Notions of who can be held accountable for a wrongdoing, and why, have shifted over time, but a key condition of responsibility is personal autonomy, the sovereign mind. Naffine (2019), pp. 150–3.

p. 212

The capacity to make free, rational choices is what confers not only humanity, but also responsibility. Ngaire Naffine, 'The Body Bag', in Ngaire Naffine and Rosemary J. Owens (eds), *Sexing the Subject of Law* (LBC Information Services, 1997), p. 81.

p. 213

A jurist named Gaius, in a textbook for law students known as *The Institutes* (AD 161), imagined a fictitious heir, a figure who could be employed by an unclaimed son to initiate legal proceedings. Gaius, *The Institutes* (AD 161), Book II, 252.

NOTES

p. 214

Imaginary defendants and complainants go by the names of Jane Roe or John Doe Christopher Janowak et al., 'Who is John Doe? A Case-Match Analysis', *American Journal of Surgery*, vol. 83, no. 8 (2017), e294–296.

p. 214

But in the nineteenth century, a new kind of fiction was required as standards of civility shifted. Lindsay Farmer, *Making the Modern Criminal Law: Criminalization and Civil Order* (Oxford University Press, 2016), p. 234.

p. 214

The man mirrored his era, and was imagined to be fair-minded, informed, careful and nosey but unexceptional. John Gardner, 'The Many Faces of the Reasonable Person,' *Law Quarterly Review*, 131 (October 2015), 1–38.

p. 214

In the early 1900s, he became known as 'the man on the Clapham omnibus'. Gardner (2015), p. 18.

p. 214

This figure was a Victorian social archetype Simon Stern, 'From Clapham to Salina: Locating the Reasonable Man' (2022), https://papers.ssrn.com/sol3/papers.cfm?abstract_id=4292274

p. 214

In another personification from the 1930s, the reasonable man 'took magazines home' and 'in the evening pushes the lawnmower in his shirtsleeves' Stern (2022).

p. 215

First used in civil law, by the 1950s the standard was being employed in criminal law. Gardner (2015), p. 3.

p. 215

Over time, the character has been reformed and blanked out Naffine (2019), pp. 24–9.

p. 215

Today, the person appears across UK legislation, from stalking and

self-defence to alcohol sales and the use of sun beds. Gardner (2015), p. 3.

p. 215

who inhabit what's been called the 'legal village'. *Helow v Advocate General* [2008] 1 WLR 2416 at 2417-8 per Lord Hope, https://publications.parliament.uk/pa/ld200708/ldjudgmt/jd081022/helow-1.htm

p. 215

Because, according to the standard, this normal, fair-minded, average person is justified. Gardner (2015), p. 4.

p. 217

It conjures a fiction of careful, fair-minded, reasonable people Katherine Angel, *Tomorrow Sex Will Be Good Again: Women and Desire in the Age of Consent* (Verso, 2021), p. 67.

p. 219

Gramsci, writing from prison in 1930s fascist Italy, considered the complicated roots of collective knowledge Kate Crehan, *Gramsci's Common Sense: Inequality and Its Narratives* (Duke University Press, 2016), pp. ix–xii.

p. 219

Countless studies have shown juries' susceptibility to rape myths Leverick (2020).

p. 219

It is impossible to know what actually happens in the deliberation room, because in the UK a jury can never be asked to explain how a decision was reached. Jury service, Gov.uk, https://www.gov.uk/jury-service/discussing-the-trial

p. 220

A second step was added to the new Sexual Offences Act asking, was a defendant's belief in consent 'reasonable'? Caroline Derry, 'Consenting to Sexual Activity', in Lisa Claydon, Caroline Derry and Marjan Ajevski (eds), *Law in Motion: 50 Years of Legal Change* (The Open University Law School, 2020).

NOTES

p. 221

This final part of the test is meant to offer jurors a specific tool, the yardstick of reasonableness. Sharpe (2018), p. 41.

p. 222

Every culture has rules, the most ancient and unvarying of prohibitions being incest. Maurice Godelier, *Forbidden Fruit: An Anthropologist Looks at Incest*, tr. Nora Scott (Verso, 2023).

p. 222

'People do not show their sexuality freely . . . To conceal it they wear a heavy overcoat woven of a tissue of lies, as though the weather were bad in the world of sexuality.' Sigmund Freud, 'Five Letters on Psychoanalysis' (1909), in Roy Schafer, *A New Language for Psychoanalysis* (Yale University Press, 1981).

p. 223

For Freud, the objective of psychoanalysis was to understand 'the id', to discover ourselves and our desires rather than to judge, repress and deny. Frank Tallis, *Mortal Secrets: Freud, Vienna and the Discovery of the Modern Mind* (Abacus, 2024).

p. 223

For BDSM, the shift in attitude was very recent (and indeed is ongoing), following changes to its definition in the *Diagnostic Statistical Manual of Mental Disorders* in 2013. Merissa Nathan Gerson, 'BDSM Versus the DSM: A history of the fight that got kink de-classified as mental illness', *The Atlantic* (13 January 2015), https://www.theatlantic.com/health/archive/2015/01/bdsm-versus-the-dsm/384138/

p. 223

'[T]here is no norm in sexual medicine for what our levels of sexual desire should be . . . Karen Gurney, *Mind the Gap: The Truth About Desire and How to Futureproof Your Sex Life* (Headline, 2020), p. 58.

p. 224

The method of discovering what's average, normal, emerged in the nineteenth century. Barry Sanders, 'The Decline of the Average Mind', in *Cabinet* Magazine, issue 15, The Average (Fall 2004).

p. 224
By the 1830s, he'd come up with the term 'the average man' Paul Fleming and Theodore Porter, 'Life on the Bell Curve: An Interview with Theodore Porter', *Cabinet* Magazine, issue 15, The Average (Fall 2004).

p. 224
Quetelet hoped this figure could help novelists and poets to create characters appropriate for their age. Fleming and Porter (2004).

p. 225
The bell curve became popular among race scientists Sanders (2004).

p. 225
Bodies once figured as 'vile', 'unnatural', 'monstrous' See Alex Sharpe, *Foucault's Monsters and the Challenge of Law* (Routledge-Cavendish, 2009), p. 43.

p. 226
Feminist legal scholars have sought to reveal his suppressed qualities. Naffine (2019), p. 2.

p. 226
These persons 'come in a closed body bag' Naffine (1997), p. 85.

p. 226
In law, cohabiting or sharing a body bag, is disruptive to Western notions of bodily integrity and autonomy, which are seen as a natural right. *Re A (conjoined twins)* [2001] 2 WLR 480, in Sharpe (2009), pp. 112–20. Judgment by Robert Walker LJ, Court of Appeal, 2002, https://e-lawresources.co.uk/Re-A--conjoined-twins-.php

11   Storytelling on the Stand: Fiction

p. 230
Sexual offences law is public, but it's also intimate law Naffine (2019), p. 25.

p. 230

Lengthy seduction novels employed the epistolary format, following characters day by day, almost in real time, creating a 'reality effect' Roland Barthes via Lynn Shepherd, 'Samuel Richardson's Clarissa – one of the great masterpieces of European culture' (25 October 2020), https://lynnshepherdbooks.wordpress.com/2020/10/25/samuel-richardsons-clarissa-one-of-the-great-masterpieces-of-european-culture/ ; Samuel Richardson, *Clarissa or, The History of a Young Lady* (1748; Penguin, 2004).

p. 230

The author's technique of presenting the novel as letters written between his characters was dazzling to contemporary readers William B. Warner, 'Reality and the Novel: Latour and the Uses of Fiction', *The Eighteenth Century*, vol. 57, no. 2 (2016), 267–79.

p. 231

'the most interesting seducers are actually rapists'. Elizabeth Hardwick, 'Seduction and Betrayal', *The New York Review* (31 May 1973), in Elizabeth Hardwick, *Seduction and Betrayal: Women and Literature* (NYRBC, 2001).

p. 231

Then she is a 'maiden no more'. Thomas Hardy, *Tess of the D'Urbervilles* (1891; Dover Editions, 2009), pp. 77–9.

p. 231

Hardy himself claimed it was 'a seduction, pure and simple'; Alec thinks so too. Carol Iannone, 'Ask a Scholar: Rape or Seduction in Tess of the D'Urbervilles?' (18 May 2008), National Association of Scholars, https://www.nas.org/blogs/article/ask_a_scholar_rape_or_seduction_in_tess_of_the_durbervilles

p. 231

The term 'date rape' emerged in the 1970s. Brownmiller (1975).

p. 232

In the 1980s, the feminist researcher Diana Russell conducted a new study of rape, examining in particular 'acquaintance rape' Diana E.H. Russell, *Rape in Marriage* (1982; Indiana University Press, 1990), pp. 57–73.

p. 232

In the same era, the journalist Robin Warshaw, using another study on sexual assault, wrote a book on date rape, which she called a 'hidden epidemic'. Robin Warshaw, *I Never Called It Rape* (1988; Harper, 2019), pp 77–8.

p. 232

'we cannot legislate what happens on a date.' Camille Paglia, 'Rape and Modern Sex War' and 'The Rape Debate Continued', in Camille Paglia, *Sex, Art, and American Culture* (Vintage, 1992).

p. 232

(Other feminists such as Lynne Henderson responded by saying that date rape is unacceptable Lynne Henderson, 'Rape and Responsibility', *Law and Philosophy*, vol. 11 (1992), 127–78, pp. 160–1.

p. 233

'A rapist, in the twentieth century, would take the trouble to drive the victim to her home, dropping her off politely at her doorstep,' Bourke (2007), p. 315.

p. 233

This idea was reflected in psychiatric theories, emerging in this period, in which rape was conceived as a 'courtship disorder' – that is, a 'flawed performance' of normal courtship. Bourke (2007), p. 300, citing Kurt Freund, 'Courtship Disorder: Is this Hypothesis Valid?', *Annals of the New York Academy of Sciences*, vol. 528, issue 1 (1988), 172–82.

p. 233

'For me the rape was a clearly defined act . . . Mary Gaitskill, 'The Trouble with Following the Rules: On "Date Rape", "Victim Culture", and Personal Responsibility' (1994), in Mary Gaitskill, *Somebody with a Little Hammer: Essays* (Pantheon, 2017).

p. 234

'Deceptions, small and sometimes large, have from time immemorial been the by-product of romance and sexual encounters.' McJunkin (2014), p. 23, citing *R v Cuerrier* [1998] Supreme Court of Canada.

NOTES

p. 234

'end of romance' Henderson (1992), p. 161.

p. 234

Since 2003, under the Sexual Offences Act, there has been a patchwork of judgments Sharpe (2018), pp. 31–9.

p. 235

When is it an 'ordinary seduction' (as one judge memorably put it), a minor wrong? McJunkin (2014), p. 21, citing *State v Rusk* [1981], in which a judge identified 'ordinary seduction' (defined as 'a female acquaintance who at first suggests her disinclination' in a ruling of 1981) as outside regulation.

p. 235

Some deceptions feel wrong – the Spy Cops, for example The full extent of the undercover deployments is still to be disclosed; the ongoing Undercover Policing Inquiry, set up in 2015, will publish its final report in December 2026, https://www.ucpi.org.uk/

p. 235

In the public forum, the conversation can lead to binaries See Amia Srinivasan, 'Sex, Carceralism, Capitalism', in *The Right to Sex: Feminism in the Twenty-First Century* (Farrar, Straus and Giroux, 2021), pp. 149–80.

p. 236

Rape by deception has been described as a 'riddle', which 'drives a stake through the very heart of modern rape law' Joseph J. Fischel, *Screw Consent: A Better Politics of Sexual Justice* (University of California Press, 2019), p. 102.

p. 236

To win her man, Bertram, she must complete the tasks William Lawrence, *Shakespeare's Problem Comedies* (Macmillan, 1931), p. 57.

p. 238

The sentencing range for this category is from five to thirteen years. Sentencing Council, 'Assault by penetration, Sexual Offences Act 2003, Section 2', Guideline effective from 1 April 2014, https://

www.sentencingcouncil.org.uk/offences/crown-court/item/assault-by-penetration/

p. 240

Scores of films have been released over the decades *18 Again!*, dir. Paul Flaherty (New World Pictures, 1988); *Freaky Friday*, dir. Mark Waters (Buena Vista Pictures, 2003); *The Swap*, dir. Jay Karas (Disney Channel, 2016).

p. 240

Locke went on to argue that a person goes where their consciousness goes John Locke, 'An Essay Concerning Human Understanding' (1694).

p. 242

That's when the stranger starts talking about the body swap movie *17 Again*. *17 Again*, dir. Burr Steers (Warner Bros., 2009).

p. 246

Their diaries and letters, examined by prosecutors, were full of codes and fictions, making them difficult to interpret. Graham (2013), p. 30.

p. 246

In the run up to the trial, the best friends had confessed, and the only possible defence was madness of two, *folie à deux*. Graham (2013), p. 30.

p. 247

'**The lone paranoiac makes slow progress**' Graham (2013), p. 204.

p. 247

'**There is little silence, but much that is silenced**,' Derry, *Lesbianism and the Criminal Law* (2020), p. 14.

p. 248

Anonymity rules are outlined in the Sexual Offences (Amendment) Act 1992 Sexual Offences (Amendment) Act 1992, https://www.legislation.gov.uk/ukpga/1992/34

p. 248

'**jigsaw identification**' Independent Press Standards Organisation

(IPSO), 'Sexual offences: Guidance for journalists and editors' (updated 12 July 2023), https://www.ipso.co.uk/media/2420/sexual-offences-guidance.pdf

p. 250

'missing bits of the jigsaw . . . It was a moment of the most intense relief, a vindication,' Trevor Grove, *The Juryman's Tale* (1998; Bloomsbury, 2000), p. 183.

p. 251

'Writing cannot be done in a state of desirelessness . . . if the writer actually didn't care one way or another how the things came out, he would not bestir himself to represent them.' Janet Malcolm, *The Silent Woman: Sylvia Plath and Ted Hughes* (Granta, 1994), p. 204.

Epilogue

p. 255

The advocate Alex Sharpe records at least ten prosecutions since 2012. Alex Sharpe, '"Deception as to Gender": A Review of Proposed Revisions to CPS Legal Guidance on Rape and Serious Sexual Offences', *The Journal of Criminal Law*, vol. 89, issue 1 (3 October 2024), https://journals.sagepub.com/doi/full/10.1177/00220183241283223

p. 255

Two such trials took place in English courts in 2023 *R v Blade Silvano* [2023] Cambridge Crown Court and *R v Georgia Bilham* [2023] Chester Crown Court.

p. 255

The 2022 consultation focused on one area in particular: deception as to gender. CPS, 'Consultation on the Deception as to Gender section in the Rape and Serious Sexual Offences (RASSO) legal guidance' (26 September 2022), https://www.cps.gov.uk/consultation/consultation-deception-gender-section-rape-and-serious-sexual-offences-rasso-legal

p. 255

The consultation received over four hundred responses CPS, 'Consultation on Deception as to Gender: Summary of Responses' (13 December 2024), https://www.cps.gov.uk/publication/consultation-cps-guidance-deception-gender-summary-responses

p. 255

Mermaids (which supports gender-diversity and trans rights) Mermaids: https://mermaidsuk.org.uk/frequently-asked-questions-2/ and https://mermaidsuk.org.uk/wp-content/uploads/2023/01/Mermaids-Consultation-Response_-Deception-as-to-Gender_-proposed-revision-to-CPS-legal-guidance-on-Rape-and-Serious-Sexual-Offences-1.pdf

p. 255

Sex Matters (which campaigns for birth sex rights) Sex Matters: https://sex-matters.org/resources/equality-act-faqs/ and https://sex-matters.org/wp-content/uploads/2022/12/CPS-deception-as-to-gender.pdf

p. 255

Alex Sharpe, writing in October 2024 before the guidance was published, expressed cautious optimism about the proposed revisions. Sharpe (3 October 2024).

p. 256

'considerable row back' Alex Sharpe, 'A long thread on the recent CPS Revised Guidance on Deception and Gender', Bluesky (20 December 2024), https://bsky.app/profile/alexsharpe.bsky.social/post/3ldqiuyrnys2n

p. 256

The new guidance is dense and guarded CPS, 'Rape and Sexual Offences – Chapter 6: Consent' (updated 13 December 2024), https://www.cps.gov.uk/legal-guidance/rape-and-sexual-offences-chapter-6-consent

p. 256

This was a revision proposed by Sex Matters in response to the consultation. Sex Matters, 'Response to consultation on Deception as to sex: proposed revision to CPS legal guidance

NOTES

of Rape and Serious Sexual Offences (19 December 2022), p. 5, https://sex-matters.org/wp-content/uploads/2022/12/CPS-deception-as-to-gender.pdf

p. 256
At its most basic level, the case asked what 'sex' means in law. Phil Sim, 'Supreme Court hearing case on definition of a woman', BBC News (27 November 2024), https://www.bbc.co.uk/news/articles/ckgv8v5ge37o

p. 256
One side, representing For Women Scotland (supported by Sex Matters), Scottish Legal News, 'Sex Matters to intervene in Equality Act case at Inner House' (3 October 2023), https://www.scottishlegal.com/articles/sex-matters-to-intervene-in-case-on-meaning-of-sex-in-equality-act

p. 257
The other side countered these claims, describing sex and gender recognition as a 'fundamental right' UK Supreme Court, 'For Women Scotland Ltd (Appellant) v The Scottish Ministers (Respondent)', hearing dates 26–27 November 2024, judgment date 16 April 2025, https://www.supremecourt.uk/cases/uksc-2024-0042

p. 257
The case was decided in April 2025. Angus Cochrane, 'Supreme Court backs "biological" definition of woman', BBC News (16 April 2025), https://www.bbc.co.uk/news/articles/cvg7pqzk47zo

p. 257
The Supreme Court judges unanimously sided with For Women Scotland The judgment will be challenged in the European Court of Human Rights. See Good Law Project, 'Help us challenge the Supreme Court's judgment on trans rights' (April 2025), https://goodlawproject.org/crowdfunder/supreme-court-human-rights-for-trans-people/

p. 257
This judgment disproportionately affects trans people Diego

Garcia Blum and Timothy Patrick McCarthy, 'Understanding the Implications of the UK Supreme Court's Ruling Defining "Sex" in the Equality Act' (18 April 2025), Carr-Ryan Center for Human Rights, Harvard Kennedy School, https://www.hks.harvard.edu/centers/carr-ryan/our-work/carr-ryan-commentary/understanding-implications-uk-supreme-courts-ruling

p. 257

In an attempt at synthesis, the network recommended in its final chapter the creation of a new and bespoke offence for deceptive sex to be added to the Sexual Offences Act. 'Inducing a person to engage in sexual activity by deception', Criminal Law Reform Now Network, 'Final Recommendation: CLRNN Reform Proposal' (2023), pp. 110–11, http://www.clrnn.co.uk/media/1031/clrnn3-deception-report.pdf

Acknowledgements

This book would not have been possible without the support of family members, friends, writers, editors, artists, lawyers, academics and others, who believed in the project, shared their knowledge and their network, suffered my rambles, challenged me and questioned me, offered me time and feedback, and who, in innumerable ways, shaped my thinking and encouraged me to continue.

Thank you.

My family, Georgia Kersh, Skye Arundhati Thomas, Rosanna McLaughlin, Kristian Vistrup Madsen, Sophia Seymour, Kevin Brazil, Constanza Dessain, Katie Duncan, Emily Wright, Ilona Kohanchuk, Isabel Munoz-Newsome, Emily Bradley, Harriet Moore, Poppy Hampson, Clare Drysdale, Helen Garner, Elizabeth Kersh, James Drake, Elizabeth Huang, Alexa Sidor, Max Clarke-Parker, Tessa McWatt, Isobel Roele, Sam McBean, Brian Dillon, Katherine Angel, Sita Balani, Nisha Ramayya, Aman Aheer, Taushif Kara, Kimberly Arms, Florence Keith-Roach, Hannah Dee, Jordan/Martin Hell, Kole Fulmine, D. Mortimer, Sophie Cundale, Susanna Davies-Crook, Ruth Broadbent, Isabel

Buchanan, Sadakat Kadri, Mike Conning, Harry O'Sullivan, Felice McKeown, Laura O'Donnell, Tamsin Shelton.

I am also grateful to the Society of Authors and the Robert B. Silvers Foundation for work-in-progress support.